HEGELIAN REFLECTIONS ON THE IDEA OF NUCLEAR WAR

Hegelian Reflections on the Idea of Nuclear War

Dialectical Thinking and the Dialectic of Mankind

Hayo B. E. D. Krombach

M
MACMILLAN

First published 1991

Published by
MACMILLAN ACADEMIC AND PROFESSIONAL LTD
Houndmills, Basingstoke, Hampshire RG21 2XS
and London
Companies and representatives
throughout the world

Typeset by Footnote Graphics,
Warminster, Wilts.

Printed in Hong Kong

British Library Cataloguing in Publication Data
Krombach, Hayo B. E. D.
Hegelian reflections on the idea of nuclear war:
dialectical thinking and the dialectic of mankind.
1. Nuclear warfare. Ethical Aspects.
I. Title
172′.42
ISBN 0–333–52531–0

To the memory of my father

Contents

Wo aber Gefahr ist, wächst
Das Rettende auch.
Hölderlin

Preface

The aim of this book is to reflect in a Hegelian philosophical manner upon the nuclear age. Its more specific purpose is of a two-fold nature. It is to acquaint the reader with the principle of dialectical thinking as it manifests itself in three different though related experiences: in the unfolding of human discourse, in the conceptualisation of scientific methodologies, and in the historical development of self-consciousness. But, because the meaning of method is mainly demonstrated in its application, the objective of the book is also to use dialectic in the effort to comprehend the idea of nuclear war within its historical context. The intellectual appeal and relevance of the inquiry lie in the philosophical approach to thematise a life in danger of committing suicide, and particularly in the way it interprets and to this effect employs Hegel's principle of historical dialectic.

The book grew out of a doctoral dissertation which was written at the London School of Economics and Political Science under the supervision of Philip Windsor. It was examined by Leszek Kolakowski of All Souls College, University of Oxford and the University of Chicago. I would like to extend to both my warmest thanks for their advice and encouragement to make the material available to a wider audience.

However, in the course of preparing its publication the original thesis had to be substantially condensed and revised. The result is a carefully laid out analysis of dialectic. Not only is the classical Greek tradition accorded in-depth consideration. The reasons are also explained why the concern with dialectical thinking has assumed different forms at various historical junctures, and why we can learn from an intellectual device that is part of our philosophical heritage.

The origin of the ideas which underly the present text goes back to my studies in philosophy at the University of Toronto in the 1970s. The emphasis on the close reading of primary sources, ancient and modern, and their meaningful rendering in the light of different historical horizons was one of the most valuable moments in those early years of academic life. I am therefore much indebted to my former teachers, in particular to R. E. Allen, Allan Bloom, D. P. Gauthier, C. B. Macpherson, R. G. McRae, Graem Nicholson, T. M. Robinson and K. Schmitz.

I became aware of the importance of applying the dialectical method to thinking about one of the most difficult problems of international relations during my graduate studies at the Institut Universitaire de Hautes Etudes Internationales at the University of Geneva. I owe special gratitude to Curt Gasteyger whose enlightening and thought-provoking seminar in Strategic Studies made me realise that, apart from the need for thorough empirical research, there is an even greater urgency to ponder the increasingly global implications of inter-state politics and the attendant threat to the integrity of mankind in a way that allows for their philosophical comprehension. After having nearly changed the world beyond recognition, we must again reflect and learn to wonder.

It was then in subsequent years at the LSE that I was offered the opportunity to work with Philip Windsor in the Department of International Relations. Being a truly inspiring educator, whose human wisdom and philosophical insight into the afflictions of the world exert a deep and lasting influence over his students, Mr Windsor provided me with unfailing moral and intellectual support and guided me patiently through an as yet uncharted field of rumination.

A more direct debt, however, is due to those who have read the final product either as a whole or in part. I have greatly benefited from comments made by Elie Kedourie, Donald McRea, Tom Nossiter and Cyril Smith from the LSE. I would also like to thank Dieter Henrich from the Institut für Philosophie at the Maximilians Universität in Munich for his sincere interest shown in my work. I have profited much from his erudite writings on Hegel and on the ethical problems which the idea of nuclear war poses. These are not only a comment in themselves, but even more so an encouragement to pursue the path of my reflections. A rather distinctive contribution was made by Cyril Smith. In regular and highly rewarding conversations we approached the philosophical problematic of dialectic from a Marxist and Hegelian point of view. Without the dialogue we would not have become aware of our differences. But without the disagreements we would not be united in history either.

For kind permission to quote from *Hegel's Science of Logic* (trans. A. V. Miller, 1969) and from *The Complete Works of Aristotle* (ed. John Barnes, 1985) acknowledgement is made with thanks to Unwin Hyman Ltd. and Princeton University Press, respectively.

Introduction

Though we have learned to expand ourselves in space, we have also begun to withdraw from its time. We have created the means to destroy the natural world of man, and yet we can hardly imagine that we might one day sever the spiritual history of mankind as well.

The writing of this book was guided by a concern with the question as to the intellectual implications of the *idea* of nuclear war. Past wars affected the life-world of man in particular states and regions, or they involved the whole world without, however, destroying it. Past wars still differentiated between life and death. But Hiroshima and the possibility ever since of a nuclear war suggest the extended possibility of a threat not just to the survival of states and regions alone. Most fundamentally, it indifferently threatens that in which they are embedded: natural mankind and the relations of its spiritual humanity. This prospect is what thinking has discovered, and it constitutes the absolute turning point in the effort of man to find his self-image in history.

The idea of nuclear war, therefore, poses a very great problem for philosophical reflection. It presents a challenge of enormous intellectual complexity. The one particular task that is assigned to us is to come to terms with and, indeed, to account for, the dialectical principle of the part-whole relationship. All thinking, because of its intrinsic historicality, is in its expression dialectical. And so our theme is not one that ought to involve only those who feel subjectively affected by the idea of atomic warfare. It is an issue which objectively is the very essence of what man has thought out for himself. And if reflective thinking is the activity which distinguishes man, then what threatens mankind is clearly of concern for us all.

Now, while all activities of international import – and, in particular, those with adverse consequences for man's global environmental habitat – must today take cognisance of this dialectical perspective, the idea of nuclear war affects its study in a rather ultimate and urgent way. In the context of our present purpose we see this relationship exemplified by the connection between the states and mankind in whose notion they are unified. In and of itself this statement may sound formal. But when considered from a historically concrete and organic point of view, it becomes immediately apparent that we are today living at a unique juncture of our human existence.

And this is for two reasons. One is that in the course of time the states in their plurality have developed and increased in number in such a way that they now form a system that is quantitatively complete or universal. In this sense of *universality* the system can be said to be identical with mankind. But mankind, in turn, is recognised also as the spiritually organic or qualitative principle which manifests itself as what we shall call *individuality*. The dialectical principle (dia-logos) which is applied to the part-whole relationship, or to the identity between universality and individuality, will in our notation be described as the life of mankind (logos) as it appears phenomenally in and through the history of the states-system and, hence, in and through the history of itself (dia).

The second reason why we think our present historical juncture is unprecedented is explained by the peril of global suicide. It is the states that would wage nuclear war and thereby threaten our survival. But because individual mankind is identical with the states the nuclear act would, logically speaking, be mankind's free act of self-inflicted finality.

It is with respect to this prospect that the part-whole relationship can now be examined in two further questions: what is at stake, and how are we to think about what is at stake in the nuclear age? An answer to the first of these issues is treated in many different theoretical and moralistic ways in a wealth of literature in science and the humanities. But an adequate philosophical description of a historical and hence mutually relational pair of extremes such as the parts and the whole is nearly absent from the minds of modern men. It may be that *homo modernicus*, practical and all too busy as he is, has sundered his calmer vocation for thinking.

In a not-so-different historical context, Hegel once explained the renunciation of speculative thought by saying that it was because of 'the cry of modern educationalists that the needs of the time demanded attention to immediate requirements, that just as experience was the primary factor for knowledge, so for skill in public and private life, practice and practical training generally were essential and alone necessary, theoretical insight being harmful even'.[1]

Hegel had hoped in his own time to re-establish the spirit of speculative wisdom, of the 'holy of holies'.[2] But while thinking about the historical relationship between the many needs of the time and the one philosophical reflection, he began to be filled with doubts as to the destiny of his effort. And so he wrote that in the face of the greatness of the task he:

> had to content himself with what it was possible to achieve in circumstances of external necessity, of the inevitable distractions caused by the magnitude and many-sidedness of contemporary affairs, even under the doubt whether the noisy clamour of current affairs and the deafening chatter of a conceit which prides itself on confining itself to such matters leave any room for participation in the passionless calm of a knowledge which is in the element of pure thought alone.[3]

This commentary needs no further interpretation. Its truth was clear then when it was written, as it is obvious today.

And yet we must try. It would be presumptuous, however, to believe that at this moment we could also engage in a similar endeavour to found a new philosophy that carries within it its own future development. Instead, all we intend to accomplish is to reflect upon our concern in at least the spirit of Hegel. It is only with the philosophical disposition which Hegel has bequeathed to us that we can at all hope to understand the dialectical complexity of history and its self-consciousness.

We shall attempt, then, to approach our question with the philosophical device which allowed Hegel himself to comprehend the meaning of the relationship between the one and the many. This method of reflection is historical dialectic. Though we shall later explicate and apply the logic of this method to our query, it is pertinent already now to ask what this dialectic involves. It is more important still to ask why we are convinced that a strenuous effort must be made to think about the idea of nuclear war in a dialectical manner. In other words: why is dialectic necessary?

Before venturing a preliminary answer to this question, let us seek to elucidate the term *dialectic* itself. In a broad sense it describes that medium in and through which parts relate to the whole to which they belong. In antiquity this method was employed to define words, ideas, or scientific propositions within the medium of the dialogue. In this usage the hypothesised objects to be defined were the whole, the questions and approximative answers to them its parts. However, that which the dialogue sought to name was regarded as being external to or separated from the interlocutors. No true knowledge of such ontological referents could therefore be established. Since the dialogue was to arrive at a definition, and since a definition *qua* itself permits of no alteration, the result of deliberation was an ahistorical term. This accorded principally with the innocent Greek *paideia* in so far as the ancients had a theoretical grasp of history only in its physical being (historia). And, because Greek philosophical language lacked the notion of a historical past, the changes of natural phenomena were understood in terms of a pattern which assumed the form of a presupposed eternal return and everlasting present.

But once the mind was forced into the divine and secular future, once it was forced to externalise itself during a score of centuries and to step into the questioning challenge and task of history, dialectical thinking began to involve the notion of spiritual history. In Hegel's philosophy history sublates all language and its dialogic manifestations. From the vantage point of Hegelian modernity, which became sceptical of promised futures whatever their credentials, it gradually acquired a novel meaning: the meaning of the present to be clarified through its past. History is not mere form; it has a content, namely its own internal, spiritually organic development from one formative moment to the next. Hegel's dialectic describes the medium between such moments in terms of relations. But these can be expressed only as ideas and not as facts. The ideality of relations suggests moreover that history becomes manifold and differentiated praxis, and that philosophy is its unified and holistic comprehension. Accordingly, history cannot be without philosophy, and true philosophy is not without its history. The one and the many are not separated but are the same. Only that which has a past and, therefore, is concrete can be grasped philosophically. And only a present can in a dialectical and reflective manner comprehend its history. The subject-object relationship is now an immanent and self-referential one. History is the object necessary for the subject whose self-consciousness is the result of reflection upon its history. Hegelian philosophy thinks of self-knowledge as mediated through its historical content and not with reference to metaphysical assumptions or the prescribed and projected future content of a providential millennium. Though we presuppose a future, its specific development can never be predicted or regarded as necessary. But a future which is hypothesised only as an abstract possibility does not yield philosophical knowledge in the strict sense. The present, on the other hand, is life as historically concrete result, and only in its result is philosophical cognition demonstrated. Hegel argued that much when he wrote that 'we must hold to the conviction that it is the nature of truth to prevail when its time has come, and that it appears only when this time has come, and therefore never appears prematurely'.[4] In other words, philosophy reflects upon life and the manner in which it comprehends itself in the full and free consciousness of itself.

This transformation – from the notion of the static present to that which has turned it into the dynamic becoming of the present – has basic implications for the way we seek to fathom the depth of dialectic. For today the medium of dialectical comprehension is not simply a particular and binding dialogue that benignly deliberates on guiding definitions. It is the push and urge of universal yet differentiated history that in its ceaseless activity not only questions faith in definitions, but also tends to break through the hopeful answers inscribed in dialogues. Since it can alter its possibilities for self-comprehension, history has rendered difficult the discourse of man. History itself provides the most cogent argument for philosophical dialectic.

The consequence of this is that man's emerging self-consciousness is discontinuous. The seemingly sovereign fragments of the spiritually organic life-world now reign as parts that lack the sense of mediating perspectives and the vital courage to reflect upon and act towards their unity. Man revolves about himself. But in his solitary freedom he now is skidding precariously on the surface of unrelated presentness.

It is this renunciation of historical consciousness which makes the study of dialectic of utmost importance in an age whose own characteristic reductionism is the fear of shrivelling space and time. We live in the reciprocal relationship between states and mankind, and both are still sublated through their one and only history. But dialectic may fail. What a nuclear war threatens is the possibility that particular states destroy the whole of the humanity of mankind and its principle of life – spiritual history.

In our effort to grasp the meaning of self-consciousness philosophically we cannot escape this relationship. We are responsible for reflecting ourselves in it, because history and its manifestations constitute the object of dialectical thinking. And responsibility is the *quintessence* of dialectic. Because mankind itself is self-conditioning dialectical history, it is therefore ultimately responsible for mediating its own self-consciousness and for its own destiny. And this implies that we must respond to the immanent expression of dialectic without taking recourse to an alienating transcendence or the gods of our fictions. But to learn to understand history dialectically is to realise also the danger man has become for himself. It is to be aware of the greatest existential predicament: the possibility that dialectical life inverts itself into death. Not the natural death of each individual, but the artificial death of mankind. History is henceforth contingent and may come to a close.

With the fire of Prometheus man has for ever burnt the stigma of consciousness into his conscience. At the beginning of true history Polybius wrote that it now becomes an 'organic whole', and that 'all events bear a relationship and contribute to a single end'.[5] Must the beginning of the life of the whole unconsciously imply already what its self-conscious development in the nuclear age makes all too explicit? The one single and victorious blow of war, of which Clausewitz could muse only in the conditional mood,[6] has meanwhile become the indicative mode of preparatory practice in our time. But if it ever came to its realisation, could we still live with human dignity beyond its lie and blasphemy? We may want to, we may even be able to avoid such finality. This is a psychological issue which, however, has no bearing on philosophy.

In the light of these remarks we wish to point out at the outset that the purpose of the book is neither to write this history nor to dwell once more on the imagined horrors of nuclear realities and the way we might conceive of their prevention. We are not proposing politically viable ideological, technical and military answers to the dialectical dilemma which has become the awesome human condition. Although expressing the genuine hopes of man, who is forever in conflict with himself, all such proposals would, in any case, be dialectically modified and subjected to historical judgment. No futures are determinate. Our interest lies foremost in finding a reflective and heuristic way into the question of dialectic itself and of how one might apply its understanding to the idea of nuclear war. Dialectic is the reason for and through which everything is. But it is also that because of which there might not be anything any more in the future. The experience of doubt is most irritating to the rational mind that longs for divine or secular redemption. In the past these remote points of reference used to define the essence of man. Today, however, this essence is intellectually indeterminate, a situation which affords little guidance for our actions. And yet it is within such uncertainty that we have to find a new grounding for the intentions of our life and thinking. To this extent, then, nuclear war is not the object of our discussion. Rather do we see in its *idea* a justification for reflecting upon a philosophical question which such a possibility poses for the intellect.

The subject of dialectic will be dealt with from various points of view. In order to establish and explain the relationship between the different planes of dialectical thinking, we shall with illuminating and guiding references to Hegel unravel hermeneutically some pertinent aspects of the ancient and modern tradition, and focus on a detailed exegesis of its written testimony. This approach is warranted on at least two grounds. One is to do with a particular attitude towards reading itself. Patient and conscientious work with primary though difficult texts is not seldom met with scepticism. It is not only believed that the interpretation at one time of a text written at an earlier period can never be truly adequate, but that it for that reason must also teach each present something different from what it may have taught previous times. This argument is not without strength. However, it is equally apparent that the reluctance to go back to the sources is symptomatic for those who do not trust that great thinkers in fact meant what they said and consequently reduce complex ideas to the level of their own imbecility.[7] There is no 'royal road to Science', says Hegel convincingly, and hence it is not enough merely to read reviews of philosophical works, or perhaps to content oneself with perusing prefaces and first paragraphs.[8] And the other reason for our method must be seen in the light of the observation that the assumptions of much of academic empirical and theoretical praxis are philosophically unreflected and, therefore, remain of little educational value. While there is no thinking without its objects, no practical activity should take itself for granted either. After all, praxis is praxis only if it is recognised and understood as such.

Since every chapter has its own preface, we shall confine ourselves here to only a few preliminary words about the structure of the book. It begins with an account of dialogic dialectic as it was thought through by Plato and Aristotle. The sections will discuss the problems which the method of the dialogue raises for arriving at an objectivity of metaphysical truths and premises for logical reasoning. In addition, we shall address Hegel's comment that in antiquity, unlike in modernity, the subject itself, or the member of the dialogue, was not made a theme for critical inquiry.

The investigative aspect of Aristotle's analytical thinking underwent continuous specification over time, but is distinctly qualified in contemporary theories of science. Appropriately, therefore, we shall in the second chapter deal with such writers as Popper, Kuhn and Feyerabend, for instance, and assess their tendency to remove dialectic from dialogic responsibilities altogether, and to reduce it to mere positivistic, paradigmatic and even anarchical means. We shall

shall also underline how, at the hands of science, dialectic has clearly suffered the loss of its erstwhile holistic intent.

Following the discussion of scientific dialectic we take up again, in Chapter 3, the issue of a comprehensive dialectic. With Hegel we shall relate the question of knowledge to the subject itself and show that the possibility of a holistic answer is conditional upon the subject's will and ability to mediate its self-consciousness in and through the medium of its own history. In order to clarify Hegel's method of self-reflection, we shall explicate in great detail some textual features of his writings, an exercise which is necessary for aquiring an intellectual sensitivity for the dialectical idiom of the part-whole relationship.

In Chapter 4 the method of historical dialectic will be systematically applied to the idea of the subject. In connection with our study this subject is taken to be the life of mankind which we see as objectifying itself in the historical medium of the states and the system they have developed into.

The book continues in Chapter 5 with a few thoughts about the effects of the idea of nuclear war on dialectic. We shall argue that what has come to an end with Hegel is not history, but the philosophical assignment to reflect upon man's highest historical good. This good is freedom. But what might come to an end with a nuclear war is history itself with all that which is embedded within it, of which the power to comprehend history philosophically is its own highest good.

The problem of the dialectic between war and peace will be briefly considered in the final chapter. Here we shall look at Hegel's distinction between the idea of war and its actual occurrence, and deduce from this our task to approximate dialogically the meaning of peace itself. The conclusion will be that since not only mankind is differentiated but also the language with which we seek to articulate its humanity we can at most hope to preserve the dialogue and learn to act responsibly. Such a sustained possibility, however, requires an educated awareness of the principle of dialectical relations, for it is in and through them alone that a sense of holistic selfhood is created of which mankind is the ultimate embodiment.

What guides us throughout is the conviction that a philosophical framework is needed if we do not wish to lose sight of that which we want to absorb into our reflections.

Part I
Scientific Dialectic

1 Antiquity

Plato and Aristotle show in very comprehensive arguments the possibilities and rational limitations of the dialogic form of dialectic. In this chapter we shall address the question of why the dialogue has these features, and elaborate on the subjective and personal requirements such as hope, courage and responsibility that Plato, for instance, feels need to be fulfilled if a dialogue is to be a valuable method for attaining truth. Genuine philosophy is experienced in the discourse of men. A discussion of an early Platonic form of a more conceptual analysis of the part-whole relationship will then lead us to an assessment of Aristotle's more objective and rational approach to the method of dialectical deduction.

Yet what in both thinkers, according to Hegel, becomes already apparent is that subjective dialogic reflections make ultimately assertions which future history alone can demonstrate. This result is not only confined to the ancients. Because of their presentness knowledge claims cannot be proved. Since the dialogue and its uncertain theoretical and practical consequences are the essence of the human condition, it manifests itself at all times. It is only in our age, however, that we have come to realise that a particular consequence of dialogue may very well incinerate its holistic reason and final origin. It is the danger of nuclear war which in itself justifies a detailed examination of the dialogue and its dialectic, and which makes necessary some inquiry into the beginnings of our theoretical scientific thinking. The conclusions we arrive at speak for themselves and need no further elaboration, except to state the obvious, namely, that in case of war a dialogue will have broken down, just as the assumptions upon which the sciences base their reasoning will have proved spurious and fatal. And yet, in brief, what the early tradition of dialectical thinking teaches us, or ought to teach us, is a sense of moderation. And this in the way we rely on *first principles*, whose assumed validity can always be questioned, and in the way we apply our activities to the idea of a whole which is jeopardised and which, therefore, needs the caring of reflective minds. Care, however, is essentially to be taken within the dialogue itself because its language is the expression of our human self-understanding.

PLATO'S DIALECTICAL DIALOGUE

Dialectic is a philosophical method which makes possible a correct treatment of speech in a discourse. But if there is a right way to employ speech there must also be a wrong one. However, the determination of such criteria cannot be sought in the dialogue itself. Neither are they to be taken as formalistic truth and falsity. Dialectical viewpoints are not in this sense opposites or contradictory. To challenge them is not necessarily to refute their underlying assumptions. They are rather to be understood organically because they seek to encompass the dialogue as a philosophical unity whose parts form a coherent development of one another and of the whole itself.

In this section we shall first discuss the practical application of dialectic. We shall elaborate the methodological aspects of the dialogue and some of its objective and more subjective elements. In the latter part, the relationship between the philosophical objects of the dialogue, that is, the ontological ideas or forms, and the dialectical method will be commented on. We shall conclude our examination of Plato by citing some of Hegel's own critical remarks on the dialectical defectiveness of the dialogue.

But apart from thematising the dialectic of the dialogue the general purpose of treating it goes beyond this attempt. For, by implication, we also wish to argue that the very need to engage in a dialogue is in the nuclear age perhaps more urgent than at any previous time. What is at stake in our era is the freedom of humanity. But only through the dialectically guided dialogue can the idea of this highest good for mankind be approached in any meaningful way. In other words, the primary experience of humanity manifests itself within the practised dialogue. An understanding of its teleological nature is therefore of paramount importance if at least the possibility for a humanity is to be established. That humanity is initially only a possibility and not a given conceptual certainty is due to the insight that it not only begins as hope, but that the fulfilment of its hope develops historically and hence reflectively only. This is true with respect to the idea of humanity as it is for all other ideas, metaphysical forms or concepts for which we seek a definition and to which the logical structure of the dialogue is indifferent.

Although we shall not give an empirical account of the discourse as it is pursued in our life-world, we believe that Plato's philosophical description of its eternal essence can induce contemporary interlocutors to ponder the dialogue as such and the content of its problematic outcome with more dialectical circumspection and with the greater mutual respect its requires.

Now, dialectic itself is for Plato a method of reflection which must be observed if one seeks intersubjective knowledge of the principles of holism or of oneness, that is, of the '*idea* of the good'.[1] It is a 'guide on the voyage of discourse'.[2] If used correctly, it helps to point out which discursive contributions are consonant, and which are incompatible with one another. Such a method or guide is based on the 'royal warrant of reason'[3] which, according to Plato, elevates 'philosophy' to a 'science' or, more precisely, to a 'science of dialectic'.[4] Plato, in fact, places dialectic 'at the top of the studies like a coping stone', and declares that 'no other study could rightly be set higher than this one'.[5]

But dialectic as a method is not separated from the dialogue, it is not independent of it. On the contrary, for the theoretical method to be meaningful, it is required to prove itself in its practical application, that is, in conversation.[6] Method and application, therefore, turn into the dialectical dialogue, a manner of writing which Plato himself employs for the development of his thinking. It is in respect of this holistic relationship that he speaks of a science.

The cognisance of philosophical science, moreover, leads to the attainment of *freedom*. Understanding the science of dialectic, writes the ancient, is the 'free man's knowledge',[7] because through it one can free oneself from the fetters of fixed and one-sided opinions.[8]

Beyond these general remarks we must also ask how the dialectical dialogue unfolds itself concretely. In order to explicate this development we shall interpret the dialectical procedure of the Platonic dialogue from the point of view of the *give and take* of *question and answer* of the logos, or of reason.[9]

The Platonic dialectic is characterised by the way the participants in a dialogue engage in the 'give-and-take of arguments'[10] in order to ascertain the ontological status of a transcendent object of thought. Thus its method is teleologically linked to an intended system. What is dialectical in a dialogue is the reciprocity of coherent and complementary accounts of the logos. The holistic logos is created within the dialogue in which the particular accounts are offered in a spirit of partnership and prevalent mutuality.[11]

To engage in a dialogue is to ask questions and to give a reply to them. It is an attempt to leave the state of ignorance as it expresses itself in opinion (doxa) and to enter the realm of truth that manifests itself as knowledge (episteme). What transforms and synthesises one into the other, what leads out of ignorance and into knowledge, is for

Plato *education*. It is the attempt 'to make out the truth after a complete course of discipline'.[12] 'Education', he writes, should consist in teaching the ability to 'question and answer most knowledgeably',[13] because, as he clarifies elsewhere, the study of a subject must be accompanied by a heuristic inquiry into what is false and true in it, and 'must be carried on by constant practice throughout a long period'.[14] Hence the issue discussed in the dialogue is not, and ought not to be, decided by a unilateral decision. It is neither stated arbitrarily, nor is it based on authoritative instruction.[15] What is put forward as an account by one participant, then, is not the truth of the matter but merely an opinion about it. It is through dialectic that the account presented is questioned. The 'given' is 'taken' again and thought through in its implications. It is opened up and dissolved,[16] and subsequently developed into more precise statements. We shall return to this point towards the end of this section.

Furthermore, the dialectical dialogue does not only take place on a horizontal plane as is the case, for instance, with disputations. Here the disputants remain seemingly autonomous and self-referring selves who, in their separateness, heap upon one another aggregates of arguments. In their unreflected sophistry they run to and fro, in merely talking they say nothing, and their verbiage remains without substance and development. In engaging in a 'shadow play of discourse' they create only 'illusions'.[17] Rather, in a dialogue the horizontal movement is sublated, and the interlocutors advance vertically from a low level of comprehension towards one another in the attempt to meet in a mutually agreed definition of the real being of the logos. Plato critically reminds us that the 'isolation of everything from everything else means a complete abolition of all discourse, for any discourse we can have owes its existence to the weaving together of forms'.[18]

This directed and upward movement, which expresses itself in form of relations, makes the dialogue dialectical. Accordingly, it is he 'who knows how to ask and answer' who is called a 'dialectician'.[19] In other words, dialectic, once its structure and theoretical method is learned and has become familiar, is *constitutive*[20] of a properly conducted and practised dialogue. What is constitutive should lead to what is projected as necessary. And what is necessary ought to be associated with truth. As we shall see below, however, this constitutive and apparently objective aspect of the discourse will have to be considerably qualified. But for now let us see how it is possible at all that question and answer come together.

In a dialogue questions and answers are issue-bound and this, as we have said, in a double sense. There is a two-fold relationship, one between the participants and the other between them and the issue. The horizontal and vertical direction form a triangular structure whose top is the cognition of reason. It is then this very issue of reason which prompts the speakers to give their accounts of it, but which also unites them in their effort to understand it together, that is, as community. Philosophically speaking, this is to say that it is the idea of the whole which conditions the developmental movements of its parts.

Yet connected with this is another very important and somewhat unexpected point. The Platonic dialogue does not take place among equals.[21] The form of dialogue we have in mind is between the philosopher, who thinks pure thoughts, and the sophist, who opines about appearances. It is for this reason rather discontinuous in the way it moves forward.[22] Wisdom is not something that flows without interruption from one person to the other.[23] It is not something one is by nature endowed with, but an attribute whose attainment requires a mutual and sincere effort.

This asymmetrical movement of a dialogue raises in our troubled time of international discourse the uncomfortable question as to whether a symmetrical inquiry into an issue can be pursued between equal partners, and whether subjectively perceived parity in status does not rather stifle the dialogue and force it to become a mutually reinforcing disputational confrontation. A tentative answer might be that while a dispute may not force an issue, an issue, however, can bind the dialogue. Yet because of the homonymous treatment of topics this is not obvious either. Though interlocutors may very well feel equal to one another, their argumentation often also originates from different primary conceptions whose formative conditions may vary considerably. The likely result of such a situation is that the discussion of a common problem, which they profess to share, is not only a cognitively self-serving, but also an action-oriented self-interested exercise.

In other words, the question arises whether one can envisage a successful dialogue whose homonym is approached from points of view which are incompatible with one another or which are mutually exclusive. The broad diversity of geographical constants and more contingent cultural contexts, for example, or the narrow dogmatism of ideological enclosures, do not easily, if at all, secure a synonymous grasp of a problem at hand. But the notions of diversity and dialectical hierarchy, as will be made more explicit in later chapters, are the necessary differentiation of the unitary principle of mankind. The possibility of a dialogic reconciliation in the strict sense is therefore difficult to entertain unless, perhaps, the interlocutors can conceive of the nuclear threat in such a way that it transforms their fixed though also spurious self-understanding into the focus of the common cause of survival, a cause to which both are related with equal necessity.

But to return to Plato. Let us assume that within one differentiated unit a dialogue in difference, as it were, can be conducted. In such a conscientious conversation, then, it is the leader himself who speculates on question and answer. The philosopher is even asked to do so by the interlocutors whom he has irritated with his challenges to think things through. He is urged to refrain from plunging them into difficulties and, instead, to keep his 'promise' and do the job for them.[24]

Thus the dialogue contains, apart from the element of freedom, also that of *responsibility*.[25] Responsibility lies mainly with the questioner himself. And he is the philosopher. It is the philosopher *qua* questioner who takes priority over the respondent and his answers. He therefore also experiences the questioning more as a *passion* (Erleiden) than an action, because the questions that press on him can no longer be avoided.[26] It is for him to discern the dissonance in what is communicated in order to bring out the real strength of an argument. The presupposition, of course, is that the questioner *qua* questioner has already within himself a synoptic overview, and that he comprehends the dialectical development of the dialogue, while the answering interlocutor merely replies with the external reflections he hopes to bring to bear on the problem which both seek to scrutinise. And this suggests that the former guides and educates the latter.

But in the dialectic of the dialogue the issue is actually not as such known. The philosopher does not, and does not claim to, know. It is the sophist who knows, albeit only in pretence. If the philosopher had full cognisance, no discourse would be required about anything, for what underlies the beginning of a dialogue is not knowledge but the need for it. The attempt by the philosopher first to think things through alone does not mean that he possesses a full understanding of the correspondence relation between thinking and the object thought about. It simply refers to the mental process which manifests their vagueness.

The internal reflection is a quiet one and one that requires time. The pause within the dialogue is provided by the answer to be given by the interlocutor. Thus the dialectical dialogue unfolds and enfolds itself in time. The essence of dialectic is its history. First, explains the thinker I 'begin with myself and my own original supposition'.[27] Once this is done 'I shall get a moment's rest while he is answering',[28] that is, while his partner is making his own point. The reflection of the leader of the dialogue can thus be interpreted as a *monologue*.[29] 'Thinking', Plato says, is a 'dialogue of the mind with itself'.[30] The 'process of thinking' is a 'discourse that the mind carries on with itself about any subject it is considering'.

> when the mind is thinking, it is simply talking to itself, asking questions and answering them, and saying yes or no. When it reaches a decision ... we call that its 'judgment'. So I should describe thinking as discourse, and judgment as a statement pronounced, not aloud to someone else, but silently to oneself.[31]

Thinking is an activity whereby the mind of the questioner refers to itself. But in the dialogic monologue the internal relationship between a particular consciousness and its object of concern produce reflectively a consistency in argumentation, which in the extraneous meeting of interlocutors is more difficult to accomplish. On the other hand, the monologue and its closed deliberation are only a first approximation of understanding, which in the dialogue comes into the open, and is there pursued freely. Hence the dialectician is involved in a double dialogue in which he attempts to grasp the 'reason for the being of each thing', that is, 'to give an account of a thing to himself and another'.[32] This very connection between monologue and dialogue indicates that the philosopher's freedom, that the idea of freedom, is not a singularly given but a social *task* to which he is dedicated. It requires the disciplined effort to overcome and sublate that upon which it depends and without which it cannot be spoken of, namely, its opposite. The philosopher, in order to become free, needs the interlocutor whom he takes with him in the ultimately communal endeavour to attain freedom. Without such a dialectical mediation of opposites freedom cannot be. In other words, what is philosophically envisaged as a whole necessarily conditions the parts, but now also is for its realisation contingent upon them.

We have said earlier that the dialogic form of dialectic has to do with the give and take of arguments. Its striving towards the logos is necessary for, as the philosopher asks his interlocutor: 'was it ever your opinion that men who are unable to give an account and receive one will ever know anything of what we say they must know?'.[33]

As indicated above, two aspects of this question need to be noted. First, knowledge seems to reside within the logos, but this same logos is, secondly, also given and taken by individual members of the dialogue. In a way it is the epistemic pull of the logos that demands from the dialecticians that they come together in the first place. But, at the same time, the Platonic dialogue cannot in and of itself sustain and fulfil such a requirement. Its methodological objectivity is carried out and developed according to the principles of dialectic only if the relationship between the interlocutors has been established on the basis of a subjective condition, namely the confidence (*con-fides*) that both of the partners in fact follow and *trust together* the theoretical precepts inscribed in dialectic.

The method of give and take is thus in a crucial way also contingent upon 'trust'.[34] That is to say, the attempt to ascertain the logos depends ultimately upon the appeal by the participants to trust each other. The functioning of the principles of dialectic presupposes the agreement on a rather uncertain commitment. In the dialogue it is a personal sentiment that either supports or weakens the effort to fathom the being of the logos. That the requirement of trust be met is due to the fact that the seemingly sovereign speakers are separated one from the other. The dialectical logos is with Plato still modified by a subjective element. A dialogue, however, that operates on the basis of such a plea can render reason only as a constant *aporia* or as a persistent problem. The physical separation of individual minds is not necessarily overcome even by a declared common intellectual concern. Any one definition is, from a dialectical point of view, limited and temporary. The search for truth is subject to the secular faith in the individually at most correct account of the logos. The true logos is in need of trust. Real trust alone is the basis for giving and taking the logos.[35]

The necessity of trust presupposes in turn, however, that trust be tested. Trust is a concept that implies community within which it is disclosed and demonstrated. But if one wants to win trust can one at the same time question it? Does the additional demand of an examination not rather undermine the very meaning of trust? At first sight it may seem so. But then again, to use an analogy, we cannot necessarily rely on our eyes either when we apply sight to objects. Apart from merely natural sense-perception, we also wish to extend it and employ more rational means and methods for investigating the structure and texture of phenomenal objects.[36] And just as it is with things, so it is with trust. But, as we shall learn below, unlike material things, trust, which is a disposition of the soul, cannot in the same manner be objectively tested. Consequently, there is no sure criterion for ascertaining and guaranteeing the truth of the logos.

In a dialogue abstract thoughts manifest themselves through the spoken language. In the act of speaking thinking is externalised and becomes concrete. Once a statement is made, a name or word uttered, a definition given, their formerly implicit and indeterminate reference to the logos of truth becomes transparent and explicit. Thought and word are dialectically identical. Through speaking reason is mediated, but also mediates itself to itself as the unified self. The interlocutors approximate the logos through the dialectical movement of ever clearer, though mutually contingent, statements about it. As Plato admonishes and advises us: 'True belief with the addition of an account (logos) [is] knowledge, while belief without an account [is] outside its range. Where no account [is] given of a thing, it [is] not "knowable"'.[37] In other words, the logos requires the application to it of a dialectical method. Without this method the interlocutors will not be able to arrive at an agreement on the understanding of their object of deliberation.

Without the praxis of the dialogue the abstract word, for instance, is without a clarified content and hence remains meaningless. In this case, Plato lets one speaker say to the other, 'all that you and I possess in common is the name. The thing to which each of us gives that name we may perhaps have privately before our minds, but it is always desirable to have reached an agreement about the thing itself by means of explicit statements, rather than be content to use the same word without formulating what it means'.[38] 'Playing with words, but revealing nothing'[39] is not only likely to lead to a mutual misinterpretation of their signification, it also does not help the dialectic of the dialogue to develop coherently. It rather causes it to be stagnant. Lest, then, the dialogue loses itself in groundless chatter, the interlocutors, precisely because truth is not known, must nevertheless *dare* a definition of it.

To speak the logos is thus to dare within uncertainty to take a stance. It is to 'dare to assert' and to try the truth.[40] But because the logos is subject to differentiated accounts, the interlocutors seek to overcome and to reconcile the doubts about their respective statements. Due to the hierarchical structure of it, however, it is incumbent upon the listening philosopher to question the claims of his opinionated sophist. And it is in his own daring that a sincere concern for the logos is manifested.[41] He therefore reminds his partner that 'our whole conversation from the outset has been an inquiry after the nature of knowledge on the supposition that we did not know what it was ... Then, doesn't it strike you as shameless to explain what knowing is like, when we don't know what knowledge is?'.[42] The philosopher's courage is thus, unlike the one of his brazen fellow speaker, thoughtful. He takes the logos upon himself, responds to its dialectical requirement, and dares his responsibility for it.

Abstract language is pretentious and yet vacuous, static and sterile. The concreteness of expression, however, is in its development dynamic and daring. And it is in a dialogue, which makes language fluid, mediative and alive, that we can find their moderated unity. The meaning of the dared and asserted word is mediated to its logos through utterance. The duration of the dialogue is the *medius terminus* that develops between the interlocutors and the truth they seek to attain.

It is precisely because the dialectical essence of the spoken word is mediation that it can be challenged. If a word is mediated it means that the necessary meaning of it is conditioned by time. A contingent word, however, does not express truth, it merely attempts to do so. In the mediating act of the dialogue the word then *becomes* rather than is the logos. It comes about through the dialogue because it is dialectically mediated through (dia) its internal language (logos). Dialogic truth always assumes the shape of a result even though a defective one. And in dialectical parlance this means that it is merely correct but not true.

To question a statement or to give the logos of it is to bring its assumed unity into differentiation with itself in order then to bring it back to itself in a higher unity to which it belongs.

What is problematic in the logos is the tension between question and answer. Inherent in the definition of the word is its dialectical division. The word appears in its differentiation because its utterance exposes it to the critique by the interlocutor. Differentiation and contingency belong to the concretisation of the abstract issue. They are the presupposition of the dialogue.

Through questions and answers the dialogue demonstrates the many epistemic aspects of the word. Though 'knowledge taken in its entirety will seem to be a plurality in which this knowledge is unlike that',[43] the interlocutors undertake to bring such difference into harmony. 'For I imagine', writes the philosopher, 'we are not striving merely to secure a victory for my suggestions or for yours; rather we ought both of us to fight in support of the truth and the whole truth'.[44] Here we have a clear example of how in a dialogue the joint venture is teleologically conditioned, not only by the logos, but also by the friendly atmosphere which prevails in a dialogue. A merely competitive and contentious dispute does not know such a striving for the sake of finding universal truth.[45]

The plurality and differentiation of knowledge is the origin of *hope* within the dialogue. Though the dialectic guides it towards the home of truth, hope cannot be truth itself. The companions, because of their subjectivity, limp always behind the objectivity of truth. What they agree upon in the end is not of more than partial validity. But because of this there also opens the path of hope between the speakers and the truth. Truth is hoped-for truth, an image of that which can only be imagined.

Up to now we have described the dialogue in general terms, and we have interpreted some of its more salient features. What still needs to be discussed, however, is the way in which the art of dialectic manifests itself in the dialogue. It is to the question as to how *method* proves itself in application that we turn in the remaining pages of this section.

As we remarked above, the participants in a dialogue become dialecticians through their proper mastery of the art of questioning and answering. This art needs to be understood as a method. But a method, as we have likewise pointed out, proves its worth only in its application. How then does the dialectic of the Platonic dialogue work?

Let us note first with Hegel that it is often 'external' considerations which exercise an influence upon the dialectic.[46] The mind that seeks to determine its objects is applied to them from without. It thereby does not reflect itself but something else, that is, something on which it depends. It is not, says Hegel, a 'self-producing activity' of the mind.[47] It is in the language of dialectic externally conditioned consciousness without yet having historically achieved the notion of internally self-conditioned self-consciousness. The consequence of this is that, on the one hand, the philosopher's free knowledge, referred to earlier, is less than free, that is, it is contingent and, on the other, that the dialectic itself turns out to be defective. Thought that is unmediated in and through reflected nature and history remains unfree. The freedom of the mind exists only, to quote Hegel, 'in a return into itself; the undistinguished is the lifeless; the active, living, concrete universal is hence what inwardly distinguishes itself, but yet remains free in so doing'.[48]

Bearing this in mind, there are then basically two related ways in which the dialectic operates. The earlier method is the *synoptic* one, the other, the *diaeretic* approach which Plato develops at a later stage.

The first, the synoptic method, proceeds by reciprocally hypothesising or assuming the existence of an 'absolute' form or idea.[49] The architectonic movement consists in an ascending series of proposed definitions or names[50] of such universal oneness precisely because at the beginning of the discourse opinions are vague at most. It is the dimness of understanding which drives itself towards the endeavour to realise more adequate knowledge. In this striving, questions and answers will alternate until the highest agreeable assumption – and it is nothing more than an assumption – has been reached. Plato dismisses the dogmatist who recognises no need to question his one-sided propositions. This is even true of mathematicians who can only 'dream about what is', for they leave their hypotheses 'untouched' without giving an account of them.[51] But definitions of this sort are dialectically untenable and, therefore, must be subjected to critical evaluation. 'If anyone should fasten upon the hypothesis itself', he says, 'you would disregard him and refuse to answer until you could consider whether its consequences were mutually consistent or not. And when you had to substantiate the hypothesis itself, you would proceed in the same way, assuming whatever more ultimate hypothesis commended itself most to you, until you reached one which was satisfactory.'[52]

But what is satisfactory is not to be taken as a final and singular form of definition. What is satisfactory is not yet fully adequate. The task of the dialectical dialogue is to gain an 'insight into the community and relatedness of things'.[53] But the things Plato is talking about are not of an empirical or historical reality. These do not constitute the content of thoughts. What the philosopher ponders are words, representations of reality, thoughts, which the mind produces in the realm of ideas or forms.[54] It is the 'ideal', according to Hegel, which for Plato is 'the most real'.[55] His objects are the hypotheses of thinking and not their scientific application. Plato treats thoughts alone, 'making no use of anything sensed in any way, but using forms themselves, going through forms to forms, it ends in forms too'.[56] In this way he 'is able to separate out the *idea* of the good from all other things.[57] That the result is a plural instead of a singular means that the open-ended, though not boundless, dialogue brings into view at most an *aporia*, a problem, to which one can continuously address questions, but for which no solution can be found. Dialectic is directed against the form of the finite. And since the finite passes into its opposite, it is not what it is. The result therefore is, what Hegel calls, a 'negative' one.[58]

It is because of the hermeneutic openness of questions and the humbling lack of the one ultimate answer, that the dialectical method of the dialogue is also educational. As we have already mentioned, it provides a means for the inner eye to see and thus to comprehend things in a synopsis, in their speculative and perspectival coherence, for, as Hegel clarifies, 'it is left to speculative thought alone to bring the thoughts together'.[59]

Plato's thinking reflects a concern with the part-whole relationship and the question as to how the consciousness of representation can be raised from a level where it thinks particular thoughts to the level where it becomes aware of their internal relationship. This growth of consciousness is dialectical education. 'Education', he therefore teaches us, 'must be integrated into an overview which reveals the kinship of these studies with one another and with the nature of that which *is*'.[60] And 'the man who is capable of an overview is dialectical while the one who isn't, is not'.[61] The objective of the synoptic dialectic then is to find out whether or not some particular thoughts partake in their one and holistic thought, whether they cohere in the logos as a dialectical universal.

It is significant to point out that when Plato speaks about material things and immaterial thoughts, he does not really distinguish between them, but merges them into the part-whole description of a neutral something. For him hypotheses state 'that *something* is many and one, not that unity is many or that plurality is one'.[62] Plato's science deals with the nature of thought and not with thought about nature. More specifically, it treats universal ideas rather than particular empirical phenomena.

The second method, however, which Plato employs, that is, the diaeresis, can be regarded already as an early form of a more conceptual and didactic approach. This is also an approach which Aristotle will adopt, and from which he will develop the scientific tool of a logical organon for understanding particular areas of scientific discourse.

The issue of the synoptic and upward movement of participation is replaced by the downward specification of the form which assumes the status of the genus.[63] The Platonic diaeresis implies the notion of 'division' or the art of 'discerning and discriminating'.[64] It is also the beginning of the application of the dialogue to dissolving and rendering fluid the hypothesised and inferential unity of a word, definition, or form.

In the previous mode of dialectic Plato examined a methodical reflection upon questions which were directed *towards* answers. Now he initiates a method of investigating the elements of forms. He is interested in the nature of a more deductive inquiry which starts *from* answers. These answers, however, are already accepted as preliminary definitions or propositions. It is a movement not merely towards immediacy or the *genus*, but from it to its constitutive parts or *species*. While synoptic dialectic thinks things together, diaeretic dialectic thinks them apart in order then, however, to mediate them back into a deeper understanding of their original unity.

Accordingly, unlike the synoptic one, the diaeretic method itself consists of two procedures. One is the *synagogue* which is the way of bringing a 'dispersed plurality under a single form, seeing it all together – the purpose being to define so-and-so, and thus to make plain whatever may be chosen as the topic for exposition'; the other is *diaeresis* or the method which enables us to 'divide into forms'.[65]

The 'science of dialectic', says Plato now, is:

> dividing according to kinds . . . and the man who can do that discerns clearly *one* form everywhere extended throughout many, where each one lies apart, and *many* forms, different from one another, embraced from without by one form, and again *one* form connected in a unity through many wholes, and *many* forms, entirely marked off apart. That means how to distinguish, kind by kind, in what ways the several kinds can or cannot combine.[66]

Though Plato's is not yet a conceptual thinking in a strict sense,[67] the combination of kinds, however, suggests the living coherence between species and their genus, that is, their concrete wholeness. A unity is *concrete* when its *differentiae specificae* have *grown* into it *together* (*con-crescere*). And this relational movement from particulars to their unity indicates a 'speculative', that is, a positive result, even though, according to Hegel, it is produced on the basis of external reasoning alone.[68] The diaeresis then is not the formal, artificial and merely arbitrary carving up of something so that the individual parts have little meaningful relation to the whole. On the contrary, the connection between particulars and the universal must be seen in a communal sense, that is, in the sense of the living, of the organic, where species of necessity relate and belong to the genus since in themselves, apart and in isolation, they cannot subsist.

Thus to divide is not 'to hack off parts like a clumsy butcher'. Rather, by division we understand the species differentiation within a genus, that is, within a 'single natural body with its pairs of like-named members'.[69] The best way to divide a living body is to differentiate it 'into twin sections',[70] that is, 'where there is a real cleavage between specific forms. The section must always possess a specific form ... [It] is dangerous ... to chop reality up into small portions. It is always safer to go down the middle to make our cuts. The real cleavages among the forms are more likely to be found thus'.[71]

A genus is to be divided into species or members. It has no mechanical parts or portions. The living genus has natural sub-divisions which are necessarily linked to the body as a whole. The relationship between genus and species is that while a specific 'subdivision must necessarily also be a portion of the total class of which it is declared a subdivision ... the converse is not true since a portion is not necessarily a true subdivision'.[72] Thus the 'right method' is this: 'whenever it is the essential *affinity* between a given group of forms which the philosopher perceives on first inspection, he ought not to forsake his task until he sees clearly as many true differences as exist within the whole complex unity – the differences which exist in reality and constitute the several species'.[73]

We have said that a dialectically conducted dialogue is possible only when there are species differentiations, but that the meaning and the objective of the dialogue is to sublate such growth differentiations in the genus. The new dialogic agreement can therefore be understood as the dialectical reconciliation of internal differentiation.

Given the organic nature of forms, it is clear that the dialectical dialogue rests on the principle of the impossibility of there existing a formal contradiction within the idea of the living. 'It's plain', Plato states, 'that the same thing won't be willing at the same time to do or suffer opposites with respect to the same part and in relation to the same thing'.[74] This statement is very Hegelian in that it refers to the principle of the organic differentiation of that which is by nature dialectical. A fuller discussion of this, however, we must defer to later chapters.

Let us at this point, then, end our review of the Platonic dialogue and merely add a few concluding remarks. In diaeresis we have a logical criterion, that is, the downward movement from genus to species. This criterion implies the necessary immanence of deductive differentiation. We also concluded that there is no similar objective symbol for testing the dialectic in the dialogue of inductive hypotheses, in which the object was to gain an overview of forms. Because of its subjective circumstances this discourse remains contingent.

However, in both procedures a dialectical method is applied to the dialogue, and a Platonic dialogue is in its very nature contingent. There is no necessarily neutral reason why people should gather and enter into a dialogue. The language in it, for instance, which is to open up towards understanding and knowledge, is much more instrumental in character than an end in itself. Concrete truth, as Hegel suggests, is not only to be found in the dialectically practised ideality of the word, or for its own sake.[75] The function of the dialogue, therefore, as Habermas might want to supplement Hegel's critique of Plato, must itself perhaps be examined in terms of the *interests* which the participants bring into it and which also inform and contribute to its outcome.[76] Yet if a conversation does take place, it remains also conditioned by the subjectivity of trust, daring and responsibility. No matter how rational the method is held to be, its successful application depends on the effects of irrational elements which manifest themselves in mutual deliberations.[77] To be 'faithful' to the 'appointment'[78] that one wants to meet in order to speak sincerely with one another, or even the offering of the 'right penalty', namely, 'that he who strays from tune should be brought back to it',[79] are no absolutely certain criteria for an operative dialogue.

The willingness to discuss a problem, the preparedness to subject oneself to question and answer, are no guarantee that the new agreement is a true one. Nor can it be said to be logical according to a kind of diaeretic reasoning within which is brought together what has been separated. The dialectic of the dialogue cannot be objectively tested because the dialogue has no clear and immanent criterion of testing its method of giving and taking the logos of truth. It cannot demonstrate an advance into a lasting and accordant unity. Contrary to Plato's ontological intentions its result is defective and hence negative. It is what it was in the beginning, an opinion and not positive knowledge. As long as there is not laid down a premise regarded as true and primary, there cannot be expected an equally necessary epistemic conclusion. But this is what Aristotle will demand in his rational attempt to overcome the one-sidedness of Plato's external thoughts.

With Plato, however, begins the speculative dialectic, the method to determine more fully and more concretely the transcendent and holistic forms which subjective consciousness posits. And yet these external object determinations are produced as pure abstractions and thus remain empty. It is only when dialectical thinking has, with Hegel, become the 'activity of self-reflection',[80] and has passed through its own particular stages of historical development, that it will be truly concrete and therewith also positive. Though Plato's dialectic is devoid of the reflective history of the subject and is for this reason incomplete, it contains, Hegel comments, already at least the 'source' of the concretisation to come.[81] This concretisation will be the subject's communal comprehension of itself in and through its history which is its immanent object of reflection.

But the dialogue does not come to an end with the development of historical dialectic. As we shall see towards the end of our discussion of Hegel's philosophy, the continuing necessity to reflect upon humanity and the difficult practice of its never certain dialogic realisation is rather reinforced in a time where the idea of nuclear war suggests the possibility of the mutual annihilation of its interlocutors and thus of the negation of their effort to preserve the life of mankind.

In conclusion, therefore, it may be equally necessary to counsel that if, in general, a whole is likely to be adversely affected by the activities of its parts, an educated awareness of the intellectual uncertainty we have discussed ought to precede any irresponsible attempt to force the premature expectations of such particular actions. This inference concerning the part-whole relationship, which we can now also restate as the dialectical relationship between practice and thinking, is clearly justified through our interpretation of Plato's wisdom and sense of moderation. It is not a plea for inaction but for a dialogue that conscientiously seeks to reflect upon the ultimate consequences of our praxis.

ARISTOTLE'S DIALECTICAL DEDUCTION

Dialectic is a pre-philosophical method of discourse which is employed for establishing the working principles of the various empirical sciences. Unlike Plato, who identifies dialectic itself with a holistic philosophy, Aristotle reduces its applicability to particular scientific judgments. The reason for this demotion of the logos is to be found in the distinction between ontology and an organon, or between metaphysical forms and logical functions. While the development of the former propositions is furthered by historical reflections, the latter are said to be premises which are not vulnerable to dialogic questioning. Instead, their logical status is regarded as being necessary.

In order to clarify Aristotle's attitude towards dialectic, we shall first situate it in its historical context. As we have seen in the previous section, Plato discusses dialectic only in relation to transcendent forms. Aristotle, however, sees in it a distinct mode of concrete historical development. This will be followed by a description of the difference between dialectic and demonstrative deductions and by an appraisal of Aristotle's disregard of dialectic. A few pertinent comments by Hegel on Aristotle will sum up this section.

But as in the case with Plato, so behind the account of Aristotle lies a concern that goes beyond the immediacy of our limited analysis of his understanding of reasoning. The implication of Aristotle's theoretical concept of science is that the application of thinking results in the fragmentation of the life-world. Yet this means, more importantly, that scientific thinking itself is no longer involved with gaining a holistic grasp of the philosophical meaning of man's status in the environment which he apperceives. We believe, however, that our time is in need precisely of a mode of dialogic reflection which relates scientific reasoning to that which its practical employment can destroy in the nuclear age, namely, the life-world and all that it embodies. It is with this reading in mind that we regard Aristotle's treatises as containing the seed of a problem which has become ever greater in the course of the scientification of man's life-world.

Let us begin, then, with Aristotle's view of history and its implication for scientific thinking. Aristotle interprets history (historia) as a cyclical continuum of natural manifestations.[1] The cycle is a process of generation and destruction,[2] for 'there is an order of all things, and every time (that is, every life) is measured by a period'.[3] The idea of history implies change which takes place in law-like fashion, and the natural history of man is no exception to this. Thus historical research is an attempt to understand the static though recurring patterns of natural events.

One of such phenomena is man's effort to preserve the life of his body, whose function is determined by the continuous sameness of needs and their satisfaction. This eternal phenomenon, which expresses itself and is practised within some form of institutional arrangement, drives him to invent the arts and sciences requisite for it. But, in addition, other things are created which help satisfy lesser needs. It is true indeed, writes Aristotle, that scientific discoveries and political institutions 'have been invented several times over in the course of ages . . . for necessity may be supposed to have taught men the inventions which were absolutely required, and when these were provided, it was natural that other things which would adorn and enrich life should grow up by degrees'.[4]

But not only observable physical and biological occurrences have a cycle. The nature of intellectual and theoretical activities as well is characterised by a similar regularity. An inquiry into the past, for instance, makes plain that 'the same ideas . . . recur in men's mind not once or twice but again and again'.[5]

However, it is of fundamental importance to realise that, apart from the cyclical formation of ideas, there is also a progressive development of them. A discovery, for example, may continue to be of value for subsequent generations and thus establish for them a tradition. But the ideas handed down are attempted answers to a different sort of question. They transcend the immediacy of needs and refer to the perennial endeavour to find ultimate truths. Aristotle tells us that 'our forefathers in the most remote ages have handed down to their posterity a tradition'[6] of questions and answers concerning the origin of the universe. The dialogue which evolves around this issue leads thus to the socio-historical transition of cognitively more refined explanations. The difference, then, between, on the one hand, the natural and static and, on the other, the intellectual and dynamic needs of man is this: 'while probably each art and science has often been developed as far as possible and has again perished, these opinions have been preserved like relics until the present. Only thus far, then, is the opinion of our ancestors and our earliest predecessors clear to us'.[7] Theoretical knowledge (theoria) of that which supports all praxis develops within a tradition of question and answer.

Though even when natural necessities have been overcome with the employment of practical means, the theoretical questions about the origin of cyclical phenomena and their truthful essence persist. New and clearer ideas are added to the inadequate opinions of the past. Knowledge thus increases; or, to be more precise, since it is subject to historical mediation, episteme becomes knowledge of knowledge. It is not a fixed view of the world. Insight grows gradually with better defined concepts of reasoning and understanding. It is this kind of knowledge which Aristotle calls philosophy. And philosophy is science of *first principles*. 'It is right also', he says, 'that philosophy should be called knowledge of the truth. For the end of theoretical knowledge is truth, while that of practical knowledge is action (for even if they consider how things are, practical men do not study what is eternal, but what stands in some relation at some time)'.[8] And what dominates the present of man is first the need to sustain his life.

Theoretical knowledge, which occupies itself with pure thought, is not in the same way guided by necessity but by 'the accounts and the causes' in the sense of the stable and unaffected 'good and that for the sake of'.[9] 'In the silent regions of thought', adds Hegel in this context, 'which has come to itself and communes only with itself, the interests which move the lives of races and individuals are hushed'.[10] Comprehending the telos is not a practical science of production. And yet, according to Aristotle, the earliest philosophers progressed, for they 'advanced little by little' in their effort to transform the wonderment of seeing into the tranquility of philosophical thinking.[11] Consequently, its acquisition 'must in a sense end in something which is the opposite of our original inquiries', it must end in a 'better state' of understanding.[12] Therefore, epistemological learning is not a circular movement; it develops with groping curiosity.

But the historical progression of knowledge is not knowledge itself, it is not identical with it. The voyage towards truth is a philosophically reflective activity and not a historiographic or fact-finding one that only passively applies its theoretical tools. Whatever is established in that history, however, is merely suggestive of truth, but is not truth itself. 'No one', Aristotle cautions the all-too-zealous and dogmatic minds, 'is able to attain the truth adequately, while, on the other hand, no one fails entirely, but every one says something true about the nature of things, and while individually they contribute little or nothing to the truth, by the union of all a considerable amount is amassed'.[13] Thus, while we can acquire a particular part of it, the whole truth, however, poses great problems.

An inquiry into the historical development of the diverse though cognitively enriched opinions about truth is helpful for understanding philosophical questions which, for Aristotle, are actually those of the sciences. It is instrumental for it 'because the ability to puzzle on both sides of a subject will make us detect more easily the truth and error about the several points that arise' in the attempt to define concepts.[14] Questions and answers may point out the argumentative difficulties that are involved in the search for true propositions. But what kind of difficulty is Aristotle talking about?

Not unlike Plato, Aristotle states that the answer to the question of truth or falsehood depends on the right or wrong way of articulating the genus and the species of individual things, things which are not, however, teleologically related to anything superior. In other words, it depends on the way one applies the diaeretic principle of combination and separation. Yet this is an activity of the subjective mind and its faculty of judgment. 'The combination and the separation are in thought and not in the things', that is, the question and answer of truth is 'some affection of the thought'.[15] And he, concludes Aristotle, 'who thinks the separated to be separated and the combined to be combined has the truth, while he whose thought is in a state contrary to that of the objects is in error'.[16] It is thus in the correspondence relationship between the inquiring subject and its object of cognition that the pursuit of truth becomes problematic. Aristotle, however, clarifies the difficulty by deciding that it 'is not in the facts but in us'.[17] An opinion about the truth is merely an opinion, and a partial one at that precisely because it depends historically upon previous dialogic reflections. And among the people who have advanced ideas in this manner are 'those whose opinions we may share, but also those who have expressed more superficial views; for these also contributed something, by developing before us the powers of thought'.[18]

The attainment of truth thus involves two procedures which are ranked according to their functions. One is the establishment of a method of inquiry into the basic propositions of science, the other is the systematically formulated knowledge of an object on the basis of the application of these primary terms. But Aristotle contends further that conclusive thinking presupposes the prior communal acceptance of such theoretical assumptions for they are the origin of all coherent reasoning. In other words, 'one must be already trained to know how to take each sort of argument, since it is absurd to seek at the same time knowledge and the way of attaining knowledge; and neither is easy to get'.[19] Hence, before dealing directly with the problems of a particular science, Aristotle seeks to establish the scientific working-principles.[20] What he is saying is that while the problem of the natural law of things is to be settled in the last analysis by the direct examination of the things concerned, the issue of how to investigate them, however, turns on difficulties related to ratiocination. But unlike the sameness of nature, the intellect is ever more enriched through its dialogic tradition.

The subjective search for objective knowledge implies then not only the application of underlying presuppositions of inquiry, but, more fundamentally, a method with which these epistemological principles can be established in the first place. This amounts to what Aristotle calls the crucial 'difference between arguments from and those to the first principles'.[21] Arguments *to* principles are historically conditioned and consequently inconclusive, those *from* principles are not. The former are pre-scientific deliberations, the latter are scientific and therefore truly philosophical judgments. But it is nonetheless with the tradition that scientific questions are first approached and formulated. 'While we must begin with what is familiar', Aristotle explains, 'things are so in two ways – some to us, some without qualification. Presumably, then, *we* must begin with things familiar to *us*'.[22] And we must commence with them not only because in human language they are intrinsic to us, but also because they are the theoretical devices for practising science. Hegel makes the same point when he says that though things may be familiar to us in perception they are not for that reason already 'cognitively understood'.[23]

It is the historical acquaintance with the way others have tried to define scientific presuppositions which allows for the establishment of principles which the scientist subsequently applies without questioning them any further. Aristotle writes accordingly that:

> when the objects of an inquiry, in any department, have principles, causes, or elements, it is through acquaintance with these that knowledge and understanding [are] attained. For we do not think that we know a thing until we are acquainted with its primary causes or first principles, and have carried our analysis as far as its elements. Plainly, therefore, in the science of nature too our first task will be to try to determine what relates to principles.
>
> The natural way of doing this is to start from things which are more knowable and clear to us and proceed towards those which are clearer and more knowable by nature; for the same things are not knowable relatively to us and knowable without qualification. So we must follow this method and advance from what is more obscure by nature, but clearer to us, towards what is more clear and more knowable by nature.[24]

But, as it will turn out, the natural way is not only the method of eliminating the dialogic differences so that science can be founded on the basis of universally agreed propositions.[25] Aristotle, in his quest for truth, will almost disregard the historical method altogether, and supplement if not supplant it with a form of scientific judgment whose internal logic he considers proven.

It is this all-important distinction between *from* and *to* principles, between logic and history, which can also be expressed in terms of demonstrative science or philosophy, on the one hand, and of dialectic, on the other. While both are deductive methods,[26] their truth-related purpose, however, differs. Science is said to demonstrate conclusively but in a one-sided way its first principles.[27] In this it foreshadows the axioms of modern positivism. Dialectic may also seek to account for such principles but, because of its dual nature of giving answers and questioning them, it argues against their assumed objectivity as well. For dialectic nothing simply is, but everything remains in a state of *becoming* other than what it is understood to be. And this, by implication, means that dialectic is rather 'critical where philosophy claims to know'.[28] Thus, while for Plato the dialectician and the philosopher are identical, Aristotle rather rejects this identification. Philosophy must be put into a fixed position from where it can secure knowledge. And only a syllogistically rigorous science, which brings formal mediation to a close, offers this certainty. Dialectic, as we have seen in our discussion of Plato, ends up only with knowledge which is problematic. But it is this which elevates dialectic to a philosophy of thinking. Science, on the other hand, arrests the effort of reflective thinking. It locks and then applies the thought concepts which reflection has produced.

At the same time a connection does exist between the two in the sense that science is grounded in philosophy. There is no demonstration in theoretical science without prior dialectic,[29] for, as Aristotle himself states, dialectic is essentially a 'process of criticism wherein lies the path to the principles of all inquiries',[30] that is, of those that deal with demonstrative proofs. This is the value which dialectic uniquely possesses.[31] Its goal is to find the methodological foundations which are the necessary starting points for the scientific investigation into the question of how things are. This cannot be done by science itself since it must always reason *from* and not *to* its own foundations. Demonstration, by contrast, is that method which teaches how objects of nature are in essence. Hence, in the order of things, the aim of demonstrative analysis originates in the dialectical reflections upon its explanatory assumptions. Though Aristotle concedes this much, he justifies knowledge claims demonstratively only, and leaves dialectic behind.

Accordingly, being in this way separated, demonstration and dialectic do not make the same kind of propositions, either. Science begins with a demonstrative and didactic proposition. This differs from a dialectical and interrogative one, 'because a demonstrative proposition is the assumption of one of two contradictory statements (the demonstrator does not ask for his premise, but lays it down), whereas a dialectical proposition depends on a choice between two contradictories'.[32] While the demonstrator asserts truth or falsehood, the dialectician can argue both sides and therefore finds them at most plausible. Scientific propositions are said to be objective premises, while those of the dialectical dialogue remain subjective questions and answers.

Furthermore, a proposition is a 'demonstration, when the premises from which the deduction starts are true and primitive . . .; and it is a dialectical deduction, if it reasons from reputable opinions'.[33] Now, 'things are true and primitive which are convincing on the strength not of anything else but of themselves; for in regard to the first principles of science it is improper to ask any further for the why and whereof of them'.[34] Opinions, on the other hand, are not apodictic in this sense, they express no obvious necessity. Rather, they are only propositions which are accepted either 'by all, or by the majority, or by the most notable and reputable of them'.[35] This amounts to saying that a demonstration is true in and of itself, and not because of an opinion, no matter how enlightened it may be.

The class of scientists who investigate natural phenomena on the firm basis of premises are those who work with mathematical units.[36] These more than any other kind of proposition adequately reflect reality. A mathematical proposition is an immediate one, and an 'immediate proposition is one to which there is no other prior'.[37] In other words, if the premise of a syllogism is held to be true and primitive like a mathematical term, the demonstration develops as a logical 'deduction from what is necessary'.[38]

Because of the epistemological importance he plays, Aristotle places the mathematician at the top of philosophy, unlike Plato, who puts him below the dialectician. For Plato the model for philosophy is dialectic, for Aristotle it is demonstration. Mathematics for Plato cannot fully construct knowledge of metaphysical reality. But Aristotle sees in its technique of inference the very paradigmatic framework for all epistemological inquiries into the individual natural and physical realities.[39] Dialectical propositions are therefore held to be philosophically inferior to the demonstrative premises.

Hence Aristotle is only consistent when he does not mention ontology or metaphysics as one of the purposes of dialectic.[40] In his *topical* work he nowhere alludes to first philosophy as a science of supreme principles.[41] Instead he declares that it is employed in relation to the 'principles used in the several sciences'.[42] The idea of a dialectically thought-out transcendent unity has been replaced with the logical description of a manifold of judgments about empiricial research areas. For Aristotle the Platonic type of heuristic dialectic can serve at most as a propaedeutic of philosophy, but cannot be philosophy itself.[43]

What one must conclude from this perspective of dialectic is that it has suffered an almost appalling loss of status.[44] Plato, we may recall, thought it to be the synthetic 'art of weaving', the 'kingly art'.[45] Yet his successor dethrones this ideal and reduces its role to that of a handmaid to the analytical sciences.[46]

Aristotelian dialectic, like Plato's, is concerned with opinions which are expressed in the intersubjective practice of the dialogue. But with dialogic dialectic itself one cannot operate scientifically and with a view to satisfying empiricial knowledge claims.

Plato regards dialectic as indeed the only method that promises the transformation of opinion not into empirical but into metaphysical knowledge. Aristotle critically suspects that it cannot accomplish this. The method of dialectic is therefore defective and its goal unattainable because it creates only epistemological illusions. True science, however, is analytic and leads to deductively necessary conclusions. And such a 'deduction is a discourse', writes Aristotle, 'in which, certain things being stated, something other than what is stated follows of necessity from their being so'; that is to say, 'no further term is required from without in order to make the consequence necessary'.[47] Thus the above-mentioned little advances that opinions make in the course of their history, but which cannot go beyond their epistemological limitation, are now superseded by the logic of ahistorical syllogisms. It is with the introduction of a minor middle premise that a proposition is incontrovertibly mediated and, therefore, advanced to its proof.[48] With reference to such a logical structure and to such a structure alone can truth be said to be self-contained.

The dialectical method is the procedure of *diaeresis* whose purpose is to establish definitions for scientific activities. A definition, as we have said earlier, is arrived at through a reflection upon a genus and its *differentiae specificae*. But, Aristotle argues, 'dialecticians seldom address their inquiries to these by themselves'.[49] What he means is that the Platonic dialectic is mainly concerned with diaeresis in relation to ontological questions. Yet the limited role Aristotle assigns to it is merely that which examines the internal logical compatibilities of definitions alone.

Consequently, and true to his scrutinising spirit, Aristotle uses the disputational *topoi*, or points of dialectical argument, against those Platonists who posit 'ideas'.[50] According to the instruction that 'the one should be made into many',[51] he employs them for destructive rather than constructive purposes.[52] While negatively dialectic can demolish claims to knowledge, positively it is unable itself to produce it.[53] But, as if this were not already damaging enough, and as we have just elaborated, Plato's expectations concerning dialectical designations are subjected to an even more rigorous treatment through the logical test of demonstrative reasoning. After all, Aristotle lectures: 'Those people are silly who think they get their principles correctly if the proposition is reputable and true ... For it is not what is reputable or not that is a principle, but what is primitive in the genus about which the proof is; and not every truth is appropriate'.[54] What is asserted in dialectic and in demonstration are thus two different things. An argument in the former remains open-ended, scientific reasoning in the latter terminates in proof.

Plato's vertical diaeresis discusses the hierarchy and relations of metaphysical forms. His philosophy is the logos of universality. It is concerned with the question of the whole. In Aristotle the empirico-scientific version of division is dealt with from a purely functional and horizontal point of view. His philosophy is the logic of individuality or of parts. Its subject matter are the mundane sciences and the principles proper to them. In other words, what Aristotle has taken over from Plato is the logical scaffolding of the diaeresis, not at all the ontological or metaphysical edifice that is to be erected with the language of the dialogue.[55] It is then not a coincidence either that he does not express himself through the medium of the dialogue but, instead, expounds a theoretical 'treatise' about it.[56]

Aristotle's formal interpretation of dialectical diaeresis also betrays a rather liberal attitude towards the purpose of philosophy as he understands it. Its scientific nature is now restricted to classificatory inquiries into, or the consistent ordering of, natural phenomena. With this he has quite clearly changed the original meaning of diaeresis. The Platonic diaeresis tries to describe the complex structure of holistic being, the idea of the unity of *ontos*, or of that which generally underlies all the sciences. Aristotle drastically severs the link between analytical logic and synthetic ontology. His scientific thinking treats the parts rather than the whole. The kinship between the one and highest form and the many forms partaking in it is now completely secularised into the preoccupation with a multitude of *material substances* and skills which are no longer mediated and harmonised with one another.[57]

But Aristotle has not only relegated the dialectical diaeresis. He has equally abandoned the principle of its organic division. This division suggests the belonging of members to a more coherently developed idea of unity. In the abstract Platonic scheme it is connected with the 'nurturing of living creatures', and as such stands for the 'structure of reality'.[58] The species are the lower *differentiae* of the highest and ideal genus. Aristotle, however, does not discuss species in relation to anything transcendent. Species and genus do not form an organic but a 'numerical unity',[59] which is the technical expression of a concrete and empirical order rather than an answer to man's deeper metaphysical queries. Thus, while Plato's dialogic questioning keeps the logos of the forms fluid, in Aristotle's treatise the logical relations between concepts begin to harden. They are already the answers which have been widely accepted as such. Rigid principles are dominant in the realm of theoretical science. It is here also that we find an attempt to formulate an *autonomous logic*,[60] a logic which is fully developed only with the discovery of the laws of syllogisms.[61]

Aristotle is sceptical about the ontological forms as separate cognitive objects. And yet he, too, as we have seen, believes in true and primitive principles which are placed at the top of scientific deductions. The original Platonic intention of an ideal philosophy is thus preserved, even though in largely modified form.[62] To this ideal he must hold fast, 'for to demonstrate anything is impossible unless one begins with the appropriate principles'.[63] But since these, in turn, are based on the opinions of the 'wise',[64] one must conclude rather disappointingly that demonstrative knowledge itself is at most just that – a wise opinion. The first principles of the philosophy of science are merely 'assumed'[65] to be true, but not known to be so. And in this, Aristotle's enterprise does in the end not differ from Plato's. Scientific research has to start from somewhere, but this does not mean that its premises ought to be regarded as self-evident. Both, ontology and formal logic, are determined by the dialectic of the dialogue and neither is, strictly speaking, proved or demonstrated independently of it. Demonstrative premises, like dialectical propositions, are theoretical research criteria. But since, as rational objects, they are externally posited by a community of deliberating subjects, their epistemological claims with respect to an intellectual advance remains questionable. This has particular weight. It is not clear at all, and Aristotle does not seem to show, how the *first principles* of science, which are approached in the dialectical manner, can in fact contribute to the study of the sciences.[66] It could be argued, for instance, that demonstrative principles do not only not refer to transcendent objects, but that they do not relate directly to those of nature and historical appearances either, but only to themselves. What they lack, in other words, is, according to Hegel's discussion of Aristotle's logic, an empirical content.[67]

It is therefore small wonder that Kant critically remarks, as well, that the general logic of the ancients, 'which is merely a *canon* of judgment, has been employed as if it were an *organon* for the actual production of at least the semblance of objective assertions, and thus has been misapplied. General logic, when thus treated as an organon, is called *dialectic*'.[68] But this dialectic is nothing but a 'logic of illusion', a logic whose method uses 'its *topic* to conceal the emptiness of its pretensions'.[69] Such a logic, however, Kant maintains, 'teaches us nothing whatsoever regarding the content of knowledge, but lays down only the formal conditions of agreement with the understanding'.[70] Demonstration, then, leads to less than a proof.

Formal dialectic itself, by virtue of its cognitive restriction, does not promise true knowledge. Though its method is diaeretic, it is used merely as the preliminary to the various scientific inquiries. With respect to the latter it is interesting to note also that Aristotle frequently refers to science in the plural rather than in the singular, because he believes that the knowledge of everything cannot be 'the province of any single study; for possibly the sciences are infinite in number, so that obviously demonstrations may be infinite too'.[71]

This pluralistic conception leads inevitably to the principle of *departmentalism*.[72] There is something intellectually disturbing about this fragmentation and the shift of emphasis from the ideal of the educational university into an instructive multiversity, as it were. Common sense obscures holistic vision. And it has its own portentous consequences which do not at all make obsolete the quest for more coherent and reflective thinking about the premises and purposes of science. For once, it is difficult to assess the relevance of the individual subjects in relation to one another. But, from a dialogic point of view, the general implications of this disintegration are still more far-reaching. Who or what choses the problems to be discussed with respect to the consequences scientific activities have for man? Is this answer decided by one interlocutor, is it the result of an accord between partners, or is it even imposed upon them from without?[73] External necessity could alter the free unfolding of the dialogue. And in this connection it has rightly been commented and judiciously advised, with an implicit reference to both antiquity and modernity, that while there may be no limit to man's capacity for separating and departmentalising subjects, it is pertinent from time to time to wonder how far the subjects themselves can endure such departmentalising without suffering damage in their substance.[74] And this task may perhaps have to be assigned to a philosophically holistic dialectic which, in the mould of Hegelian wisdom, comprehends and sublates at least the spirit of the Platonic sincerity of dialogue and the Aristotelian clarity of demonstrations.

With Aristotle dialectic, when interpreted with respect to the pluralistic sciences, has turned into a mode of intellectual training which lacks an overall direction. Not being situated in a mediating and binding framework, it runs the risk of deteriorating into eristic or contentious argumentation for its own sake. This, however, needs to be qualified in the sense that Aristotle's dialectic does seek to secure individual propositions for the sciences. A dialectic that aimed only at converting arguments could hardly show a great philosopher's ideas in the making.[75] At the same time, it is equally the case that while for Plato dialectic belongs to the one single science of philosophy that covers everything, for Aristotle it contents itself with being 'no definite science' at all,[76] thereby also covering everything but in another sense. Though it creates no dome of comprehension, the method of dialectic begins to assume the status of universal applicability. 'All men', Aristotle writes, 'attempt to discuss statements and to maintain them, to defend themselves and to attack others'.[77] But this is for him an almost trivial observation which has no resemblance to the exact exposition of a syllogism whose compelling judgment is mediated formal logic.

Dare we say that no conclusions are conclusive? And least of all those that fall through the vacuity of instrumental reasoning about subjective propositions which are devoid of any natural or historical content? Though the 'critical philosophy' of antiquity, Hegel chimes in with Kant, has 'turned metaphysics into logic', its determinations are given an essentially 'subjective significance', with the result, however, that such a philosophy remains 'burdened with the object' it has avoided.[78] In order to overcome this one-sidedness, he suggests therefore that one brings to bear upon reflection the 'speculative proposition',[79] with the intention of revising and sublating the separation of the logic of scientific method from the art of engaging in the logos, that is, in the dialectical dialogue.[80]

According to Hegel, a proposition is rooted in history, and it is the task of speculative philosophy to work out the concrete insight into this history. True recognition is historical and is mediated through the medium of language. But it is precisely the exclusion of dialectic from demonstration which renders Aristotle's apparently rigorous philosophy of science itself problematic. It deals with a series of independent judgments only, without ever bringing them into a unity.[81] Individually, however, these judgments have 'little truth'.[82] Speculative thinking seems to be nonsensical to the logician. But, as Hegel critically remarks, 'once the dialectic has been separated from proof, the notion of philosophical demonstration has been lost'.[83]

Hegel, therefore, argues that Aristotle's logic 'really requires recasting, so that all his determinations should be brought into a necessary systematic whole – not a systematic whole which is correctly divided into parts, and in which no part is forgotten, all being set forth in their proper order, but one in which there is one living organic whole, in which each part is held to be a part, and the whole alone as such is true'.[84] And in the Hegelian philosophical scheme, as we shall see, this whole is the dialectic of history itself which in its full concretion sublates all formal judgments.

Let us in conclusion to this section reiterate what we have said at the outset, namely that with Aristotle begins the theoretical particularisation of philosophical holism and the formation of primary principles of the sciences. These, however, remain unmediated to one another because reasoning according to rational precepts is fundamentally analytical. It separates what history alone holds together dialectically. If interpreted in the light of the question of what is at stake in the nuclear age, then this approach to reflection has obviously much wider but today also more ominous implications. For not only does scientific thought tend to break the thinking towards harmony – with the scattered pieces it may even destroy its memory.

SUMMARY

Dialectical thinking is concerned with the articulation of the part-whole relationship as it reveals itself within the dialogue. It is in antiquity, according to Hegel, that philosophers first become familiar with this issue and analyse its theoretical implications. The *aporia*, which the subjective Platonic dialogue necessarily results in, leads Aristotle to restrict its applicability to the, however, no less problematic establishment of objectively held scientific propositions which are to precede the various forms of deductive reasoning.

The wedge of analytical rationality that is slowly driven into the idea of metaphysical holism splits it up completely in modernity and replaces it with a theoretical examination of fragmented empirical research areas. The false consciousness of such particularistic intelligence rejects the idea of meaningful purpose and intellectual coherence. It is to the dialectical argument of modern theories of science that we now turn.

2 Modernity

The purpose of this chapter is to discuss the modern legacy of the ancient mode of dialectical thinking. What we have to consider is the problem of dialectical movement as it exhibits itself in three different though related theories of science. We thematise their respective assumptions partly because the modern self-image of man is increasingly determined by his scientific dissection of the natural and social world. But our approach is justified also on the ground that the aim of analytical inquiries is of a particularistic, practical and experimental nature. The scope of knowledge which can be obtained is thus limited, if not even defective. The tradition of the search for holistically epistemological reflections is given little credence in a thoroughly scientificated life-world.

The way in which the Aristotelian view of objective science is modified by modern dialectical methods exemplifies this significantly Hegelian critique of a fragmented and unmediated intellectual culture. Attempts to theoreticise scientific activities such as Popper's seemingly serious falsification theory, Kuhn's already paranoid paradigms, and Feyerabend's incoherent but all the more dadaistic anarchism attest to the breakdown not only of the idea of a rational system of knowledge, but also of the dissolution of a consistent method to arrive at cognitive understanding. That Feyerabend professes that this liberation from investigative strictures is medicine for epistemology merely begs the question as to what is to be healed. What is at stake in the nuclear age, and what is therefore entrusted as an assignment to thinking, is an ecumenical whole. It is the subject mankind and its global environment. Yet this is an idea which the playfulness with theories of science is adverse to contemplate. The anarchical attitude, like the paradigmatic and positivistic ones, is unable to comprehend the humanisation of eschaton. But in our inquiries into the internal functioning of theories and their application we shall suggest that we must engage in a Hegelian-inspired holistic thinking about the subject. For otherwise the fractured relationship between the subject mankind and its scientific objects and their technological employment cannot be healed and reconciled. In universal death, which could well turn out to be the consequence of such a failure to reflect, no harmony is recognised.

While it is acknowledged that the scientific conceptions under consideration merit a much broader analysis than can here be attempted, their brief treatment, however, will at least point at a variety of philosophical problems which they pose for dealing with the last things mankind is confronted with.

POPPER'S OBJECTIVE DIALECTIC OF FALSIFICATION

Dialectic is a theoretical method whose negative principle of falsification is applied to the problem of the teleological growth of scientific knowledge. Epistemological claims, however, are weakened by their tentative nature.

In this exposé we shall outline Popper's own method of explanatory deductive reasoning, and discuss his problematic interpretation of Hegel's dialectic. Some thoughts about the implications of his positivistic theory of science for the life-world of man and for the idea of war will end the section. Our concern with the latter, in particular, is affected by Popper's alienating concept of falsification which permits of no holistic reflection.

Concerning the theoretical argument, let us point out that for Popper the base of scientific method is no longer taken to be a system which derives its legitimacy from merely accepted but also asserted premises or axioms. 'There can be no ultimate statements in science', he says, 'there can be no statements in science which cannot be tested, and therefore none which cannot in principle be refuted'.[1]

In Aristotle, as we have seen, the dialectic of the dialogue is positively employed for establishing scientific propositions which are then, without any rational justification, simply laid down as given premises for demonstrative scientific deductions. Unlike the ancient, Popper uses the rational logic of a negative dialectic in order to dissolve just such premises.

At the end of a long tradition of epistemological research, these primary concepts came to be formulated, as in the case of Carnap, for instance, in terms of so-called empirical protocol sentences which were held to be irrefutable.[2] It is to the claims of the logical positivist that Popper initially addresses himself. He declares that the problem of scientific principles or of metaphysics can be reformulated into the problem of scientific method.[3] That is to say, that theory has to prove itself in practice. The procedure is to clarify the ontological status of observation statements. Since sense experiences always take place against the background of conjectures, or are cognitively unified only 'in the light of theories',[4] it is the knowledge claim inherent in such hypotheses which must be subjected to critical and even falsifying tests. It is this practical and dynamic method which transforms the tradition of static models.[5] A premise is no longer a given but has become a task, a problem for epistemological inquiries.

But if formal logic of reasoning can yield only a problem, the question 'on what does our "knowledge" rest?' seems to be irrelevant, and we must instead ask: 'how do we test scientific statements by their deductive consequences?'[6] Popper denies the possibility of conclusive inductions, and he replaces it with a 'deductive modus tollens'.[7] This method teaches us that though we are 'not justified in reasoning from an instance to the truth of the corresponding law . . . we "are" justified in reasoning from a counterinstance to the *falsity* of the corresponding universal law'.[8] However, though this approach rests on the decisive criterion of 'negative instances',[9] Popper concedes that, just as no theory can be positively constructed on the basis of observation statements, as is maintained by Carnap,[10] a theory cannot be 'conclusively disproved', either.[11] Theories, whatever their provenance, must remain 'tentative forever', for they contain no absolutely certain or demonstrative knowledge.[12]

Consequently, if one wants to retain a criterion of scientific objectivity, it can no longer be found in either premises or conclusions. Objectivity now develops within an activity which is the refutation of theories through a falsifying experience. From the point of view of Popper's general logic of methodology, experience has therefore a negatively restricting and not a positively expanding function. This critical aspect is reminiscent of Kant's employment of the principle of the *a priori*, not as a doctrine, but as a transcendental critique of reason. The purpose of this critique is 'not to extend knowledge, but only to correct it'.[13] In other words, the critique of transcendent knowledge claims is a reflective act of transcendental subjectivity.[14]

But Popper goes further than Kant's theoretical questioning. His practical method of falsification is not only to be a criterion of demarcation from the claims of an objective reason, but also from the *a priori* categories of the subjective understanding. Experiences are not synthesised by presupposed categories. The static term category itself is now of a different meaning, namely, that from which one can posit at most tentative hypotheses. And because such hypotheses are devoid of any *a priori* givenness, they have no objective validity.

They can be infinitely criticised, overthrown and replaced with better ones. It is the method which 'destroys, changes and alters'.[15] Transcendental synthesis thus loses its formerly dogmatic associations. Since the object theory and the subject that posits it are now dissolved into indeterminacy, Popper argues for an alternative approach to understanding a subjectively arrived at objectivity. The one method of philosophy can only be 'rational discussion'.[16] In other words, objectivity does not lie in fixed foundations but flows as movement.

The renunciation of a rationally rigorous objectivity and the recognition of objectivity as movement suggest the possibility of a directed growth of knowledge. For Popper the method of falsification is not an end in itself. It functions as a means towards an end. Popper claims that science is in need to grow, in need to progress, and 'it is the way of its growth which makes science rational and empirical'.[17] And he adds that this ideal of the growth of knowledge is a 'historical idea'.[18] Knowledge is knowledge only of knowledge, that is, it is based upon previous knowledge. It implies a teleological movement towards the approximation of truth or verisimilitude.[19] Why this should be so, however, remains unexplained. Nonetheless, long after the positivistic approach to understanding science was propounded, Popper simply situates this goal in a Platonic-like 'third world' whose 'autonomous' status he describes as a 'theory of the Objective Spirit'.[20] The objective spirit is to comprise scientific theories and other intellectual constructs. By the approximation of truth is not meant a genetic accumulation of knowledge. Rather, by the elimination of non-viable hypotheses the logical content of knowledge alone is said to be continuously enriched until it corresponds to its ideal of non-contradiction.[21] Hence the tradition of epistemology serves only the rational method of falsification, and historical situations have merely logical functions.[22]

Though falsification is a logical procedure for discovering and then removing inter-theory dissonances, the logic itself is activated by a community of scientists which discusses and decides on what hypotheses to advance which promise to falsify an antecedent theory.[23] What settles the fate of theories, therefore, is not an objectivity that stands over and above the researcher but an intersubjective judgment whose ultimate indeterminacy, however, is for Popper the new constituent of scientific objectivity. And since for him comprehensive and theoretical rationalism is untenable,[24] he now explains his understanding of objective rationalism in terms of the 'practical attitudes' of scientists who can only have an 'irrational *faith in reason*'.[25] This also evokes a comparison with Kant. He, too, 'found it necessary to deny *knowledge*, in order to make room for *faith*'.[26] The difference again, however, is that because of his *a priori* assumptions Kant speaks of a rational belief in reason, while Popper's denial of transcendental categories leaves room only for an irrational belief in it.

We have so far outlined the objective logic of falsification and the subjective phenomenon of decision. But these two aspects of Popper's scientific methodology are structurally related to one another through the principle of formal dialectic. Positivistic dialectic requires the elimination of logical contradictions. It is the application of a negative rule which is to have a positive effect upon the epistemological endeavour to allow knowledge to grow.

Popper's theory of critical analysis is the method of trial and error.[27] This method implies that a scientific thesis is put forward tentatively and tried out empirically. If the outcome of a test does not correspond to the expectations the problematic, because contradictory, thesis has to be discarded and another one, an anti-thesis, offered and subjected to the same procedure. The normative aim of this method is to arrive at a stage where subjective expectation and objective experiment no longer contradict one another. The goal, in other words, is to find a new unity of knowledge. But since that aim is indeterminate, and the possibilities for critical discussion are infinite, thesis and anti-thesis will never terminate in a rationally necessary and final synthesis. A method which could establish such an external end-point, according to Popper, does not exist.[28]

The man of practical action always has to 'choose' between alternatives,[29] and hence will always end up with a problem. The choice to be made focuses on the logical relations between hypotheses. And since science is a practical activity, it should therefore also be visualised as nothing but 'progressing from problems to problems'.[30] Thus the growth of knowledge, which is to be sustained by the teleological direction of critical theory, can then be understood only in terms of a new, though perhaps more precise, articulation of the old problem. The area of theory incompatibility, which is the source of a theoretical problem, is merely narrowed but not determinately overcome. It is for this reason that Popper's negative dialectic declares at the same time the elimination of any possibility of a rational synthesis of knowledge.

Popper's instruction that one removes contradictions is dictated by his attitude towards dialectic which he recognises only as a formal logical device of the understanding. But we immediately have to ask as to the status of such positivistic logic, if neither verification nor falsification can be made conclusive. Does it not turn out to be useless for coherent philosophical reflection? Notwithstanding this proviso, however, Popper's employment of formal logic may be an indication that his seemingly dynamic theory has its justification in a rather static logic. Accordingly, he sharply contrasts this negative and functional dialectic with Hegel's positive and historical dialectic of reason. And he maintains that, for Hegel, the result of the struggle between thesis and anti-thesis does not lead to elimination but to synthesis, and even to the preservation of contradictions.[31] Several points need to be made in this context in order to clarify Popper's own view of dialectic and his unwarranted criticism of Hegel.

To begin with, it has been argued that Popper simply undervalues or even misjudges the heuristic and positive function of theoretical contradictions as instructive for research and progress.[32] That contradictions be maintained for a considerable time is simply demanded by the principle of testability of theories, because it is very unlikely that the discovery of a discrepancy would at once lead to its correct interpretation.[33]

A much more severe objection, however, is justified with respect to Popper's careless and unconscientious rendering of Hegel. The rational theoretician has here completely misread and misunderstood Hegel's philosophy of reason. Though we shall in the following chapter describe some of the features of this philosophy in detail and in their textual context, an indication of the differences between the two thinkers may, nonetheless, be in place at this point.

Let us first make a general remark. The concept contradiction can in our view be thought through only in relation to the notion of unity. And the dialectical method of overcoming contradiction is meaningful only if its telos is a systemic unity. To put it differently: the idea of the whole is recognised in and through its parts, and vice versa.

Bearing this preliminary comment in mind, we may now better highlight the positions of Popper and Hegel. Hegel's philosophy is best described as a reflection upon life. Popper, by contrast, presupposes life and hence restricts the activity of thinking to the application of its formal concepts to particular cognitive objects within the purview of life. And while in Hegel's philosophy life is a necessary and mediated result, in Popper's epistemology the theoretical efforts never end in a reasoned conclusion which is apodictic but in one which, though open, remains indeterminate. For Hegel, life immanently comprehends itself in the knowledge of its historical becoming. Historical life is consequently the life of self-consciousness. In Popper, and again differing from Hegel, theoretical consciousness refers to external and separate objects only. Though knowledge of them grows, it can never be understood as such within a context because no legitimate criterion of objectivity is ever available.

Popper may be right in claiming that on the basis of the principle of non-contradiction the overcoming of the opposition between thesis and antithesis cannot lead to a synthesis. But he distorts Hegel's reflections when he ascribes to him these triadic terms. Hegel nowhere refers to his dialectical approach as involving the relation thesis-antithesis-synthesis.[34] The contradictions Hegel is thinking of are not static theses and their proposed opposites. They are more appropriately to be comprehended as the growth differentiations of the principle of organic or historically concrete life. And life is, and is preserved, only in its developed unity. It cannot be the synthesis of rational fragmentation and logical elimination.

Hegel's reflections on this are unequivocal. Finite things, he writes, that is, the growth differentiations, 'in their indifferent multiplicity are simply this, to be contradictory and *disrupted within themselves*'.[35] Not only is everything 'inherently contradictory', but 'something is therefore alive only in so far as it contains contradiction within it, and moreover is this power to hold and endure the contradiction within it'.[36] Life is only in that contradictions are worked through and sublated within its historical context.

Thus, for Hegel, the idea of eliminating historical moments of life is simply inconceivable and utterly nonsensical. It leads to nothing but the fragmentation of consciousness. Discussions whose revolutionary criticism aims to destroy what they try to establish can hardly be taken seriously. The meaning of life does not consist in denying the possibility of becoming conscious of itself. Life is the courage to reflect upon its holistic history. Popper's preoccupation with theoretical scientific parts, which are to compete in eliminating each other, is therefore very problematic. The open society which in piecemeal fashion is to be engineered according to such precepts turns out to be the most closed-minded one. It promotes little more than the fetishism of individualism which, however, lacks the sense of individuality.

History is the history of the relationship between the individual and the community. But in his psychological fear of history Popper withdraws from it philosophically. His theory of science and ideas of society are a telling testimony of the spiritual impoverishment of modernity. Hence also his attempt to treat his one-sided and ahistorical rationality as an alternative to Hegel's comprehensive reflections is also wrong and futile. Not only, as we shall see, can Popperian rationality and Hegel's notion of reason not be separated one from the other, but Hegel's philosophy, in fact, includes and subsumes the theory of Popper. Hegel therefore writes about the positivists of his time, and in sure anticipation of those to come: let them 'try to argue as much as they like without philosophy – without it they can have in them neither life, Spirit, nor truth'.[37] And to this we can add, paraphrasing an Aristotelian comment made earlier, that, though Popper expressed more superficial views, he too contributed something by developing a method of how to think[38] – or, more critically, not to think.

But Popper's negative dialectic has yet other awesome effects. He at one point states that the trial and error method, which he identifies with the ability to 'learn from our mistakes', is the 'criterion of progress'.[39] And he substantiates this by arguing that a linguistic formulation of theories allows us to criticise and eliminate them 'without eliminating the race which carries them'.[40] Though Popper believes he has made the validity of theoretical assertions contingent upon the outcome of practical measures, his analysis of purely logical relations has no bearing whatsoever on and is in no way related to praxis and its own consequences. His scientific considerations of functional rules do not amount to a concern with man's changing and even jeopardised life-world. And in this sense they are a sure criterion of regress.

For if one were to relate Popper's positivistic rules of falsification to the world of practical application, how would both fare? This question imposes itself immediately when one thinks about the idea of nuclear war. Can one, for instance, regard mankind as a laboratory for testing nuclear strategies through the method of conjectures and refutations? Has it not been cautioned that if war came there would be no opportunity for learning through trial and error?[41] Must and, indeed, can we learn from our mistakes? And who are, can be, or ought to be the learners when Popper's interest is not merely in the theory of scientific knowledge but rather in the theory of 'knowledge in general'?[42]

In our view this knowledge today must mean an *educated* understanding of the historically mediated part-whole relationship. It can no longer be confined to the merely instructed skills employed in research areas. Moreover, Hegel's dialectic of sublation clearly challenges Popper's liberal optimism about the abstract and, therefore, falsifiable freedoms of individuals, be they people or the states. If we philosophically comprehend the harmful consequences of such prescriptions in the nuclear age, then we can see how Hegel's wisdom remains the more truthful and sensible guide for action than Popper's wishful projections of the infinity of formal progress. For is it, on reflection, not also the case, in contradistinction to Popper's rational logic, that 'what experience and history teach us is this – that nations and governments have never learned anything from history or acted upon any lessons they might have drawn from it'?[43] It is Hegel's grasp of history which urges and warns the thoughtful mind into the realisation that the parts can live and survive only if they preserve the whole through which alone they weave together their existence.

KUHN'S SUBJECTIVE DIALECTIC OF PARADIGMS

Dialectic describes the psychology of paradigmatic activities. Science grows slowly and inductively and, therefore, can be said to pursue a positive principle. Though paradigms change through the alternation of normal and revolutionary science, they are no longer teleologically directed towards theoretical truth expectations.

Kuhn questions the validity of the prescriptive rationality of any theoretical method. The doubt concerning the explanatory strength of formal logic and the peculiar internal characteristics of paradigms signify an important break with the tradition of epistemology. The weakness of Kuhn's alternative view, however, is that the relationship between paradigms bears no resemblance to a Hegelian-like dialectic of historically determined knowledge, and is for this reason an unsatisfactory account. In addition, as will emerge from our brief study, and as Kuhn himself concedes, a paradigm, whose function is to elucidate activities in the sciences, cannot apply itself to and therefore cannot reflect upon the more profound philosophical disquiet of man in the nuclear age.

In the foregoing discussion of Popper we have seen how he uses historical situations only in order to substantiate the logical function of the theory of falsification. If one accepts the positivist assumptions, it is still possible with this method to make knowledge claims. Now, what distinguishes a Kuhnian paradigm is not its concern with external objects of cognition but with the subjective belief structure of a group of scientists. A paradigm does not inform us at all what knowledge is supposed to be. It merely seeks to describe socio-psychological behaviour without ascribing to it any epistemological purpose or positivist orientation.

If Popper's explanation for practical falsification has already softened rational knowledge claims, Kuhn's paradigm weakens them still further. For while Popper deals with theoretical questions, Kuhn takes the heuristic idea of praxis, which manifests itself within the historical context of normal science, more seriously. He is a historian of science[1] who describes the inner 'process' of particular research areas rather than explains the logic behind methodological prescriptions.[2] Kuhn thus blunts the sharp rationality of critical theory. What therefore remains to be done if science is deprived of any internal necessity is an inquiry into the contingently personal and historical accidents of paradigmatic activities. The principle of dialectic is then no more realised between a historical situation and a meta-theory to which the logical interpretation of the former is to correspond. It rather exhibits itself between the subjective agents within a paradigm alone. It follows a horizontal rather than a vertical pattern of knowledge acquisition. But if the idea of dialectic is this much reduced, the question arises as to how the behavioural processes of paradigms can yield 'progress'?[3]

Kuhn wants to make the point that Popperian revolutions cannot be the whole of science. Something different, namely, normal science, must necessarily go on in between.[4] Normal science is an accumulative, a fact-finding, and therefore basically an empirical activity whose objective is to establish 'particular coherent traditions'.[5] It suggests an inductive rather than a deductive approach to understanding science.

A paradigm is a tool for research. But since it is as such also the equivalent of a community of scientists, it is a self-applicatory framework or foundation for practical studies. Kuhn takes the communal paradigm for granted.[6] In fact, a paradigm takes itself for granted. No rational explanation, however, is given for why it should function as a fundamental unit. But the absence of a criterion of appraisal turns the question of self-justification into a question of subjective faith and hence into circularity.[7]

The irrationality of a paradigm is compounded by the incomprehensibility of its size. The area which it inquires into is 'minuscule'.[8] Kuhn emphasises the 'one-to-one identification'[9] of a community with a scientific subject matter. The life-world of a paradigm is thus circumscribed by a rather 'drastically restricted vision'.[10] Its myopic consciousness is confined to a 'single monolithic and unified' domain of research.[11] And there can be 'no standard higher' than the scientific community itself.[12] But Kuhn qualifies the one-to-one correspondence when he writes that 'a paradigm governs, in the first instance, not a subject matter but rather a group of practitioners'.[13]

With this shift in emphasis paradigmatic dialectic assumes a one-sidedly subjective and self-referential characteristic. And for this reason it may be of no consequence whatsoever for anyone who seeks to make sense of the world that extends beyond a particular research community. What can a paradigm convey if it withdraws not just from an admittedly questionable rational objectivity but from the life outside its boundaries as well? Kuhn insists that the worth of a paradigm lies in it being recognised as having an 'independent existence'.[14] But is the idea of independence not a rather naive one when the interrelatedness of scientific activities is considered? The part-whole relationship cannot be severed by artificially drawing perforated lines between the paradigms, on the one hand, and between them and the holistic concept of science, on the other. And not only that. If a paradigm deals only with itself, it is meaningless for somebody else's self.

The merely subjective and psychological life-world, which is claimed to be most important in paradigmatic science, thus clouds the dialectical scientific enterprise as a whole. Kuhn never really resolves the crucial question of the relationship between a paradigm and its constituent theories.[15] He evades the issue by arguing that with micro-paradigms the earlier difficulties of critical theory are likely to vanish.[16] The smaller the paradigm, the less is there a need to take recourse to theoretical generalisations. But since in the case of knowledge transition dialectical reflections can hardly be avoided, what is likely to vanish is the very concept of normal science itself.[17] For not only are the communities small. Even a so-called scientific revolution 'need not be a large change'.[18] In fact, they can be 'micro-revolutions' which occur regularly.[19] Kuhn's scientific thought involves, not unlike Popper's permanent revolution, a *revolution in perpetuity*.[20] Yet within a subjective life-world even such a minute change will be helpful only if one makes it absolutely clear in precisely what sense it is to be regarded as a unit of change in an intra-paradigm transition.[21] Kuhn, however, subscribing to no objective ontology or meta-theory, cannot give such explanatory elaboration.

Another issue is the following. It concerns the relationship between paradigmatic communities. Kuhn admits that, because of the 'narrow and rigid education', professional communication across group lines is sometimes arduous, and often results in misunderstanding.[22] Being a rather *closed society*,[23] at least in intent, a paradigm is isolated and separated from its community neighbours. It is no wonder, then, that, when thought through, the pluralistic and diverse world of paradigms is utterly discontinuous. It is a world that is on the verge of splitting asunder into innumerable special interests or research activities. The Kuhnian paradigmatic world is completely fragmented. It is not at all imbued with a spirit of co-operation, purpose and unity. The language of its intellectually paranoid practitioners does not transcend its self-imposed subjective confines.

Now, what does paradigmatic research actually consist in? Fundamentally, it is about problem-solving. And it is in this area that Kuhn wants to go further than Popper in the sense that while for the historian it is a practical issue, for the rationalist it is instrumental for theoretical purposes only. Though both interpret the historical function of problems differently, it has been remarked that, if science is basically a problem-solving activity rather than a purely epistemological enterprise, only Popper and Kuhn treat this method in one way or another.[24]

This issue can best be discussed, perhaps, when one relates the concept problem to that of facts. Let us regard a fact as a universal, and a problem as a particular. And let us assume also that once solved, a problem may lead to a new fact. What the difference refers to is this: while the particular implies activity and, hence, time-consciousness, the universal does not. That is to say, the problem may change historically, the fact not. The fact, expressed in form of a theory, is held to be a constant and cannot be transformed. A problem, on the other hand, is paradigm-immanent and does not reside in the theory itself. If the scientific community becomes aware of an inconsistency between a theory and the object it purportedly relates to, it is ultimately this consciousness which has created this problem. Hence the issue of correspondence has its origin in the psychological subjectivity of the paradigm and must be tackled and worked at within that framework. In other words, if a theory of science seeks to elucidate the nature of its subject-matter, it has to deal with the classical distinction between scientific progress and scientific rationality. For while progress is an unavoidably temporal concept, rationality has tended to be viewed as an atemporal one.[25]

Kuhn realises the dilemma which the relationship between problems and theory poses. He therefore withdraws from the task of solving problems and, instead, undertakes to treat scientific 'puzzles' for which there is the 'assured existence of a solution'.[26] This certainty is explained through the pre-knowledge one already has of the puzzle as a whole, into which the particular pieces must fit. Unlike a puzzle, however, a problem is continuous and open-ended, and no form of rationality allows it to be interpreted holistically. But without even a modicum of logical guidance for solving puzzles, what can a solution of a puzzle refer to? If science is paradigmatic, its result cannot yield epistemologically arrived at knowledge. And Kuhn himself says that perhaps knowledge is the 'wrong word' to use in the context of a paradigm.[27] Since knowledge is only attained through practice and cannot be articulated explicitly, that is, assessed with respect to an explanatory theory, 'we have no direct access to what it is we know, no rules or generalizations with which to express this knowledge'.[28] The empiricism of paradigms is bottomless and vacuous. But if this is the case, and if science nonetheless ought to remain related to the question of knowledge and its progress, then paradigm changes turn out to be simply irrelevant and devoid of interest.[29] Paradigmatic research is shallow. It does not enrich but impoverishes further the quest for truth and philosophical reflection.

But what, in fact, is a change of paradigms? What is a change from so-called anomalies, that are accumulated in normal science, to a crisis that is to bring about a revolution of insight? For Kuhn the essential clues to the success of science are quantitative techniques of measurement.[30] And what is to be measured are the recurrent puzzles which violate paradigm-induced theoretical expectations. Hence progress is not based on the 'single simple act'[31] of logically removing contradictions, but of factually counting many similar ones. It is a practical and, in this sense, positive, not a theoretical and negative activity. Kuhn has no rules for research or for testing paradigms, because paradigms are deemed to be prior to theory building. He explicitly disavows the identification of experiments.[32] Hence in the final analysis it is the subject scientist rather than the object theory that is of interest. But then we must ask: how does the scientist determine the crisis point itself that is to lead to a new and qualitatively different theory? An answer to this question may be redundant because, since no paradigm ever resolves all its problems, for there are always anomalies, we have the paradoxical conclusion that *all theories stand refuted at all times*.[33]

With Popper we don't know what actually goes on when a transition of theories takes place. He only says that it is a logical necessity. Kuhn, however, describes this process more fully. He compares theory transition to a spontaneous, one-directional and irreversible *gestalt* switch.[34] It is because of this behavioural aspect that he sees in science a *psychology of research* rather than a *logic of discovery*.[35] But why should a psychologically describable shift of intellectual vision constitute progress? Kuhn answers his own related question as to what happens at the final stage of such intuitive immersion into another paradigm by saying that it must remain 'inscrutable and may be permanently so'.[36] In other words, a paradigm cannot demonstrate an increase in knowledge.

Psychological paradigm transitions are unstructured and, because they are subjective, depend also on values and on choices. But here again, to the query of how a value-based enterprise can develop a science that is progressing, Kuhn has 'unfortunately no answer at all'.[37] Therefore, if no criterion for judgment and paradigm comparison is established, one cannot even do justice to Kuhn by invoking the image of a Hegelian-type dialectic where a later theory preserves and accommodates the former. If, because of paradigm discontinuity, no communication is possible, the relationship between paradigms is that of abrupt polarity.[38] Such a polarity cannot be rationally overcome. Therefore, Kuhn writes in a mood of scientific despair, only death seems to be the final exit out of the dilemma of paradigm incommensurability. If there are no good reasons for convincing each other to accept a new scientific idea, if one does not see the light, nature will lend a helping hand.[39] Nature's necessity resolves all the problems of contingent rationality and paradigms.

Though Kuhn's spurious dialectic purports to clarify the subjective procedures related to theory transitions, he is obviously in no position either to say whether one theory is in fact superior to its competitor. There is no objective criterion that could function as an arbiter. 'The superiority of one theory to another', he says, 'is something that cannot be proved'.[40] There is no objectivity to be approximated, not even a Popperian verisimilitude.[41] There are 'no external standards', there is 'neither a decline nor a raising of standards, but simply a change'.[42] Thus, though Kuhn clings at times to the assertion that paradigm transitions 'must inevitably be progress', he immediately qualifies this untenable claim to 'a sort of' progress,[43] for, after all, it refers only to numerical measurements and a mere refinement in articulation and specialisation. There is no pretence of any theoretical interpretation. This, surely, is not the same as saying that with such improvements one also moves teleologically 'closer and closer to the truth', a notion which Kuhn is likewise quick to 'relinquish'.[44]

One may, of course, wonder whether science, even a paradigmatic and non-epistemological science, is at all conceivable without a concern for ontological truth?[45] Must starting somewhere mean the impossibility of going anywhere? Must we not aim at truth even if the truth cannot be known? In the light of these considerations it seems, therefore, that an evaluation of Kuhn's paradigmatic understanding of science may depend partially on the extent to which this tension is in fact bearable.[46]

But not only is there for Kuhn no longer any telos. The Kuhnian paradigm, as a closed and minuscule scientific community, has other disturbing implications, as well. Kuhn declares that there are assured solutions to puzzles because the scientist works 'only for an audience of colleagues'.[47] He is isolated and disinterested in problems that lie outside his field. The scientist is insulated from 'socially important problems that are not reducible to the puzzle form, because they cannot be stated in terms of the conceptual and instrumental tools the paradigm supplies'.[48]

What importance does this have for our reflections upon the problem of war? Popper says that since war cannot be completely explained, no rationally holistic solution to it is possible either. Only by means of systematic piecemeal engineering can society hope to construct something like peace.[49] Popper at least proposes a method. Kuhn questions the possibility of any rationally founded outcome of scientific activities. For if the prescription of falsification were to be practised and followed through, all peace would undoubtedly fall to pieces. But he even denies the applicability of his own paradigmatic thinking to problems of war and peace. He writes, for instance, that it is no criterion of goodness in a puzzle that its outcome be intrinsically interesting or important. On the contrary, the really pressing problems, such as the 'design of a lasting peace', are often not puzzles at all, largely because they may not have any solution.[50] It is because a paradigm is taken for granted, that it can be assumed to have solutions. Other problems are 'rejected as metaphysical, as the concern of another discipline, or sometimes as just too problematic to be worth the time'.[51]

These lines speak for themselves. They show the limitations of a scientific paradigm when it comes to a reflection upon opposing political and philosophical concerns that are of much wider dimensions and of considerably greater consequences for humanity. Restricted and specialised research assumes responsibility only for the consequences within its own particular domain. It is a form of reductionism that has abdicated from that kind of Hegelian reason which reflects upon perspectives and dialectical relationships. The historical reason of responsibility thinks the link between the paradigms and their responding care for coming to terms with a holistic world, between the particularity of scientific practice and its consequential universality. If paradigmatic thinking cannot be critically sublated, its practical realisation may well result in the resolution of conflict in nuclear death.

FEYERABEND'S DISSOLUTION OF SCIENTIFIC DIALECTIC

Dialectic is a hedonistic interplay of proliferated theoretical alternatives to already existing theories, and it describes in a positive manner their transitions. As we have seen in our discussion of Popper and Kuhn, dialectic is intrinsically bound to method. Both in its rational and paradigmatic form, however, method itself has become a problem because it does not lead to a fixed system of knowledge. In consequence, though Feyerabend in his critique seeks to adopt a Hegelian standpoint, he maintains that not even a method can be posited that is firmly grounded or in any way justified. The corollary of the illusion of method is the illusion of a dialectical goal itself. Hence he dissolves the idea of a determinate method of dialectic.

Feyerabend links his radically anarchic view of the tradition directly to a seemingly more humanist understanding of the life-world. Yet this raises questions of its own when related to the endemic problems of our time, of which the possibility of a nuclear war is clearly the most difficult one to absorb into our reflections.

Popper's rational dialectic refers to truth not as something which is, but as something which *ought* to become approximative truth or verisimilitude. Dialectical reasoning is still conducted through a rigidly defined logical criterion of a necessary formal premise which determines its movements towards an equally necessary conclusion or, if we take the premise to be a problem, a solution.

But the abandonment of a merely presupposed theoretical truth suggests that method has acquired a new operative status. As an organon it has begun to take the place of truth and to regulate itself. It remains, however, instrumental for the cognition of a posited object of the understanding. *Method* has become more *autonomous*, because knowledge is not simply there but must be worked out, and this can be done only methodically. On the other hand, the autonomy of function entails its own defectiveness in the sense that method and system are separated one from the other. A dialectical method which cannot result in systematic knowledge evaporates into illusion.

The status of functional autonomy is further enhanced through the paradigmatic method. Kuhn no longer assumes any rational goal, and there is no given premise from which to deduce a teleological movement. The question therefore arises as to what progress could mean in the absence of a specified goal, and whether, in fact, there need be any such expectation at all?[1]

Thus, when truth can no longer serve as a rationally guiding principle for scientific thought, method must take care of itself.[2] It has become a 'self-correcting mechanism'.[3] Since a scientific community is not interested in truth, and since it has given up all hope of establishing a correspondence between theories and the world, it is emptied of rational reason. In being merely a behavioural description, it no longer reflects upon hypothesised ontologies. Paradigmatic activity somehow revolves about itself, it is suspended and groundless.

Yet the openness of this empirical method, which has no clear direction, is of great mediative importance. It makes possible the employment of the idea of unconstrained method for different purposes. It allows for the free proliferation of a plurality not of facts but of theories. The unfolding of alternatives is for Feyerabend the multi-dimensional equivalent to Popper's uni-directional way towards verisimilitude. If method is with Kuhn no longer imbued with rational reason, it must develop its own procedural means with which it can indicate progress. In order to avoid the 'dogmatic petrification' of a theory, Feyerabend seeks to liberate paradigmatic claustrophobia by proposing the creative invention of 'many alternative theories'.[4]

With Kuhn and Popper we have seen how facts or empirical data co-determine the way a method is employed. For Popper it is one factual counterinstance, for Kuhn it is the many factual anomalies. Both settle the fate of a theory either in a logical and immediate or in a historical and eventual way. The Feyerabendian term 'theoretical pluralism,[5] however, refers to theories alone and their proliferation, and not to facts. That is to say, methodology itself is claimed to be fully autonomous because it deals with theories *inter se*. Thus the understanding, once it is stripped of its rational pretensions, allows only for theoretical knowledge. But because this is conditioned through an open historical horizon, it is not unified but remains multifarious. Feyerabend's pluralism is not a method of systematically gathering historical determinations. It is 'not a "systematic" account but a *historical account of each stage of knowledge*'.[6] History is therefore distinguished from both rationality and paradigms.

Yet this is not to say that method is separated from history. Quite the contrary, the principle of proliferation 'prevents the elimination of older theories' which contribute to the content of their rivals.[7] The material which the scientist actually has at his disposal is indeterminate and is 'never fully separated from the historical background'.[8] It is only within a historical context that pluralism is able to function as a criterion for theory critique.

The anarchical proliferation of theories somehow rehabilitates the usefulness of 'metaphysical speculation'.[9] Feyerabend argues, for instance, that we cannot discover our world 'from the inside'[10] because a paradigm cannot be judged 'according to its own standards'.[11] What one needs instead are 'external' criteria for criticism, that is, a set of alternative assumptions which 'suspend' established theories.[12] What Feyerabend does is to break open the closeness of paradigmatic dialectic and to let the understanding freely unfold itself into a plurality of alternative, though uncollected, theories. The metaphysical aspect of alternative ideas does not refer to their ontological status but merely to their instrumental and temporary suggestiveness.

Theories which are external to one another also suspend each other's truth claim. What is historical and functional cannot fulfil the quest for certainty. Feyerabend, therefore, not only drops 'the idea of *certainty*, or of *directness*, or the weaker idea of *support*; he abandons the 'demand' for certainty altogether.[13] The invention of alternatives is a 'more or less irrational act'.[14]

Feyerabend's theoretical pluralism clearly stands in opposition to the *consistency condition*. He is against methodical empiricism because there is not a single rule which is not violated at some time or other.[15] In this connection he is referring to both Popper and Kuhn when he writes that the 'idea of a universal and stable *method* that is an unchanging measure of adequacy and even the idea of a universal and stable *rationality* is as unrealistic as the idea of a universal and stable measuring instrument that measures any magnitude, no matter what the circumstances'.[16]

Demands for rational adequacy, Feyerabend fears, only encourage theoretical monism and discourage theoretical pluralism. And the paradigmatic practice of worshipping historical facts[17] justifies even less the assertiveness of methodological principles and, hence, cannot be accepted as a cognitive authority. For Feyerabend, the consistency principle is an alarming sign that no new ideas are being produced and that the activity of theorising has come to an end.[18] Monistic methodology is to be liberated from its logical and factual restrictions. The emphasis on theoretical pluralism thus indicates a shift away from the concept of unity and correspondence. 'Knowledge', according to Feyerabend, 'is not a process that converges towards an ideal view; it is an ever-increasing ocean of alternatives'.[19]

Unlike Popper, for whom the basic statements have a necessary and logical function, but in line with Kuhn, Feyerabend also criticises the principle of *meaning invariance*. The idea of meaning invariance is of Platonic origin, and it refers to 'eternal and unchanging entities'.[20] Just as Aristotle criticises Plato's philosophical forms, so Feyerabend questions the theoretical assumptions of Popper's Platonism. He argues that actual science does not always observe the requirement of meaning invariance.[21] And, therefore, if the idea of facts to which words are attached becomes problematic, then the meaning of the terms we use depends upon the 'theoretical context' in which it occurs.[22] That is to say, theories are meaningful independent of observations. Words, then 'do not "mean" something in isolation; they obtain their meanings by being part of a theoretical system'.[23]

Though theoretical systems may be mutually inconsistent and irreducible, they cannot be overcome by 'bridge-laws'.[24] Since such synthesising connectives are not available, the meanings of all terms must be elastic, and our attitude towards them should be tolerant and lenient. Too great a concern with meanings, Feyerabend writes, can lead only to dogmatism and sterility. Flexibility, and even sloppiness, in semantical matters is a prerequisite of scientific progress.[25]

Therewith Feyerabend abandons the requirement of a direct correspondence between fact and theory, and he rejects the demand that theories be consistent with one another. But then again, if the objective of science is to be the realisation of the idea of progress, what are the criteria with which to judge theories and their transitions? It is at this point that Feyerabend invokes the function of dialectical thinking in order to explain his method of theoretical pluralism. Though his understanding of dialectic is very Hegelian, he interprets it in a way that is more reminiscent of the rational Popper. However, Feyerabend's analysis will serve us here well as a last argument for a scientific though one-sided dialectic and, at the same time, as an anticipation for the discussion of Hegel's historical and comprehensive dialectic. May it therefore suffice in this section when we present Feyerabend's own view of dialectic: 'Dialectical philosophers [he writes] have always emphasized the need not to think in a "mechanical" way, that is, in a framework whose concepts are precisely defined *and kept stable in any argument*; [rather, H.K.] the development of our knowledge presupposes the existence of at least two alternative systems of thought, of a thesis and an antithesis'.[26]

That Feyerabend does not mention a formalistic *synthesis*, that sublates thesis and anti-thesis, is significant. From a rational point of view it would require a third point of reference, an at least hypothesised and external reason that would determine the movement of thought. But Feyerabend denies the assumption that thought is a '*necessary development* that occurs independently of the human will'.[27] Now, this would be a correct interpretation of dialectic if it explicitly referred to the Kantian distinction between understanding or rationality and reason. However, Feyerabend has Hegel in mind whom he quotes as saying that 'dialectic is fundamentally nothing but the spirit of contradiction that lives in every human being'.[28]

Feyerabend's rendering of dialectic suggests that it is neither based on the formal logic of syllogism nor on the unitary concept of paradigm, but on the need to propose alternative theories. 'Such a method', he says, 'cuts the ground from underneath all dogmatic philosophizing'.[29] He is, in particular, critical of the rational logic of dialectical positivism, that is, of the Popperian requirement of eliminating formal contradictions. 'Such philosophers', Feyerabend argues, 'went further than was really necessary and suggested that the principle of non-contradiction also be abandoned'.[30]

And then Feyerabend continues, and we quote him in full:

> Now they were correct in saying that the development of knowledge *negates* its earlier stages. Of course, knowledge *itself* does not automatically lead to such self-negation, and it never would if consistency and meaning invariance were retained. The appearance and self-negation is the result of a *method* that is consciously applied by thinking beings and that demands the use of mutually inconsistent alternatives, of the actual 'invention' of alternatives (which is a contingent event . . . and not something that is *bound* to

> happen), and of *transitions* between these alternatives brought about by the discovery of inadequacies. It may also be admitted that the earlier stages are not wholly eliminated, but *preserved* . . ., not preserved in exactly the same form in which they were previously held, but in the sense of being *reinterpreted* and thereby changed.[31]

If preservation is not interpreted as preservation of *meanings*, then 'the need for a special "dialectical logic" disappears'.[32]

Thus Feyerabend contends that 'contradictions can be maintained',[33] and that, in fact, the principle of proliferation 'prevents the elimination of older theories which have been refuted' because they 'contribute to the content of their victorious rivals'.[34] A 'pluralistic methodology' is to 'retain', is to 'improve rather than discard', theories.[35]

With this Feyerabend has dissolved the rigidity of Popper's critical but negative 'ratiomania'.[36] He interprets the dialectic of theory transitions as a much more fluid and positive movement. Since the logic of analytical possibilities is relativised, the rational contradictions are capable of being transformed into the method of process.

Feyerabend now tries to apply his understanding of dialectic to the problem of how paradigms change. He questions, as we mentioned earlier, that paradigm transitions are generated from within, and asserts instead that a paradigm can be criticised and therefore changed only from without. With Kuhn's account of change it is impossible to say that it has actually led to a 'better' paradigm.[37] Without an absolute the comparative is meaningless.

Since no concept of an absolute can be defined, Feyerabend removes the dialectic from the aspirations of scientific activities and translates it into a 'methodological problem'.[38] In other words, he takes normal and revolutionary science out of the context of praxis and turns them into methodological principles on the same level,[39] without ascribing to them different evaluative terms. We are dealing, Feyerabend writes, 'with a methodological problem and not with the question of how science actually proceeds'.[40] The allegiance to a paradigm, that is, to normal or factual science, follows the 'principle of tenacity', and the change of paradigms, which refers to revolutionary or theoretical science, is called the 'principle of proliferation'.[41] Their coexistence on an equal methodological level leads to the collapse of the Kuhnian tale of the separation of normal and revolutionary science. According to Feyerabend, the essential feature of the actual development of science is now the 'interplay between tenacity and proliferation'.[42]

What is autonomous is this dialectical interplay. It dissolves the extremities, lifts itself out of the fixity of empty facts, and descends from equally untenable rational premises. Science has become movement, suspended though, reasonless and without a ground. But towards what is it to progress and grow if the anarchy of its dialectical play has no direction in terms of rational meaning and epistemological purpose? Our discussion of scientific dialectic and its various aspects has now reached a point where this question can no longer be answered by science itself. Deliberations on scientific activities acquire a meaning only if they are related to that which makes science and to that which science is to serve, that is, to man and his humanity. Feyerabend, therefore, brings the argument onto a higher level of reflection.

Science treats theoretical particulars which are universalised. It is the dialectical interplay within the plurality of particulars which Feyerabend now transposes onto the realm of the interplay of human individualities and their particularistic end. This end is a version of liberalism which Feyerabend associates with a 'plea for hedonism'.[43] He believes that dialectic may be an answer to 'the most important question of all, the question to what extent the happiness of individual human beings, and to what extent their freedom, has been increased'.[44] If science and its process is linked to the progress of human happiness, then individual man must be given a free hand in pursuing his activities which are to result in the realisation of happiness. What Feyerabend advocates with pluralism is a self-centred, egoistic and aesthetic pleasure. He has a concept of individualism, of happiness and freedom, without, however, clarifying how their playful proliferation is related to the principle of directed change, if by change he means progress.

The idea of hedonism is reminiscent of Aristotle. For the ancient the activity of happiness is 'contemplative'.[45] It is *theo-ria*, implying a transcendent divine reason. But for Aristotle, too, each man is himself, and, indeed, it would be strange 'if he were to choose not the life of his self but that of something else'.[46] And the happiest life the individual seeks to pursue is the 'contemplation and service of God'.[47]

It is now interesting, within the framework of our general account of dialectic, to compare the modern with the ancient. Just as Hegel and Plato stand, historically speaking, at opposite ends, Feyerabend and Aristotle are in the same way similar and different. But both are encompassed, historically and philosophically, by Plato and Hegel.

This point we have already alluded to in our analysis of Plato's dialectic, and we shall return to it at a later stage.

Aristotle speaks of reason and enduringness. Feyerabend has stepped out of much of this tradition, never to regain its myth. His individual activity is no longer directed towards theoria. For both, however, the ancient and the modern, happiness is identified with an individualistic self-referring life. But while for Aristotle it means a highest and lasting good, for Feyerabend it is reduced to a lower, unstable and ephemeral good. Man is separated from anything transcendent which he may be able to posit, but which he neither contemplates nor binds in rational reason. For Feyerabend there is no meaning in a mediation towards truth or God. The individual, following only his inclinations, gains a strange meaning in that which is senseless.

Feyerabend believes, however, that with the dissolution of method as a dogmatic principle, the life-world of the sciences, will acquire a 'humanitarian outlook'.[48] 'The sciences, after all, are our own creation', and it is, therefore, 'good to be constantly reminded of the fact that science as we know it today is not inescapable and that we may construct a world in which it plays no role whatever (such a world, I venture to suggest, would be more pleasant than the world we live in today)'.[49]

It is doubtful whether the encouragement of unaccountable variety and pluralism has much to do with dialectic. As we shall see with Hegel, dialectic requires a guiding method and a systemic form of sublation. Feyerabend, however, replaces these criteria with his wondrous belief in the idea of 'anything goes'[50] or in the cunning of unreason. Yet if anything goes, nothing goes anywhere. Feyerabend's individualism describes a humanism that does not allow a reflection upon its relationship to a possible humanism of mankind.

Equally problematic is his scientific optimism whose unreflectedness can be appreciated only if it is read alongside his pronouncements on method. Let us conclude this section with only a few comments on this issue. Our own view is that today's science and technology have assumed a particular form of self-determinacy in the sense that, irrespective of political decisions, their development determines our life-world more than we can hope to determine it.[51] In other words, the dialectical relationship between human subjectivity and its scientific and technological object has the tendency to move in the direction of the latter. Hence we do not believe that science is inescapable. And, consequently, we do not believe either that it will be possible to construct a world in which science would play no role any more whatever.

It is true that it is our own creation. But the realisation of this has by now much weakened man's ability to enrich and preserve his consciousness of selfhood. In the nuclear age it is man's self-consciousness which is in jeopardy. Thus the scientific-technological results, intended or not, are also part of our creations and need to be reflected upon in a holistic and responsible manner. And this is required precisely because their causal relations cannot be fully ascertained by purely rational means.

Swift once described the role of science and its effects in a vivid story. Once upon a time there was a flying island of science, called *Laputa* which hovered above man and his earth. In order to reduce man to obedience its scientific community was capable of quite some methods. If a crime, for instance, deserved it, the perpetrators were 'pelted from above with great Stones'. And if they would still continue to be obstinate, the last remedy then was to let the 'island drop directly upon their Heads, which makes a universal Destruction both of Houses and Men'.[52] What was then a political satire may or may not realise itself in a nuclear fire. As our following discussion of Hegel and the historically mediated part-whole relationship will make quite obvious, it is of this and of its uncertainty that we ought to be constantly reminded.

SUMMARY

The principle of modernity is the particularisation of the life-world. Dialectic remains a form of inquiry, varied and discontinuous though it may be, to come to terms with it. In this chapter we have elucidated some of the fundamental contradictions of the assumptions of specialised scientific thinking. As we have suggested in our references to Hegel, these rational and subjective dilemmas occur in the absence of and cannot be made sense of without a comprehensive historical awareness of the relationship between science and philosophy. In the nuclear age the inability to reflect may have fatal consequences for the subject that more and more appropriates in a passive way prefabricated thought patterns. For if the particular scientific consciousness of man can destroy the presumed confidence in his holistic self-consciousness, then it is not only the former that has the force to do so. It is also the latter that may then no longer have the power to preserve itself.

It is this idea of self-consciousness which will be our theme in subsequent chapters. Modernity has raised the question as to how to reconcile the various scientific methods which rely on fragmenting reality in order to obtain only spurious knowledge of it, with a philosophical reflection on the idea of self-knowledge that seeks its completion in the historical existence of life. Hegelian dialectic provides us with a philosophical insight into such a reconciliation.

Part II
Historical Dialectic

3 Hegel's Logic of Dialectic

The last section on scientific dialectic has revealed a remarkable affinity between Feyerabend and Hegel. Despite their differences in interpreting dialectic, the recourse to Hegel only affirms his growing importance today for at least two reasons. In the first instance, Hegel's appraisal of scientific knowledge and his reflections upon the principle of historical relation clearly challenge in particular the positivist's belief in the primacy of facts. Kuhn and Feyerabend are representatives of a more critical brand of thinkers who have begun to question the static logic of formal dialectic. The second and for us even more fundamental reason for why Hegel has become so crucial is that the principle of relation has direct implications for comprehending the idea of self-consciousness. This seminal idea is related to the historical mediation of man's social and communal activities. In other words, while the world of objects has largely been thematised by positivism, the world of the subject is and can only be reflected upon by humanism. But because the former is not without the latter, Hegel's humanism prevails in significance not only over any expression of modern positivism, but in the end also over those of its recent commentators who have merely a restricted and flawed understanding of dialectic. Generally speaking, then, it is in our opinion the actualisation of the historical essence of dialectic which, more than any of its other aspects, adequately describes the relationship between subject and object. But, moreover, it is Hegel's dialectic alone which transforms a science of objects into the science of the self or of the self-knowledge of the subject.

We shall present a broad and yet thorough exegesis of the logic of Hegelian dialectic. In order to remain within the hermeneutic and contextual tradition, a very close and extensive reading not only of Hegel, of course, but of Kant and Feyerabend, as well, is unavoidable. It is with them that we can best appreciate the transition from a science of facts and things to that of relations. It is through them also that we are in a more advantageous position to explore the difficult domain of Hegel's dialectic. Much of the difficulty that arises from studying Hegel's philosophy is associated with notorious terminological obscurities. And inaccurate translations of principal words and expressions, and the lack of willingness, on the part of the reader, to work patiently and with sympathy through primary philosophical writings only compound the problem of misunderstanding a thinker and of unwarranted prejudices against his intellectual concerns. But this is not to mean that Hegel is not accessible. Once his diction has been appropriated and his technical language become familiar, Hegel's insightful philosophy will turn out to be rather concrete and very comprehensible.

Every approach to a philosopher ought to begin with the question of how he views the time he lives in and what conceptual problems underlie his reflections about it. Hegel is confronted with a period in which praxis has dirempted the relationship between historical activities and the attempt to understand them holistically. But in thinking both from a geographical and intellectual distance about the French Revolution and subsequent events of his epoch, he realises at the same time that it is through diremption and negativity that the organic need of reason arises, not once but continuously, to reconcile the differentiations in the positivity of notional unity. For only if this need, which manifests itself in the philosophical language of syllogistic or relational dialectic, results in reflected unity is praxis again possible and at all meaningful. Only in reflection is man really close to himself and free.

Hegel, as no other philosopher before or after him, has given us a veritable understanding of how to find a historical perspective within which to reflect upon a menaced time. The nuclear age, which plainly symbolises the possibility of ultimate diremption, is such a time. It is, however, also an age which, once severed from itself, may no longer be redeemable by history. In order to cope with an already factually fragmented world, it is of paramount importance that one studies Hegel conscientiously and endeavours to grasp the comprehensive logic of dialectical thinking. This logic is ultimately that of life. Since it is the life of global humanity which is threatened, the development of its notionalisation ought therefore to be our primary philosophical concern.

In this chapter we are interested in highlighting and clarifying the issue of life and the way it reflectively relates to itself by looking at various characteristics of Hegel's unsurpassed historical dialectic. The part-whole relationship will to this effect be outlined from the rather novel point of view of pairs of terms and an examination of their Hegelian meaning. A strictly philosophical appreciation of this approach presupposes some knowledge of Hegel's work. In consequence, the following sections are not as such intended as an introduction to his philosophy. Nonetheless, we hope that the depth of Hegel's reflections becomes transparent to all those readers who do not only wish to acquaint themselves with his dialectic, but who also share his humanistic concerns as they are expressed through this most profound method of thinking. We shall conclude this propaedeutic with a suggested way of applying Hegel's dialectic to our attempt to comprehend mankind as the subject of life.

UNDERSTANDING AND REASON

One way, then, of looking at the part-whole relationship is by examining first the intellectual tools that allow us to thematise the terms *part* and *whole*. This we can perhaps do best by considering the faculty of thinking which comprises two devices of reflection: *understanding* and *reason*. The modern philosophical tradition ascribes to these aspects of thinking different functions. In its widest sense, for instance, the former may be said to deal with particularity, while the latter is concerned with subsuming the concepts of particular objects under a more holistic notion. A clarification of these terms is essential before we apply the part-whole perspective to the issue of the nuclear age and its methodological comprehension.

In our discussion of scientific dialectic we have basically treated Greek and contemporary forms of dialectical thinking as they pertain to epistemological purposes. This method can be loosely described as rational, or as that which is determined by the understanding. It is with the employment of the rational mind that we seek to ascertain the truth of singular phenomenal objects external to us, that is, external to the inquiring subject. The understanding, on this account, involves thus a method which attempts to enhance the consciousness of objects, but which, by its very nature, is unable to acquire a comprehensive knowledge of the self. With the understanding alone no self-consciousness is approximated.

Here is not the place to enter into an elaborate discussion of Kant's rational critique of reason and its ancient and medieval variants. It may, however, be appropriate to use some textual references in order to bring into sharper relief the distinction he makes between understanding or rationality, on the one hand, and reason, on the other. Much of the confusion that arises in interpreting these expressions is due to the misleading association of rationality with reason. But once this problem is dealt with, we shall be in a better position to follow Hegel's reaction to the rational dilemma of Kantian idealism, and to scrutinise Feyerabend's own though deficient reading of Hegel.

Kant distinguishes between understanding and reason in the following way. The understanding, he says:

> may be regarded as a faculty which secures the unity of appearances by means of rules, and reason as being the faculty which secures the unity of rules of understanding under principles. Accordingly, reason never applies itself directly to experience or to any object, but to understanding, in order to give to the manifold knowledge of the latter an *a priori* unity by means of concepts.

This difference is illustrated in the relations below:

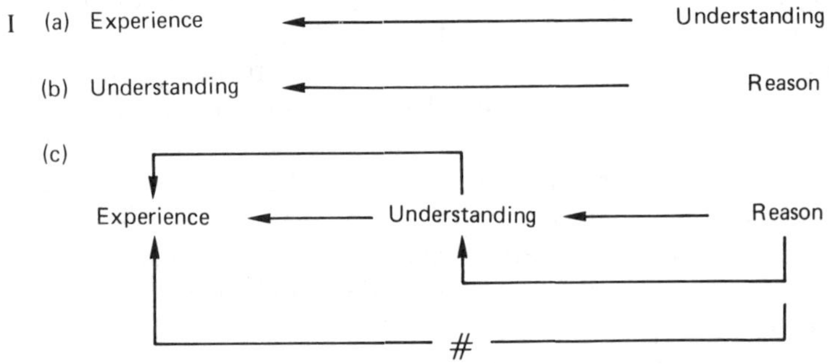

Nothing empirical corresponds to the Kantian principles of reason as a synthetic unity. These principles are transcendent ideas which dialectically serve only the understanding and its transcendental conceptual categories. At the same time, however, they serve it as its ultimate conditions for drawing inferences about the phenomenal or experiential world, the world of objects. According to Kant:

> reason is never in immediate relation to an object, but only to the understanding; and it is only through the understanding that it has its own (specific) empirical employment. It does not, therefore, *create* concepts (of objects) but only *orders* them, and gives them . . . unity . . . Reason has, therefore, as its sole object, the understanding and its effective application. Just as the understanding unifies the manifold in the object by means of concepts, so reason unifies the manifold of concepts by means of ideas.[2]

The dialectic in this scheme, however, is a one-sided and defective method because it does not comprehend the holistic relationship between reason and experiential phenomena. It does not establish a rational system of correspondence; it only determines the partial connection between reason and understanding.

The ideas of reason originate in and are posited by the transcendental subjectivity of the understanding. The understanding needs reason because its ideas give direction to the rational knowledge acquisition of the external life-world. Knowledge proceeds only *as if* there were such objective ideas. Kant is unequivocal about this. He writes that we:

> derive the object of experience from the supposed object of this idea, viewed as the ground or cause of the object of experience. We declare, for instance, that the things of the world must be viewed *as if* they received their existence from a highest intelligence. The idea is thus only a heuristic, not an ostensive concept. It does not show us how an object is constituted, but how, under its guidance, we should *seek* to determine the constitution and connection of the objects of experience.[3]

And Kant continues saying that although 'there is nothing whatsoever to hinder us from *assuming* these ideas to be also objective . . . we are not justified in introducing thought-entities which transcend all our concepts, though without contradicting them, as being real and determinate objects, merely on the authority of speculative reason'.[4] And by the latter Kant has in mind its hypothetical and not its apodictic nature.

The Kantian term reason refers to a formal, non-developed, that is, *a priori* and therefore historically contentless ground-giving unity only. Yet this highest abstract unity, 'which rests solely on concepts of reason, is the *purposive* unity of things. The *speculative* interest of reason makes it necessary to regard all order in the world as if it had originated in the purpose of a supreme reason'.[5] Thus the principles of pure reason, if properly understood, are nothing but regulative principles. But if misunderstood as being constitutive, 'they give rise, by a dazzling and deceptive illusion, to persuasion and a merely fictitious knowledge, and therewith to contradictions and eternal disputes'.[6]

Kant's treatment of the formal dialectic of pure reason leads inevitably to an antinomial dilemma. Though subjective rationality posits an absolute, it cannot hold or demonstrate it. Instead it employs it for regulative and, in this qualified sense, rational purposes only. Reason is to order the concepts which the understanding forms about the objects in the world of sense perception. The dilemma lies in this. The apparently *a priori* subjectivity, as the transcendental condition for uniting apperceived phenomenal objects, is, on the one hand, thought to be the 'pure original unchangeable consciousness' or 'consciousness of self'[7] or the 'abiding and unchanging "I" '.[8] But, on the other hand, the understanding is in no position to unify its categories. To accomplish this it must hypothesise transcendent ideas of reason. Thus the 'transcendental unity of apperception'[9] depends on a transcendent unity of that which cannot be perceived. What cannot be sensuously perceived are the noumenal ideas to which no phenomenal and that is no historically conditioned object corresponds.

Hegel now corrects the implications of Kant's problematic transcendental dialectic. The reflections on method must be thought through to their ultimate conclusions. By this we mean that a method must be such that it allows for the sublation of its immanent contradictions and their mediation into a system of coherence. For Hegel, accordingly, it is not a transcendentally given subjective ego that hypothesises a transcendent yet unreal reason whose unity is to be approximated progressively and in the future. Rather it is the principle of self-developing reason as the organic subject which for reflective purposes posits within itself the rational and mutually relational stages of its real historical becoming. And the subject *qua* history is fundamentally a communal and social becoming. It is the world of rational ideas in the past out of which historical reason produces the self-knowledge of its own presentness. The subject is conscious of an object. But for Hegel this object is now the subject's objective history. In thus reflecting upon its self-own object the subject becomes self-conscious. For Hegel the understanding does not, as is the case with Kant's rational reason, relate to an external and alienating transcendent object; it relates to the mediating and immanent objectification of the subject. Method, therefore, is not a cognitive device in the service of the understanding. Method is reason itself, and reason is the principle of the self applying itself to itself. The relations shown opposite visualise this distinction.

Kant's subjective understanding may also be regarded as a fundamentally separating and analytical *force*. This is clearly illustrated when we take the following example. The understanding has no power, for instance, to connect and ultimately unify an infinite series

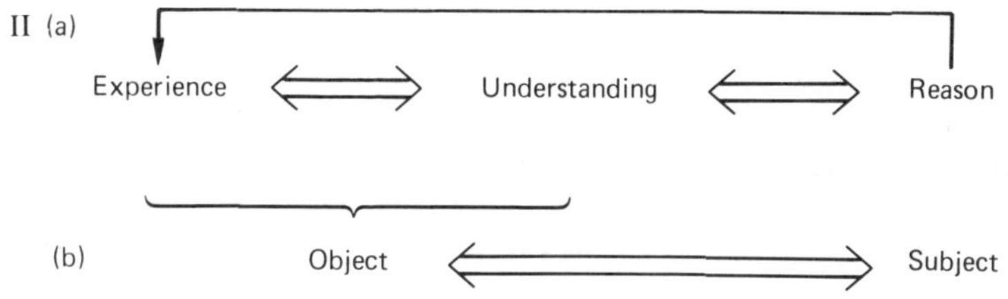

of, let us say, phenomenal points into noumenal infinity. Infinity is a symbol which only pretends to synthesise empirical data without actually creating their unity. *Power*, however, is with Hegel reason as subject. While Kant's reason lacks absoluteness because it is posited and abstract, Hegel's reason is absolute because it is produced and concrete. What is concrete is the rational content of reason's self-mediating history. Concretion is reflective becoming at the end of which reason reappears as self-created and unified result. The appearance of reason is what Hegel also calls its spirit, which is not to be confounded with an individual ratiocinating mind. Spirit, in its dialectical denotation, is a notion of social universality and historical immanence. It does not refer to anything external to the subject, but only to the subject's internal self.

Furthermore, while Kant's dialectic of reason functions formally and mechanically, Hegel's dialectic of reason operates organically and in this sense in a historical manner. In the first instance, Kant's reason is an outer, non-reflective and, therefore, passive noumenal cause. And it is an explanatory, prescriptive and normative end to be approximated. In Hegel's case reason manifests itself as the inner phenomenal cause or active *causa sui*. More to the point, the reason of the subject is for Hegel the thinking in the present about the thoughts and deeds of its past. Reason describes and reflects itself because it relates to itself historically.

Having sketched the different interpretations by Kant and Hegel of the methodological role of understanding and reason, we are now better equipped to throw some light on Feyerabend's employment of the term reason. Feyerabend's writings are of great significance in the context of this book, because they represent a rare transition from contemporary theories of scientific dialectic to Hegel's philosophical method of historical dialectic. His references to Hegel, of which we shall see more in subsequent sections, have therefore a distinct bearing on our own reflections. However, it must be said already now that, though Feyerabend adopts the Hegelian notion of reason, he gives it the meaning of understanding, or rather confuses it with rationality. He discusses Hegel's method, but tends to empty it of the dialectical soul of unified reason. But in misinterpreting the notion of reason, Feyerabend's method of dialectic invariably falls back again onto the level of conceptual rationality, a rationality whose posited objects remain not only hypothetical in the Kantian sense, but which also defy the Hegelian demand that they be historically bound. Consequently, Feyerabend's attempt to see in Hegel's dialectic a possibility to overcome the rational dilemma one is confronted with when treating the scientific question of theory transition is a sign of astute intellectual insight into theoretical problems. However, we do not diminish this estimation by also evaluating it cautiously.

Besides this critical note, the collapse of the two terms has far-reaching implications for understanding another though all-important aspect of historical reason. For not only is reason identical with the subject. Hegel discovers in it the very *principle of life* itself. Hence life is subject, and reason is its sublated history. That is, self-conscious life is only in that it is reflected history. It is self-developing and self-preserving presentness. Being historical, life dynamically idealises or permeates all those manifestations which it has in the past rationally posited and practically sought to approximate. It thereby determines or actualises its own becoming and self-understanding.

In Feyerabend life is presupposed and, moreover, taken for granted. In that he retains the term reason, but reduces it to a hypothesised reason, he uses it interchangeably with rationality. The theorist of science thus dissolves into indifference the fundamental distinction which the philosopher of history makes between understanding objects and the reason of the subject. The upshot of this is that Feyerabend also, though perhaps inadvertently, fails to distinguish between the Hegelian *notion* of life as it thinks itself through, and the rational mode of thinking about the *concept* life. But the meaning of life cannot be reduced to a form of conceptual understanding. In that life is with Hegel 'imperishable *life*',[10] it is self-related identity and as such is its self-own irreducible reflected absolute.

Feyerabend's epistemological concept of reason is the equivalent to a kind of rationality which merrily posits separate and incoherent multitudes of theories of objects. For Feyerabend reason has no direction, and nothing binds it. Instead, in its rational interpretation, it 'grants that the ideas which we introduce in order to expand and to improve our knowledge may *arise* in a very disorderly way'.[11]

Again, Hegel's philosophy cannot be limited to a theoretical, instrumental and outward-looking question of how to improve and increase knowledge of something external to the subject, in the sense of a more refined and numerical articulation of episteme.[12] Hegel's method of dialectical objectification is inward-looking. It is a reflective and holistic insight into the historical becoming of self-knowledge or self-consciousness. Science, which after all means knowledge, is fully comprehensive only as the science of the self, while the science of objects exterior to the subject is always partial and illusory. Hence science is the historically developed knowledge of self-identity. For this reason it is also the activity of a philosophical and not a theoretical investigation. The inward movement of reason, Hegel says, 'is no longer either a transition into, or a reflection on something else, but "Development"'.[13] Development implies the internal transformation of the self. To develop means that the self as subject actively *de*-envelops itself into its history, and then intentionally *re*-envelops or reflects itself back into itself in order to become and hence to be self-consciousness. It is reason's 'manifestation of itself in its process as a development of its own self'.[14] As one commentator of Hegel put it: the ultimate object is not outside reason, and therefore reason does not have to get externalised and become *transiens*. If action is understood not as a deed in the practical sense, but as an activity of the spirit, then the ultimate object is within reason, and reason is *actio immanens*.[15]

Feyerabend's less than rigorous epistemological dialectic is in the light of this reading of reason almost arbitrary and actually a misnomer. Hegel's philosophical dialectic describes reason in terms of the historical method. And reason uses this method in order to form itself into a self-preserving coherent system. Dialectic is self-mediation *through* the historical medium of the self. In fact, internal or organic *dia*-lectic is not the same as the externally hypothesised pluralism of an *anything goes*. It is open development because it opens the historical venues towards self-knowledge. Yet this dialectical openness is precisely what constitutes the subject's social unity and historical holism. Both interpretations, therefore, have also different consequences. While for Hegel the philosophical method is one that leads to determinate knowledge, namely, to the self-knowledge of the subject, Feyerabend's theoretical pluralism results neither in subjectively posited knowledge nor in mediated or produced self-knowledge.

Theoretical pluralism only serves the formal methodological relationship between understanding and reason. For Hegel reason historically demonstrates progress towards self-consciousness because it refers to the immanent past-present continuum. Yet for Feyerabend the external and future-oriented 'idea of reason accepted by the majority of rationalists . . . may prevent progress' in the sense of improvement, and, indeed, 'our chances to progress *may* be obstructed by our desire to be rational'.[16] But this rationality refers to the consciousness of an object other than the self of the subject and hence is undemonstrable.

To end this section: we make these comments about Feyerabend fully aware of Hegel's fundamental critique of criticism in general. Hegel warns, for instance, that refutation must not come from outside, that is, it must not proceed from assumptions lying outside the system in question and inconsistent with it. The genuine refutation must penetrate the opponent's stronghold and meet him on his own ground; no advantage is gained by attacking him somewhere else and defeating him where he is not.[17] We trust, however, that our examination of Feyerabend will show that he, intentionally or not, appropriates Hegel in a way that not only does not do justice to Hegel's philosophical strength, but even leads to a misconception of the method of his historical dialectic.

The difficulty we meet in understanding Feyerabend's interpretation of reason and rationality is due, here as elsewhere, to the way he employs both locutions alternately. Let us therefore follow his own reading of Hegel more closely, and look at some pertinent examples. This is at the same time an opportunity to elucidate Hegel's own philosophical dialectic, and to illustrate the part-whole perspective in terms of the historical development of self-conscious life.

FEYERABEND AND HEGEL

Philosophical thinking endeavours to comprehend the idea of holism. Theoretical epistemology, as we have already experienced through Aristotle, tries to apply this idea to the particularity of empirical research areas. Such a transposition, however, is in modernity not only problematic from the point of view of legitimacy. It also raises the question of hermeneutics and of how to interpret the dimension of reason, that is, of the manifest need for unity in the sciences and in the experience of life, respectively. We consider the unity of life, however, to be more than the sum-total of scientific cognition because, unlike science, the consciousness of life is spiritually mediated into its all-encompassing self-consciousness. Being a concrete idea that relates to itself through its immanent history, life can be adequately reflected upon only philosophically.

As we have argued earlier, the different views about dialectic between Feyerabend and Hegel lie in this very distinction between science as epistemology and science as the self-knowledge of life. And, in consequence, Feyerabend's discussion of reason is incompatible with Hegel's own reflections. This observation we wish to substantiate by means of a more expansive study of Hegel's text and Feyerabend's appropriation of it.

That Feyerabend uses the term reason the way he does may be attributed to his equivocal and incomplete reading of Hegel. For him 'one of the consequences of pluralism and proliferation is that stability of knowledge can no longer be guaranteed'.[1] Rational knowledge, that is, a subjectively posited understanding of phenomena, is an illusion. It prevents progress because of the rigidity of rationalism or because of the 'stultifying effect of "the laws of reason"'.[2]

Since scientific activity has turned against its own presupposition and is not guided any more by an objective and rigorous method, its theoretical enterprise is much more sloppy and irrational. In fact, such subjective characteristics are the 'preconditions of progress'.[3] Stronger still: Feyerabend adamantly insists that 'without "chaos" no knowledge. Without a frequent dismissal of reason, no progress'.[4] Cognitive understanding will not advance unless particular irrational attitudes repeatedly challenge the claims of a universal rational reason. This attitude, however, amounts to an advocation of episteme without logic. 'Ideas', Feyerabend writes, 'which today form the very basis of science exist only because there were such things as prejudice, conceit, passion; because these things *opposed reason*'.[5] They opposed reason as it was posited by a transcendentally categorised understanding, that is, by rationality in its strictest sense.

Reason, in this context, is employed in its rational and theoretical connotation. But Hegel would argue that philosophical reason is not an assumed and external objectivity, separated from its positing subjectivity. It is related and mediated subject/object identity. It is the identity between reason as subject and its object which is its phenomenal historical world. And it is this unity of subject and object which exists as historical life.[6] Life is not posited as an abstract idea, but is lived historically and is always concretised in the present.

While the understanding posits objective though illusory assertions into the future, reason is truly and actually objective because it is the present subject which has produced itself out of its historical past.

'No philosophy', Hegel tells us, 'oversteps its own time'; hence 'the present is the highest stage reached'.[7] Knowledge is knowledge only of the becoming of the present, to which alone it realistically relates. There is no knowledge of the future, only opinion, prediction and hope.

Moreover, his ambiguous grasp of the relationship between reason and rationality becomes particularly apparent when Feyerabend says that 'even within science reason cannot and should not be allowed to be comprehensive and that it must often be overruled, or eliminated, in favour of other agencies. There is no single rule that remains valid under all circumstances and not a single agency to which appeal can always be made'.[8] But that which acts theoretically, in the sense just described, is not reason as subject but the subjective understanding which posits its own, albeit rational, reason. The understanding attempts to comprehend the world as its object. It does this by positing a contingent and formal theory or hypothesis, to which ought to correspond something called a fact or a thing. What is here comprehensive is so merely in a contingent way. It is as such finite precisely because it derives its claim from the understanding, whose categorial scientific determinations ought to become comprehensive only on a higher conceptual level, namely, that of posited reason. In understanding a conceptual object we are conscious of something necessarily indeterminate, something that lies over and above the understanding itself.

Hegel's reason, however, describes an entirely different relation: it becomes determinate self-consciousness. It comprehends, and historically contains within the domain of its reflections, all the past determinations of the formative understanding, and mediatingly sublates and preserves them within itself. This self is always the subject in its present existence. The subjective understanding *qua* rationality itself can never be comprehensive, though it strives to become so. 'The understanding', Hegel writes, 'imitates reason in its absolute positing, and it gives itself, through this form, the appearance of reason'.[9] For Hegel the subject entails subjectivity. Reason contains the understanding as its phenomenal historical ground, or as its appearance. Thus, instead of the former epistemological endeavours pursued by Kant's transcendental and fixed *a priori*, or by Feyerabend's rationally sanctified formalism of an *anything goes*, we have with Hegel a self-determining living agent. This agent is alive only in that it reflectively reproduces itself out of the historical and hence spiritual life-world which it has posited into itself and for itself.

At this point, it may be fitting to insert a note of terminological clarification. We have made mention of both *concept* and *notion*, These terms are in German the *Be-griff* whose prefix *Be* means purposeful activity[10] or the directional comprehension or grasp (Griff) of something. It refers to the present which consciously reaches out into its past and returns from it with a richer formation of self-consciousness. In Hegel's German text no linguistic distinction is made between contingent, subjective and conceptual comprehension, on the one hand, and the necessary and notional comprehension of the subject, on the other. In both instances the word *Begriff* is employed. But in our heuristic discussion of understanding and reason we shall throughout refer to the former as *concept* and to the latter as *notion* so as to render more distinct the way these terms are applied to the relationship between the part and the whole.

It must be borne in mind, however, that for Hegel the *concept is notionalised* in the sense that the notion comprehends its concepts, or that the *Begriff begreift sich selbst*. The present reflectively comprehends its past. And in the logic of historical dialectic it cannot be otherwise. As Hegel makes it crystal clear: 'The usual practice of separating understanding and reason is, from every point of view, to be rejected. When the Notion is regarded as irrational [vernunftlos, H.K.], this should be interpreted rather as an incapacity of reason to recognize itself in the Notion'.[11] In its development the notion is history and as actuality is the present in which it knows itself as free life. Subjectivity, on the other hand, is unfree because it cannot but posit a concept from which it is alienated and which itself is not self-determining. Subjectivity does not relate to itself, but only to that which is extraneous to it. With this brief terminological interlude the theoretical and philosophical relationship between Feyerabend and Hegel may be understood better.

Feyerabend writes: 'a thinker following .... Hegel regards any prolonged stability .... as an indication of *failure*, pure and simple. Any such stability indicates *that we have failed to transcend an accidental stage of research and that we have failed to rise to a higher stage of consciousness and of understanding*'.[12] But that which induces the understanding to question its arbitrarily posited determinations is, according to Hegel, not the alienating understanding itself but innermost reason. Historical life continuously transforms the aspirations of rationality. It is this self-relating reason which frees the resisting understanding from its own conceptual and dogmatic shackles and fetters.

Feyerabend quotes Hegel and says with him that 'the more solid, well defined, and splendid the edifice erected by the understanding, the more restless the urge of life to escape from it into freedom'.[13] Feyerabend concedes, however, that:

> every move away from the status quo, by opening the way to a new and as yet untried system of categories, temporarily returns to the mind the freedom and spontaneity that is its essential property. But complete freedom is never achieved. For any change, however dramatic, always leads to a new system of *fixed* categories. Things, processes, states are still separated from each other.[14]

It is true the understanding works with categorially determined fixed concepts, and that this may engender a teleological urge or drive to escape from them into the illusion of freedom. But Hegel sublates these illusions into the historically appearing development not of consciousness but of self-consciousness. Freedom for him refers to immanent and notional, not to external and conceptual reason. In philosophical logic notional reason 'comprehends the understanding';[15] that is, philosophy subsumes and converts theory. Philosophy produces freedom, namely, the existence of life which theoretical thinking posits only as an ought. Not the concept but the notion is the 'realm of *subjectivity* or of *freedom*'.[16] This subjectivity, however, is not rationality but reason, and as such is the truly free subject or completed self-conscious history. 'The pure Notion is the absolutely infinite, unconditioned and free.'[17] It is free because in its existent actuality it freely determines its present self-consciousness out of its past through which it forms itself into a coherent, that is, non-finite or unlimited whole. It is free because it is the self-will to know itself through its self-own becoming. Knowledge is existential knowledge of the self and not knowledge of an object other than the self. But since it is relational knowledge, it is and can only be expressed in terms of its absolute idea. The future, however, lies in the as yet separated beyond and, therefore, cannot be known but only believed in. Its idea is not fulfilled and, consequently, is spurious and defective. The freedom of the future is therewith also only a possibility for the subject and its present; it is not necessity.

It is because reason is subject that that which urges and drives it forward is its organically determined history, which is its continuous life. The freedom of reason is the freedom to become and to be itself. Hegel's reason is not a hoped-for, future-oriented reason, but one that is historically always fulfilled in its present. The present *is*: it is the result that has developed out of its past. Reason is not an *ought* that still awaits completion. For Hegel it relates only to the task of present being to comprehend itself fully in and through the multiple ought of its past. It is the sublation of an alienating teleology and hence implies the freedom of produced entelechy. It is free reason because it is reason in-and-for-itself and thus self-determinate. That the understanding seeks freedom, but does not reach and comprehend it, lies in the fact that it dwells in the illusion of an extraneous concept. The conceptual object, unlike the notional subject, is freedom posited as an in-itself only. It cannot yet be philosophically treated as the produced in-and-for-itself.

Another example of Feyerabend's questionable interpretation of Hegel is the following. To the previous sentence he now adds, quoting Hegel: 'The existence of different elements, of a manifold is still "exaggerated into an opposition by the understanding"'.[18]

Again, it is right to argue epistemologically that the understanding is divided into particulars. But what happens here and why? Hegel writes, completing Feyerabend's citation:

> Thinking reason, however, sharpens, so to say, the blunt difference of diverse terms, the mere manifoldness of pictorial thinking, into *essential* difference, into *opposition*. Only when the manifold terms have been driven to the point of contradiction do they become active and lively towards one another, receiving in contradiction the negativity which is the indwelling pulsation of self-movement and spontaneous activity (Lebendigkeit).[19]

This, unlike the precepts of epistemology, suggests spiritually organic self-organisation and not an attempt to ascertain the structure of other objects.

Thus it is not merely the plurality of the conceptual objects of the understanding which still seeks its unity in a distant reason. Rather is it the one notional subject of reason which develops and dialectically transforms these objects into spiritual contradiction, or into the growth differentiations of life, until they are fully sublated in the unity of the present. Reason organically contradicts, judges or differentiates itself into the manifold historical and formative movements of its understanding. The past necessarily develops into but also only out of its present. The beginning of this cyclical process is undifferentiated *universality*, its judgment and externalisation into history is the past as *particularity*, and the present end is immanently preserved unitary *individuality*. Individuality is subject as mediated fulfilled reason. Hence its self-comprehension is actualised through the reflected manifestation of its history.

'Contradiction', writes Hegel, 'is the root of all movement and vitality [Lebendigkeit, H.K.]; it is only in so far as something has a contradiction within it that it moves, has an urge and activity'.[20] Reason is this spontaneous and pulsating activity; it is 'internal self-movement proper, *instinctive urge* in general'.[21] 'The principle of all self-movement . . . consists solely in an exhibition of it',[22] or solely in its organic differentiation. 'Something is therefore alive only', Hegel concludes, 'in so far as it contains contradiction within it, and moreover is this power to hold and endure the contradiction within it'.[23] A present is only as the perennial assignment to comprehend itself through the contradictory or differentiating moments of its becoming. It is never a given but always the positive result of contradiction.[24] And this is to say further that, unlike factual nature, which is devoid of consciousness and hence in no position to change its seasons, history's consciousness always alters the possibilities of its self-comprehension.

Feyerabend fails to notice that Hegel's reason is historically concrete and not abstract in the hypothetical sense. He misrepresents Hegel because he incorrectly translates the key terms. For instance, he renders 'der reflektierende Verstand'[25] as 'reflective reason',[26] and quotes: 'Reflective reason . . . is nothing but the understanding which uses abstraction, separates, and insists that the separation be maintained and taken seriously'.[27] This is a rather deplorable and careless language because it shows how the theoretician Feyerabend is prone to using rationality or understanding (Verstand) and reason (Vernunft) interchangeably. A more adequate translation is: 'But "reflective" understanding . . . stands for the understanding as abstracting, and hence as separating and remaining fixed in its separations'.[28]

Finally, that Feyerabend's interpretation of Hegel lacks philosophical unity and is therefore one-sided, is also seen in the way he quotes him in another though similar context concerning the categories of the understanding. The latter's activity, Feyerabend says, belongs to the 'evil manner of reflection',[29] or 'bad habits of reflection'.[30] However, he does not add the important, even crucial continuation of Hegel's sentence, namely: '. . . which demands comprehensibility';[31] '*welche nach der Begreiflichkeit fragt*'.[32] But it is precisely this notional comprehensibility within which reason binds meaningfully the manifold categorial determinants of the understanding into the actuality and existence of every dialectically determined present.

A conjectural explanation for why Feyerabend has left out the second part of the quote may be that he regards comprehensibility as a rational and hence deceptive reason. Yet what Hegel means by comprehensibility (Begreiflichkeit) is not an encompassing though contingent object of the subjective understanding, and an understanding, moreover, that operates on the basis of the presupposition of life. Rather is it present and actual reason which necessarily comprehends all rational manifestations. Life is not presupposed by a more anterior premise. The demand for comprehensibility is the demand of the dim consciousness of life for the dissolution of fixed rational categories which obstruct the task towards its more adequate self-understanding. Reason drives towards the break-up of such rigidities in order to make the task more fluid and thereby to ensure the further development of life itself. Perspectival dialectic is comprehensibility. To demand or to ask for comprehensibility is life's own urge to grasp itself notionally. To ask for life is to reflect upon oneself as one's becoming; it is to respond to one's own innermost reason. This is the search for the free unity of historically developed self-consciousness. All historical transformations are directed towards their comprehension, as long as this comprehension is a willed one.

The understanding demands posited conceptual comprehensibility, while historical reason demands itself as self-produced notional comprehensibility. Hegel very persuasively criticises the particularity of the understanding for wanting to posit and hold a multitude of single all-encompassing conceptual universals. But this critique does not persist in its negativity, for the negative is again positively sublated by the thinking activity of historical reason. It is then also because Feyerabend uses understanding and reason in the same sense that he confounds them both. He thereby reduces Hegel's dialectical meaning of reason to a categorial-like rationality that makes unwarranted claims of knowledge.

Reflection of the understanding is possible because it necessarily leads towards its own posited, that is, rational reason. The bad habit of this activity is its assumption that there are rationally valid fixed phenomena. But in the theoretical sciences of natural objects full comprehensibility cannot be obtained because, in the end, rationality still has to ask for its reason. It has to ask for its historical meaning and purpose, both of which can be articulated only by and for the inquiring subject. Feyerabend is concerned with showing what theory already may concede itself, namely, that it cannot hold its own ground and therefore must be analysed in more anarchical terms. But he does not or perhaps cannot put the question of the philosophical science of self to the implications of the theoretical rationalism of otherness.

But this is the very question Hegel asks with great conviction and pursues with the most captivating reflections. He has long ago made already this '*turning point* of the movement of the Notion',[33] or the 'turning point of the method'.[34] Here again, the notion and its method do not refer to a rational understanding. They describe the philosophical and historical method of reason to form itself into self-knowledge. The ultimate being which Hegel reflects upon is 'fulfilled being', is the '*Notion that comprehends itself*', or is 'being as the *concrete* and also absolutely *intensive* totality'.[35] This totality is holistic life as it has preserved and actualised itself in its present. Fulfilled being is accomplished only in the historical present. Future life is merely expected, and this only on the basis of a reflection on the past. But what lies in the future is not known. Only the present is known, and it is known through the dialectial mediation and sublation of the past.

The result of Feyerabend's radicalism is that he dissolves the subjective and rational models of science along with their methods which have proved to be all too removed from the life of man and his existential concerns. But with the untenable consequences of Feyerabend's escape from the rigours of positivistic and paradigmatic assertions into the unmediated conceptual playground of freedom, begins at the same time the other mode of thinking and reflecting. The search for a theory of knowledge, once it has broken down within its own demand for absolute autonomy, is replaced by a different kind of quest.[36] In a scientifically and technologically menaced time this other and primary quest can only be for the holistic knowledge of the subject as its self-own historical object. It does not revolve about a theoretical and quantifiable object. Life is not a hypothesis. The quest has intrinsically to do with man and the practical exigencies of life.[37] The life of the subject man is the fulfilment of a qualitative principle, namely, the philosophical reflection upon its praxis. This principle, which is a notion of self-consciousness, finds its expression also in the Hegelian meaning of *necessity* (Not-wendigkeit) and it refers to the subject's need (Not) to turn around and towards (Wende) itself and to reflect comprehensively on the dialectical becoming of its life.

Hegel's extraordinary and timeless insight into the shortcomings of scientific reasoning, traditional and contemporary, and his consequent inquiry into the philosophical knowledge of the subject is reminiscent of Socrates' quest for the theoretical knowledge of objects. Lest one loses sight of the whole one has to relate particular sense observations to a higher organising principle. 'I was afraid', says the ancient, 'that by observing objects with my eyes and trying to comprehend them with each of my other senses I might blind my soul altogether. So I decided that I must have recourse to theories, and use them in trying to discover the truth about things.'[38] But while in Platonic epistemology truth is to be found in the unitary form of the object, for Hegel it refers to the unified historical content of the self-knowledge of the subject. Different historical epochs, then, relate not only to the different possibilities for knowing objects. They also make different demands upon the subject.

Actualised reason is the self-knowledge of autonomous and self-producing life, and thus is the notional comprehensibility of its historical essence. Life in its ever present actuality is, to put it in more technical terms, the fulfilled *syllogism*. It is what it is because it has become what it is. The Hegelian understanding of syllogism is reflected and mediated result. It is that which *remains*, and remains alive, in and through that which *has been*, or it is *Ge-wesenes*. It is the result of history, and history is always only *oneness*. Its *con-clusion* is the present as it is reflected in the complete union *with* its historical past. The present *closes* the relation between itself and the past.

If the consideration of life is true philosophy, then philosophy is the thinking of the self-comprehending subject. Rational theory not only presupposes life, but increasingly fragments and manipulates its historical reason. And in another sense theory even alienates itself from philosophy, and the more so the more it dissolves itself into seemingly autonomous parts which do not regard themselves as *members* of an organic whole.

To conclude: Hegel may want to argue that theory believes that it no longer requires philosophy in order to constitute itself and its specialised sciences, and that it therefore has nothing to say to it any more, either. But theory may come to realise that its rational doings and undoings only weaken its self-own ground which is life itself. It may then also be at such a historical juncture, as we experience it today in the age of the atom and environmental crises, that theory might have to begin to reflect upon its reason and to respond to it as to itself. In other words, theoretical consciousness may ask for its philosophical self-consciousness. The idea of nuclear war indisputedly constitutes this juncture, and compels the human mind to reflect upon reason in its historical spirituality rather than in its soulless rational divisions. The dialectical diction, which is bequeathed to us by Hegel, is clearly more adequate for this purpose than the language of Feyerabend's anarchical hedonism.

The holism of which Hegel speaks is the subject which constitutes itself through itself. This perspective is the reflective turning point[39] within the tradition of philosophical thinking. It is the consequence that Hegel draws from the historical unreflectedness of particularising thought. In that Hegel reflects upon life, he reflects upon that which is most complete and yet has become so fragile that we must face the possibility of its destruction.

PHILOSOPHICAL SPECULATION

The interpretive distinction between understanding and reason has additional implications for the meaning of the important but often misunderstood Hegelian term *speculation*. This implement of reflection usually carries Kantian and idealistic overtones, and is suggestive of views about how the future might unfold itself, or about how rational forms of transcendence in general might be approximated. But Hegel is not in this sense an idealist. He is a realist whose thematisation of speculation makes sense only in association with his historical propositions about the subject. The subject is an agent reflecting itself in and through its own becoming. What is speculative is the comprehension of past historical moments relating coherently to one another. The history of the subject is its dialectically unified reality. The threat to life, which is the underlying topic of this book, may therefore be said to be the threat to its possibility to preserve the development of self-consciousness in its spiritual speculation. The present section considers the issue of speculation with relevant references to Feyerabend and Kant.

The reflection of the understanding is an illusory reflection because it remains locked within the limits of its own rational concepts. If we now take, for instance, a paradigm to be a form of such a reflection, we may say with Feyerabend that it cannot question its own standards from within, and that it needs an external point of reference. Feyerabend places the external or alternative point in the 'minds of the participants', that is, in the minds of those who participate in scientific deliberations, whereas Hegel is said to regard 'the idea as the subject of development, and human thought as derivative'.[1]

Two points need to be noted. Feyerabend may be right in saying that it is with the proliferation of alternative theories that we acquire more knowledge about a particular field of scientific and specialised research. And in this sense we may have become more conscious of the possible horizontal width of knowledge which we accumulate about a restricted phenomenal domain. This is what Feyerabend himself calls the expanded consciousness of the 'understanding'.[2]

But to speak of transcendence[3] in connection with theoretical understanding alone without introducing reason is to distort Hegel's philosophy. To transcend is to go beyond and outside the confines of the understanding. However, while it is not clear what it would mean to go beyond arbitrariness, to transcend *a priori* held categories can with Kant at least be taken to be the positing of reason from a transcendentally given starting-point. On the other hand, to transcend may equally refer to the proposition of an altogether different argument. This Hegelian argument would be that one moves away from an illusory rationality and instead thematises the appearance of historical reason. This means, then, that the historical reason of the present sublates the transcendent objects of the past and turns them into the immanent tool for reason itself. The existence of the subject has subjectivity for its historical essence. The implication of such a speculative turning point of philosophical reflection is that any transcendentally posited absolute itself goes through its historical transformation and development. It is not that the transcendent absolute has a definitional essence, but that the history of the absolute is its essence. Hence essence is not being but *becoming*.

No matter how much the understanding proliferates alternative theories, it could not by itself transcend its own self and establish a comprehensive rational system. Feyerabend rejects the Kantian possibility of linear progress based on transcendentalism. But he also misreads the Hegelian idea of historical reason. So, even if his point is correct, namely, that the understanding cannot achieve a system, Feyerabend presents us only with a one-sided and negative alternative because, given the philosophical tradition, he employs terms such as transcendence and consciousness too loosely, without thinking them through.

The second point we are concerned with refers to the distinction Feyerabend makes between human thought and its ideas. Feyerabend gives one the impression that the Hegelian *idea* was something unconnected with the world of phenomena to which man, who experiences these phenomena historically, belongs of necessity. But this Hegel would deny. In fact, his whole philosophical enterprise is an attempt to demonstrate the exact opposite.

Hegel's idealism is very different from the idealism of a Kant and the Enlightenment tradition, for instance. For Kant it is the understanding which *has* formal and therefore ahistorical ideas of transcendent reason. In Hegel reason is not in any conceivable way derivative; it is immanence. It is the world and its becoming and hence *is* at every present moment historically concrete. Hegel's reason describes holism. It is, to repeat, ultimately only 'one' whole.[4] And, moreover, for Kant reason can be approximated precisely because of its derivative function. However, it is never filled, let alone fulfilled. In Hegel, by contrast, historical reason is in its present existence always fulfilled and complete. And as completion it is actualised result. This speculative idea is the subject's imperishable life. Life actively idealises, penetrates and permeates the merely subjective and hypothesised ideas of its history in order to reach the natural phenomena and, in turn, to sublate them spiritually. The dialectic of the idea is only through the phenomenally real world of its historical moments. It is speculative phenomenology. The Kantian ideas in their plurality are devoid of becoming and do not relate back to the phenomena of nature. Such phenomena are and can only be historically experienced and dialectically woven into comprehension.

The historical relationship which Hegel philosophises about is called *speculation*. Kant articulates the rational or the merely speculative employment of reason. This future-oriented speculation endeavours the approximation to a concept which, however, is never actually reached. And hence Kant says of such a concept that 'it is *only* an idea. The absolute whole of all appearance . . . *is only an idea*; since we can never represent it in image, it remains a *problem* to which there is no solution'.[5] It is in this meaning of hypothesis that the Kantian idea is a rational and speculative object. It is speculative because it is unknown, and never to be known.

In Hegel speculation is not the activity of subjective rationality; it is the internal activity of reason as subject. With this difference Hegel accomplishes the dissolution of and solution to Kant's antinomial rational dilemma. It means that the idea produces itself reflectively in its phenomenal and rational otherness. It sees itself within and sees into its historical becoming. It reflects itself in its self-posited and mediated otherness, that is, within itself. This self is comprehended as history. Hence the self reflects itself through its own history. The self is always mediated self. In this sense speculation is reflection reflecting itself historically. While the understanding reflects upon external and formal objects, reason reflects itself in its internal and concrete history. Reason is insight into speculative relations. And insight is a critical and yet holistic faculty of thinking, because relations are intrinsically holistic and not particularistic. With clarifying reference to Hegel the point, for instance, has been made that what speculative philosophy teaches is a radical scepticism about one's own rational presuppositions. Genuine speculative philosophy is never merely the creation of conceptual figments which disregard the facts of natural consciousness. Rather is it a thinking which always acknowledges natural experience, but which does not take it as a given, as something unquestioned, but which seeks a standpoint from which this natural experience can question itself about itself.[6]

Thus for Hegel speculation is the method of the notional subject with which it produces itself out of its nature in such a way that it sublates the mediative rational concepts about this nature. Only through the sublation of speculative relations is development possible and does the subject become historically conscious of itself. Accordingly, we can say that while for Kant the concepts (Begriffe) are objects, for Hegel the notion (Begriff) is the subject.

Speculative philosophy argues with Hegel that the rational, that is, 'the familiar, just because it is familiar, is not cognitively understood [as reason, H.K.]. The commonest way in which we deceive either ourselves or others about understanding is by assuming something as familiar, and accepting it on that account; with all its pros and cons, such knowing never gets anywhere, and it knows not why'.[7]

Dialectical or speculative philosophy, then, disputes the justificatory grounds of our theoretical presuppositions. Historical reason questions the assumptions of the ahistorical understanding. For Hegel philosophy is not exhausted by a conceptual consciousness. Philosophy wills the notional self-consciousness which is produced through the historical sublation and preservation of the understanding and the concepts it has of nature. Nature itself is the nature of reason; it is the rationalised phenomenon of the logic. Reason dissolves and sublates the theoretical determinations of the understanding. It thereby surely irritates, but also induces it to reach a higher, more comprehensive grounding for its utterances. This higher ground is the more fully developed subject as historical reason (Grund) which develops out of its phenomenal nature as foundation

(Grund). And because reason is the subject, its higher and highest ground is the positive principle of life. 'That which enables the Notion to advance itself', Hegel says, 'is the ... *negative* which it possesses within itself; it is this which constitutes the genuine dialectical element'.[8] The 'result, grasped in its positive aspect, is nothing else but the inner negativity of the determinations as their self-moving soul, the principle of all natural and spiritual life'.[9]

And Hegel concludes: 'It is in this dialectic as it is here understood, that is, in the grasping of opposites [as organic growth differentiations, H.K.] in their unity or of the positive in the negative, that speculative thought consists'.[10] This unifying mode of thinking of the notion 'is not abstract but a living, concrete unity in virtue of the fact that in it the opposition in consciousness between a self-determined entity, a subject, and a second such entity, an object, is known to be overcome; being is known to be the pure Notion in its own self, and the pure Notion to be the true being'.[11]

Thus to negate in concrete logic is not, as in formal logic, to deny or to disregard, let alone to eliminate reason. On the contrary, reason is thought to be the subject which, in turn, does not eliminate but sublates the understanding. Only in that it historically overcomes rational utterances can it also question them. And what it challenges is the positivistic claim to justify its transcendentally posited theoretical concepts. For Hegel concepts are not developed as relations and hence remain spurious and defective.

What Hegel means by negation is that it dissolves or differentiates, and renders transparent the historical objects which are posited by the understanding. It is not to destroy the understanding itself. It is only to demonstrate to it that it is a finite historical moment within the infinite movement and development of life. Life comprehends its history, which is always sublated in the present. And the present alone is life. The contingent historical formations gain meaning only if they stand in a necessary relationship to the completed present. Meaning is immanent relation. It is the underived relationship of the part to the whole, of the past to the present. Meaning is the meaning of history.

In reflection life differentiates itself into its historical yet relational manifestations. The relationship of otherness, of contradictory manifestions, or of spiritually organic growth differentiations is for Hegel the internal self-movement and instinctive urge *in general*.[12] But within that which is *general* nothing can be eliminated or falsified in the formal logical sense. Nothing can escape from reason. But everything educates itself out of consciousness and through historical transformations into self-consciousness. Growth implies that there are antecedent stages of growth. It does not mean their elimination. Every present has a past, and this past is its tradition. If in our reflections we were to eliminate the past, no recognition of the present would be possible. If we were to eliminate the task to comprehend ourselves through our traditions, historical growth, that is, dialectical mediation itself, would end. We would lose our bearing and the speculative relationship to ourselves. Being is meaningless without its relational becoming. There cannot be self-conscious life where there is no history, because it is only through its spiritualised manifestations that life recognises itself. The ultimate meaning of life itself is thus its historical self-recognition.

This too, then, is a difference between theoretical and philosophical logic. In the philosophy of dialectic Hegel says that '*speculative thinking* consists solely in the fact that thought holds fast contradiction, and in it, its own self, but does not allow itself to be dominated by it as in ordinary thinking, where its determinations are resolved by contradiction only into other determinations or into nothing'.[13]

Therein lies the tragedy of the activities of the formal and ordinary understanding if one considers them in isolation only. The faculty of the understanding is such that it can either boundlessly multiply its manifold claims of theoretical determinations or destroy itself. In other words, since it cannot hold itself, the tragedy of asserted yet antinomial rationality is that it is inevitably non-relational, unsublatable and consequently meaningless. But if the understanding is regarded, as in Hegel, as the historically concretised manifestation of reason, then there will be a *tertium* for it. In this *tertium*, however, the understanding is no longer an extreme beginning and end. Its role is reduced to a mediating *middle term* or to a relational means for a higher and coherent purpose, namely, for the sublating actualisation of its reason. In order to understand the *tertium* in its historical context let us look more closely at its teleological meaning as it is dialectically employed not for the objective determination of things but for the reflection of the subject.

For Hegel, the understanding is the third term of the dialectical syllogism. It is the included *middle* in the teleological and syllogistic movement of reason. The middle is the historical and hence mediating content within dialectic. That is to say, the organic coherence of the subject's reflected identity is mediated through the means as 'medius terminus'.[14] What does this signify?

If we take the notion to be the subject, then the subject as 'end is in its own self the urge to realise itself .... [T]he Notion therefore repels itself from itself. This repulsion is in general the *resolution* of the relation of the negative unity to itself, whereby it is *exclusive* individuality; but by this *exclusion* it *resolves* itself, or *opens up* itself, because this exclusion is a *self-determining*, a positing of *its own self*'.[15] Only the present existence of the subject as self-end can resolve or decide (ent-schliessen) for itself exclusively (aus-schliessend) to unlock itself or to open up (auf-schliessen). In opening up it decides to free itself into the manifestation of its historical content. The free decision in-and-for-itself is the truth of the subject and as such the result of coherent syllogising (schliessen).

In true teleology, Hegel writes therefore, 'the free is the Notion in its Existence'.[16] Existence is only through the mediation of its historical concretisation. It is the notion self-judged or opened up into its history. Existence is the objective content of the notion as subject. And further, the *in-itself* of the historical rational object is the *for-itself* of the present existing subject. Hence 'in teleology ... the content becomes important, for teleology presupposes a Notion, something *absolutely determined* and therefore self-determining ...; for end [Zweck, H.K.], according to its form, is a totality infinite within itself'.[17] But the infinite is for Hegel not the infinite of the beyond; it is the non-finitude of historical coherence and thus of immanence.

The notion as subject has itself for its end. And it is because the notion is life that the dialectical judgment is for it its own living historical becoming towards its self-own syllogism as sublated life. The notion relates to itself historically. It coherently syllogises itself with itself. Accordingly, Hegel can write that 'the end-relation [Zweckbeziehung, H.K.] is more than *judgement*; it is the *syllogism* of the self-subsistent free Notion that unites itself with itself through objectivity'.[18] Translated historically this is to say that the end-relation is the present and its objectivity is its past. And it is through the mediation of the past that the present becomes syllogised actuality. Thus the negativity of the judgment is itself negated and sublated into positive unity.

This movement, which we may call the double telos or the speculative entelechy, is 'purposiveness'; it is the 'rational ['Vernünftige' = not rationality but reason, H.K.] in its concrete existence'.[19] Existence is the determined determination of reason. Reason as end 'manifests *rationality* ['Vernünftigkeit' = reason, H.K.] because it is the concrete Notion, which holds the *objective difference within its absolute unity*. It is therefore essentially in its own self *syllogism*.'[20]

The subject determines itself through its historical object. History is the means through which the subject guides itself into sublated existence. The object is the rationalised objectivity of the world. As history it is the essence of the subject and the historical becoming of its being. Essence is existence, and existence is essence. Thus the subject as 'end unites itself through a means with objectivity, and in objectivity with itself. The means is the middle term of the syllogism'.[21] Reason produces itself purposefully out of its posited understanding which it uses as its historical means.

That Hegel humbles the understanding into a means instead of, as in the tradition, respecting it piously[22] as the sole law-giver is of utmost importance for the attempt to come to terms with the difference between rationality and speculative reason, or between means and end, object and subject. About the first term of these relational pairs Hegel says this: even though

> the means is an object . . . it has no power ['Kraft'= force, H.K.] of resistance against the end . . . To the end . . . which is the posited Notion, it is absolutely penetrable, and receptive of this communication, because it is *in itself* identical with the end . . . Its lack of self-subsistence consists precisely in its being only *in itself* the totality of the Notion; but the latter is a being-for-itself. Consequently the object has the character of being powerless [machtlos, H.K.] against the end and of serving it; the end is the object's subjectivity or soul, that has in the object its external side.[23]

The object is in this manner *immediately* subjected to the end. While history drives forward with its original natural force, the subject is the spiritual power that preserves itself in that it supersedes the differentiated moments of this force. The end is, the means always has been. However, since subject and history cannot be one without the other, they are the same in their immanently coherent end-means relationship.

That the subject as end is the power over its means is possible through the application of the means as the cunning of the self-conscious end. Writes Hegel: 'But that the end posits itself in a *mediate* relation with the object and *interposes* another object [rationality, H.K.] *between* itself and it [that is, the world as nature, H.K.] may be regarded as the *cunning* of reason . . . [I]t puts forward an object as means, allows it to wear itself out in its stead, exposes it to attrition and shields itself behind it from mechanical violence'.[24] Thus the dialectic of philosophical speculation is the insight of reason into its historically antecedent rational means which it has posited and out of the struggle of which it securely produces and preserves itself. One is therefore inclined to maintain that the need of reason for unity grows in proportion to the development of the self-consciousness of ever wider spiritual circles.

For Hegel, then, the development and progress of the understanding does not move chaotically into arbitrarily proliferated directions as Feyerabend would have it. Instead the understanding is led purposefully into the focal point of reason. We interpret this also by saying that the development of particular historical moments is the development towards spiritually organic self-preservation. Thus the meaning of the teleological *towards* of rationality is its transformation into reason.

Hence the *cunning of reason* is an activity which goes beyond what is intended by the finite and limited horizon of the understanding. The cunning means that whatever a particular rationality does – it affects the whole. It refers to more, to the implications and consequences of rational actions. Thus, although individual activities are believed to be in-themselves and self-determinate, that is, to be within the real absolute circle of rationality, such activities, however, are known by reason to be *for* reason itself. And this *for-itself* is the actual, developed circle, or better: it is the fulfilled cycle of reason in its presentness. Although such particular activities may in themselves be destructive and therefore finite and negative, Hegel could in his time still firmly believe that they are for reason also and always constructive and hence positive.[25] 'Reason', he says, 'which finds the consciousness caught up in particularities, becomes philosophical speculation precisely in that it lifts itself up to itself and to the absolute which, at the same time, becomes its object'.[26] Reason becomes itself through itself. The subject produces itself as object and becomes historically and coherently identical with it as with itself. It becomes identical with its self-own otherness. And it is in this sense that the positive is through the sublation of its negative.

However, Hegel fears that such a philosophical sublation of theoretical dilemmas is almost incomprehensible for common sense which is proud of its formal and rational utterances. He argues, for instance, that 'speculation does indeed understand common sense, but common sense cannot understand the activity of speculation. Speculation as the actuality of knowledge accepts the being of knowledge only in totality; everything that is determined has for it actuality and truth only in the acknowledged relation to the absolute'.[27] And in argumentation, furthermore, common sense is irritated and reacts somewhat aggressively to being questioned and finitised. It sees no need to justify the spurious ground of rational reason, on which it stands in apparent though only deceptive security. Hegel uncovers the true nature of a cowardly but dangerous rationality. He says of it that 'not only can common sense not understand speculation, but it must even hate it when it learns of it, and if it does not deem itself in the utter indifference of security must abhor and persecute it'.[28] An isolated and merely self-referring part thus falls back upon the inferiority of pride when it is called upon to respond to the need of the whole. The part does not recognise that it is the fulfilment of the whole which in the end alone affords it meaning and security.

But in that it shuns responsibility, rationality is either not aware of its dialectical determination, or, if it is aware, is afraid of a dialectic which it cannot bear. With its blind forces it then threatens to lay waste the realm of historical reason. We have in the nuclear era at present reached the highest stage of the development of rational praxis. But this age also requires our utmost willingness and intellectual courage to gain the speculative insight into that which is actually in danger in our time and henceforth. Hegel advises us to see into the mirror of our rationality and to reflect upon the horror of its erstwhile actions and those it might still inflict upon humanity.

NEGATIVE AND POSITIVE REASON

One of the points critics of dialectic make is to say that it is a negative activity in the sense that the historical background of thought movements remains undifferentiated and non-syllogised into a positive unity.[1] Yet, in examining Hegel's organic dialectic, we have already seen in very clear language that we are dealing with the positive sublation of the subject. The subject takes the laborious journey of reflection in order to arrive at a self-understanding. But without being already actualised in its presentness the subject could not even begin to reflect upon itself. What it does in dialectical reflection is to posit consciously its negation into history and to mediate itself out of this negation into the positivity of self-consciousness.

Lest we misconstrue this crucial aspect of Hegel's philosophy, let us investigate further the part-whole or negative-positive relationship, and discuss Feyerabend's doubtful interpretation of these terms of dialectic. He employs the dialectical method in a negative and one-sided way in order to question the dogmatically held particularlistic views of formal understanding. Feyerabend does not see the organically and positively sublating dialectic of the subject. Taking reason to be rationality he asserts that 'full rationality can be obtained by extending criticism to the stable parts also', that is, to the 'fixed categories'.[2] In other words, the criterion for advancing knowledge is not the subject, but the weak or decategorised epistemological form of rational subjectivity.

For Feyerabend full rationality refers only to his principle of proliferation, a principle which involves the activity of particularising. However, since he uses reason and rationality interchangeably and in their formal sense, we would not get any farther by criticising the fixed categories of rationality with rationality itself. It would still mean a going back to the understanding and its divisional self. The result would remain a merely rational knowledge, a knowledge that is isolated and lopsided, yielding nothing but half truths, and confusing the reflection of common sense.[3]

But the problem of rationality cannot be resolved by dissolving and simply multiplying random concepts. Hegel, referring at one point to the notion's nature and spirit, or to its phenomena and rational history, writes about the impotence of nature that it

> cannot adhere to and exhibit the strictness of the Notion and runs wild in this blind irrational ['begrifflos' = reasonless, notionless, H.K.] multiplicity. We can *wonder* at nature's manifold genera and species and the endless diversity of her formations, for *wonderment* is *unreasoning* ['ist ohne Begriff' = is without the notion, H.K.] and its object the irrational ['das Vernunftlose' = the reasonless, H.K.]. Nature, because it is the self-externality of the Notion, is free to indulge itself in this variety, just as spirit, too, even though it possesses the Notion in the shape of the Notion, engages in pictorial thinking ['Vor-stellen' = rational thinking, H.K.] and runs riot in its endless variety. The manifold natural genera or species must not be esteemed as anything more than the capricious fancies of spirit in its representations.[4]

Hegel depreciates in this passage the Aristotelian view that it is owing to their wonder that men both now begin and at first began to philosophise about the heavenly stars, for instance.[5] But this eruption of light, Hegel says without much reverence for the ancient, 'is as little worthy of wonderment as an eruption on the skin or a swarm of flies'.[6] The object of subjective rationality, which, as 'wonderment is purely negative', is only 'externality' and therefore 'means nothing to Reason'; it is something 'to which Reason knows itself to be superior'.[7] Wonderment is a negative attitude because it is evocative of the understanding's consciousness of something external to it. As such it is not yet positively mediated into history and not yet sublated by its spiritual transformations into self-knowledge. It is only within the appearance (spirit) of history that reason becomes reflectively conscious of itself, and it becomes so only after having actively transformed the various historical moments of rational consciousness.

Thus neither nature nor the spirit lead to comprehension or to a system. But dialectical reason, methodically self-employed, not only criticises and destroys the arbitrariness of a rational and conceptual rigidity. It does so with the view of obtaining a more developed form of knowledge, namely, the self-knowledge and self-consciousness of itself as life. In other words, the dialectical movement negates in order to become positive again. Self-sublation is possible through the application of an internal instead of an external meaning of criticism. The essence of historical growth is to move beyond rational particularities and towards reason. Since movement as method is a dialectical structure, it forms itself coherently into a system. Method and system, the negative and the positive, *become* and hence *are* the same. Method and system are historical life. Method is only as system, and the system is only as method. We shall elaborate on this notion of coherent identity further below in the section on Method and System (p. 118ff). Here we only wish to look at Feyerabend's negative interpretation of reason.

Feyerabend says with Hegel that reason is 'the force of the negative absolute, that is, an absolute negation'[8] of the understanding or of 'science and common sense'.[9] Now, according to Hegel, this is so because for reason the 'ossified material [of the understanding, H.K.] is already to hand, and the problem is to render this material fluid and to re-kindle the spontaneity of the Notion [den lebendigen Begriff, H.K.] in such dead matter'.[10] The problem, as it were, is to notionalise the concept. In a deeper sense, it is to understand that the present is not rationally defined factual givenness. Our understanding of the present depends upon and is contingent upon our reflection on its past. It is the thinking about relations. And relations, since they are not empirical but spiritual, can only be grasped in and through dialectical thinking. What something is depends on what we make it to be. The *is* is not in any way determined from without, but we ourselves determine it completely from within ourselves. The present *is becomes is* because we have made it into what it is.

Again, it is interesting to note that Feyerabend translates *Begriffe* with 'concepts'[11] without taking account of its spontaneous characteristic, or without seeing in it its Hegelian meaning of the life of the notion. We have pointed out that this distinction is partly a problem of how to translate *Begriff*. Yet it is also a question of how to gain an insight into a philosopher's thinking and the concerns which lie at the origin of his reflection. It is, after all, for this reason that we seek to distinguish Hegelian from those other modes of dialectical thought which fail to grasp not only the purpose of knowledge acquisition, but therewith also the meaning of our age, an age which stands in an increasingly diremptive and negative relationship to itself.

Hegel reflects upon living historical life, and he is concerned with history and its continuous existence. But the notional articulation of human existence today is one of the most difficult philosophical issues to tackle. Dialectically speaking, life for man is always historical. And it is always actively and spiritually sublated and produced life. It is then also in the sense of creative and formative production that we must understand history and the following sentence which Feyerabend quotes. We must, he says with Hegel, 'dissolve the opposition of a frozen subjectivity and objectivity and comprehend the origin of the intellectual and real world as a becoming, we must understand their being as a product, as a form of producing'.[12]

Only the history of the subject produces and reproduces itself in order to become and therefore to be itself as product. The product is preserved life.[13] But the movement of life is history. And history produces in order to maintain and become itself as a self-same self. In order to recognise itself life must externalise itself and sublate this externalisation reflectively. The understanding has the force of conceptual representation. It defines and posits what Hegel calls with Spinoza a *substance*. That this substance – to be further thematised in the section on Substance and Subject, p. 113ff – is rationally posited means that it is not self-produced as reason is. With Hegel, however, the subject is reason. And reason is power, the organic power to produce itself in and through reflection.

'Everything', Hegel writes, 'turns on grasping and expressing the True, not only as *Substance,* but equally as *Subject*'.[14] That substance is *equally* subject is to say that in Hegel's view universal substance is relationally individualised into the subject. External substance, whose Spinozean definition emanates from the understanding, is to be regarded as a particular spiritual appearance of reason. Hegel thereby renders the static into a dynamic and historically living substance. Substance belongs to the subject. As we shall learn later, it is one of its historical manifestations. Hegel therefore concludes that 'the living Substance is being which is in truth *Subject*, or, what is the same, is in truth actual only in so far as it is the movement of positing itself, or is the mediation of its self-othering with itself'.[15]

As the true it is the whole[16] and since the true is absolute, the absolute is the subject.[17] Unlike substance, which negatively loses itself in its emanations, the subject positively finds itself in and through its manifestation. The subject as 'reason is, therefore, misunderstood when reflection is excluded from the True, and is not grasped as a positive moment of the Absolute. It is reflection that makes the True a result'.[18] In other words, 'reason is *purposeful activity*'[19] in that in it 'the essential nature of reflection' is to be regarded as the '*specific, original ground of all activity and self-movement*'.[20] Or, to speak with Goethe: 'Im Anfang war die Tat' (In the beginning was the deed, H.K.)[21] and not the divine word.[22] It is not that we posit God and define Him for our purposes, but that God posits us for His purpose.[23] The absolute lives as subject, and as subject it lives dialectically through its history and for itself.

Historical reason is a totality when it has become organically holistic totality, that is, when it has become preserved, fulfilled and therefore self-related actuality. The understanding with its conceptual representations contains within itself an unconnected plurality, a contentless manifold. 'Common sense', writes Hegel, 'does indeed express reflection, but its statements do not contain for consciousness its relation to the absolute totality, but remain within and unexpressed'.[24] Common sense is only negativity, and the understanding is nothing but the activity of parting. This is so because the understanding reflects on rationally posited concepts. But its 'common sense cannot grasp how that which is for it immediate certainty is for philosophy nothing'.[25] It is something merely one-sided, negative, unconcrete and therefore ahistorical. Concrete thinking, however, is with Hegel the weaving thinking of historical reason.

Hegel himself, which remains unnoticed by Feyerabend, has warned against regarding the dialectical method as merely one-sided and negative. 'The fundamental prejudice in this matter', he says, 'is that dialectic has *only a negative result*'.[26] But it is in this negative sense that Feyerabend interprets dialectic. For him 'this is how *dialectic thinking* arises as a form of thought that "dissolves into nothing the detailed determinations of the understanding"'.[27] But with the dissolution of rational structures begins the alienation of reason and therewith the beginning of the de-actualisation and possible destruction of the subject.

In contrast to Feyerabend's interest in the theoretical development of the particular sciences, or rather his lack of philosophical perspective, Hegel reflects upon the subject and its creative intentions which are directed to the holistic science of historical life. He recounts at length – and we wish to quote him in full – the positive character of reason when he says, (continuing Feyerabend's translation):

> The understanding *determines*, and holds the determinations fixed; reason is negative and *dialectical*, because it resolves the determinations of the understanding into nothing; it is positive because it generates the universal and comprehends the particular therein. Just as understanding is usually taken to be something separate from reason as such, so too dialectical reason is usually taken to be something distinct from positive reason. But reason in its truth is *spirit* which is higher than either merely positive reason [verständige Vernunft, H.K.] or merely intuitive understanding [vernünftiger Verstand, H.K.]. It is the negative, that which constitutes the quality alike of dialectical reason and of understanding; it negates what is simple, thus positing the specific difference of the understanding; it equally resolves it and is thus dialectical. But it does not stay in the nothing of this result but in the result is no less positive, and in this way it has restored what was at first simple, but as a universal which is within itself concrete; a given particular is not subsumed under this universal but in this determining, this positing of a difference, and the resolving of it, the particular has at the same time already determined itself. This spiritual movement which, in its simple undifferentiatedness, gives itself its own determinateness and in its determinateness its equality with itself, which therefore is the immanent development of the Notion, this movement is the absolute method of knowing and at the same time is the immanent soul of the content itself.[28]

But what is positive, what generates or produces, is historical life. And the knowledge of life is knowledge of itself as subject according to the Delphic principle of 'know thyself'.[29] But this ancient precept, to which Hegel himself refers, had its origin in the relationship between an individual person as subject and an externally determining object, and not between the individual community as subject and its own determining objective history. Accordingly, Hegel says, breaking with the tradition, knowledge is no longer merely a '*love* of knowing' something external which is posited by rational subjectivity or by the understanding, but is the immanent and '*actual* knowing' of the self-producing subject as reason.[30] It is no longer the philosophy of a conscious though particularistic and hence unfree antiquity, but the philosophy of self-conscious, holistic and therefore free modernity.

The subject comes to know itself in that it negates itself, in that it steps outside itself and works on its own historical otherness, which is its objective past. Thereby the subject reproducingly sustains itself in reflection. In this lies its transformative becoming, in fact, its overcoming of alienation, its positive actuality and self-consciousness. The logical principle of this change, Hegel says, is that 'the negative is just as much positive'.[31] Put differently: 'To hold fast to the positive in *its* negative, . . . in the result, this is the most important feature in rational cognition [im vernünftigen Erkennen, H.K.]'.[32] But most appropriate for our theme is Hegel's comment on the tremendous power of the negative, the negative which is the very energy of thinking. In a telling and moving passage he writes:

> Death, if that is what we want to call this non-actuality, is of all things the most dreadful, and to hold fast what is dead requires the greatest strength. Lacking strength, Beauty hates the Understanding for asking of her what it cannot do. But the life of Spirit is not the life that shrinks from death and keeps itself untouched by devastation, but rather the life that endures it and maintains itself in it. It wins its truth only when, in utter dismemberment, it finds itself. It is this power, not as something positive, which closes its eyes to the negative, as when we say of something that it is nothing or that it is false, and then, having done with it, turn away and pass on to something else; on the contrary, Spirit is this power only by looking the negative in the face, and tarrying with it. This tarrying with the negative is the magical power that converts it into being.[33]

And this power is the subject that has the strength to recognise itself through a reflection upon its history, upon that which is no more, but to which it is nevertheless immanently related in the being of the constantly developing present.

Let us end these paragraphs with an anticipatory note. Dialectical logic has for its principle the organically determined cyclical double negative which expresses the mediation of self-recognition. Though we shall in the next chapter illustrate and explain – with specific reference to the relationship between the state and mankind – the movement of the positivised negative, let us here, however, already state it in its simplified form:

I (a) (+ = − − = − +) ⟵ (b) + = +

(Dialectical coherence, not formal correspondence)

(c)

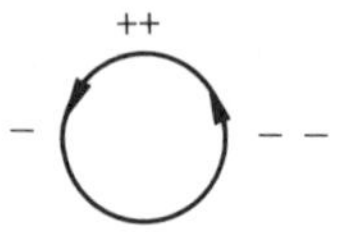

Positive reason (+) negates or judges (ur-teilt) itself into its understanding (−). In that reason then works on the understanding, it is active in a second negation. This second negation is the negation of the understanding which is the historical production of reason as the positive syllogism of the double negative. It is in the double but dialectically unified and hence cyclical movement that the life of the subject gains the fulfilment of truth as actuality and as self-consciousness. This activity of reflection is particularly assigned to us today if we do not want this age to fall asunder through the negativity of a self-contradictory rationality and its unreflected assertions.

FORMAL AND CONCRETE LOGIC

We have sought to clarify a few distinguishing facets of Feyerabend's interpretation of Hegel. With the intention to probe still deeper into the subject matter of Hegelian terminology, we now continue this exegetical exercise and relate the difference between the understanding's critique of reason and reason's critique of the understanding. For this purpose we shall allow Hegel to speak for himself and, consequently, draw largely from his writing.

For Hegel the task of philosophy is the dynamic *thinking* of reason, while a given theory is seen as the application of static *thought* and, accordingly, refers to the understanding.[1] While in the conceptual science of the understanding subjectivity hypothesises external and unknown objects, in the notional science of reason the subject produces an internal and known object. This object is its own manifestation and actualisation. It is therefore, corrects Hegel, 'not the object of thought that is the more excellent, but the very energy of thinking'.[2] Thought and thinking have therefore, strictly speaking, also a different logic.

When logic is taken to be the science of subjectivity, it is understood that such thought constitutes the '*mere form* of a cognition, that logic abstracts from all *content* and that the so-called second *constituent* belonging to cognition, namely its *matter*, must come from elsewhere', and is therefore 'absolutely independent of logic'.[3] In other words, in rational logic form and content are separated.

'Hitherto', Hegel continues the above passage:

> the Notion [concept, H.K.] of logic has rested on the separation, presupposed once and for all in the ordinary consciousness [of the understanding, H.K.] of the *content* of cognition and its *form*, or of *truth* and *certainty*. First, it is assumed that the material of knowing is present on its own account as a ready-made world apart from thought, that thinking on its own is empty and comes as an external form to the said material, fills itself with it and only thus acquires a content and so becomes real knowing.[4]

According to formal logic 'truth is the agreement of thought with the object, and in order to bring about this agreement – for it does not exist on its own account [an und für sich, H.K.] – thinking is supposed to adapt and accommodate itself to the object'.[5] Since 'the difference of matter [content, H.K.] and form, of object and thought' means that 'each is regarded as a sphere divorced from the other', the object posited by rational subjectivity, that is, the 'thing-in-itself, remains a sheer beyond of thought'.[6]

It is not an object in-and-for-itself because it is not the internal object of the subject which posits itself out of itself as its self-own object. In other words, while formal rationality presupposes the separation of subject and object,[7] historical reason produces subject/object unity. Hegel is not against difference, difference in the sense of dialectical and organic growth differentiations; he is not against the difference between form and content. What Hegel argues against is the separation between form and content.[8] Historically interpreted this means that he is against the artificial, arbitrary and formal separation of the historical content from its present actualised form.

As he emphatically says himself, 'the usual practice of separating understanding and reason is, from every point of view, to be rejected'.[9] It is present and concrete thinking which thinks about its past as about itself. A purely formal thought cannot be employed to think about itself,[10] because it is ahistorical and hence one-sided thought only. This is particularly true, as we have seen, in the case of Popper, Kuhn and Feyerabend, whose dialectical theories of science treat cognitive objects external to the subject. Theirs is not the dialectical philosophy of the subject which reflects itself in its historical objectification. That formal logic is not denied[11] is to say also that Hegel's own dialectical logic is *not* an alternative to formal logic. On the contrary, it presupposes it historically. Nonetheless, it questions its merely rational concept of truth.[12]

For Hegel the views about the theoretical dichotomy between subject and object are, however, 'errors the refutation of which throughout every part of the spiritual and natural universe is *philosophy*',[13] which as historical reason reconciles the dilemma of rationality. '*Reflective* understanding . . .', he writes:

> stands for the understanding as abstracting, and hence as separating and remaining fixed in its separations. Directed against reason, it behaves as ordinary common sense and imposes its own view that truth rests on sensuous reality . . . and that reason left to its own resources engenders only figments of the brain [Hirngespinste, H.K.]. In this self-renunciation on the part of reason, the Notion of truth is lost; it is limited to knowing only subjective truth, only phenomena, appearances, only something to which the nature of the object itself does not correspond: knowing has lapsed into opinion.[14]

Thus the understanding posits theoretical reason[15] whose object, however, can never be known: it can only be believed in. The understanding is capable only of a subjective logic, whose plural forms are taken to be fixed determinations. And these are separated one from the other and not held together in an organic unity. They are considered by Hegel to be:

> dead forms and the spirit which is their living, concrete unity does not dwell in them. As thus taken, they lack a substantial content – a matter which would be substantial in itself. The content which is missing in the logical forms is nothing else than a solid foundation and a concretion of these abstract determinations . . . But logical

> reason itself is the substantial or real being which holds together within itself every abstract determination and is their substantial, absolutely concrete unity.[16]

But what is lacking is historical consciousness, which alone renders the subject meaningful in that it unifies its concrete historical development into a reflected comprehension of itself as life.

'Absolute knowing', Hegel carries on,

> is the *truth* of every mode of consciousness because . . . it is only in absolute knowing that the separation of the *object* from the *certainty of itself* is completely eliminated: truth is now equated with certainty and this certainty with truth.
>
> This pure science presupposes liberation from the opposition of consciousness. It contains *thought in so far as this is just as much the object in its own self, or the object in its own self in so far as it is equally pure thought.* As science, truth is pure self-consciousness in its self-development and has the shape of the self, so that the absolute [an und für sich, H.K.] truth of being is the known Notion and the Notion as such is the absolute truth of being.
>
> This objective thinking, then, is the content of pure science. Consequently, far from it being formal, far from it standing in need of a matter to constitute an actual and true cognition, it is its content alone which has absolute truth, or, if one still wanted to employ the word matter, it is the veritable matter – but a matter which is not external to the form, since this matter is rather pure thought and hence the absolute form itself. Accordingly, logic is to be understood as the system of pure reason, as the realm of pure thought.[17]

These lines require little interpretation. Logic is the self-fulfilment of the notional subject. Logic is the self that thinks itself in and through its phenomenal history. Form and content together are actualised and continuously actualising history. In their coherent unity they constitute the ever present absolute. The absolute is holistic history within which all otherness is dialectically sublated and transformed into the logical self of the subject. The subject is history *in* itself, and it sublates this history *for* the sake of comprehending itself. The absolute is therefore subject which alone knows itself. It is the present which has created itself out of its past. And it is absolute because, in being ab-*solus*, it alone exists. The past is not, and the future is not yet. Hence the logical form of the present consists in its philosophical reflection about its becoming as the true content of its life.

GROUND AS ONTOLOGY AND LOGIC

The question now arises as to whether the *absolute* is an ontological concept in the traditional metaphysical sense, or whether it refers to the logical unity of the historical development of the subject. If it is the latter, the absolute is the equivalent to the notion. Hence the ultimate reason (ground) of that which exists as subject is its history. Therefore also, our understanding of the present is not mediated ontologically but through the logic of its dialectic. And with dialectic we most adequately describe the part-whole perspective, which is shown in the development from the *logic of pure being* to the *logic of the becoming of being*. We do justice to Hegel's philosophy only if we distinguish between these two expressions, but at the same time bear in mind that they are dialectically related to one another.

We mentioned the term *ground* earlier in connection with Hegel's idea of speculative philosophy. In this section we specify it further since *ground* has a different meaning in formal and in concrete logic. For Hegel logic is not so much the explication of concepts as it is the manifestation of the notion.[1] In the formal logic of the understanding the law of ground says that everything has its sufficient ground as posited.[2] But rationality cannot establish a sufficiently explanatory and external ground; it has no such explicans.

Reason, however, in its historical meaning is its own real and immanent ground. It is the developed totality of all formative moments. It is the identity of the part-whole relationship. This ground is 'inner ground'.[3] A theory cannot fully explain another hypothesised object. Yet philosophy does wholly manifest itself into itself as historical object. 'Every philosophy', Hegel says, 'is in itself completed and has, as a real work of art, an internal totality'.[4] This relationally woven totality is its historical ground.

It has been said,[5] that with theories of the understanding one *looks at* objects and tries to determine what they are in themselves. They are *draufsichtig*. Philosophical reason, on the other hand, *looks into*, or has insight into, itself. Its development is its self-own object. It is therefore *einsichtig*, that is, insightful or reasonable. And what is reasonable is the ability to relate particulars to their holistic and historical context. Or: the ability of reason to comprehend itself is its power to relate itself to itself through its becoming. The logic of formal understanding forgets to consider this principal feature of the historical perspective. Hegel criticises this shortcoming when he says of the understanding that:

> instead of entering into the immanent content of the thing, it is forever surveying the whole and standing above the particular existence of which it is speaking, i.e. it does not see it at all. Scientific cognition [that is, the dialectical logic of reason, H.K.], on the contrary, demands surrender to the life of the object, or, what amounts to the same thing, confronting and expressing its inner necessity.[6]

Thus, while any subjective and rational ground remains contingent and removed from the considerations of its life, the ground of the subject as reason is its historical essence. The problem of *ground* is in the philosophical tradition a problem of rational and passive ontology. For Hegel the ground is the active *issue itself* (die Sache selbst) of logic.

The modern Kant, for instance, wrote about the ancients that their formal or general logic is merely a '*canon* of judgment'. 'Employed as if it were an *organon* for the actual production of at least the semblance of objective assertions' it is as such 'misapplied'.[7] And he added that general logic, when thus treated as an organon, is the 'logic of illusion'.[8] It is a logic, moreover, which when produced dogmatically is the tool of 'metaphysical jugglers'.[9] According to Kant, 'logic teaches us nothing whatsoever regarding the content of knowledge, but lays down only the formal conditions of agreement with the understanding'.[10] On the other hand, Kant concedes that there exists a transcendental dialectic, an even 'natural and unavoidable dialectic of pure reason', a dialectic, however, whose characteristic it is not to cease to 'play tricks with reason . . . even after its deceptiveness has been exposed'.[11]

Unlike Kant, for whom a critique of pure transcendent reason is a rational critique of dialectical tricks, Hegel thinks of the dialectic of historical reason not as something playful or ontological, but as 'method'.[12] And this method is not rationally or arbitrarily employed in order to establish an illusory ontology. Rather is method the necessary self-employment of reason in the dialectical logic of its becoming. The subject *qua* subject exists only in and through its organically developing spiritual history. To this history it relates of necessity because the idea of developing self-consciousness implies the necessity of relation.

The question as to whether Hegel's philosophy constitutes an hypothesised ontology or whether it is the description of the logical manifestation of reason is, indeed, a controversial one. There are those who think that Hegel's is an ontology of logic,[13] that activity is an ontological category,[14] that process is the central category of a new ontology,[15] that logic is an unbroken or complete ontology,[16] or that it is an ontological theory.[17] We have suggested that such terminological interpretations can be challenged and modified. Another and different view, therefore, holds that *logic is not an ontology but that, instead, ontology is logic.*[18] It is this reading of Hegel which we have here adopted. The dialectical dissolution of ontology expresses most succinctly his philosophical task to sublate the formal strictures of reasoning both in antiquity and modernity, and to convert them into the timeless flow of actuality.

The problem under consideration may perhaps just be a semantic controversy. Yet it may likewise reflect a debate over a much more fundamental philosophical difference. In order at least to throw some more light on the question let us, therefore, see what is traditionally meant by ontology, and what Hegel's logic itself stands for. With ontology we have in mind a meta-theory or a formal-logical concept which, through a rational doctrine of method, is externally applied to the world in order to ascertain its *ontos*. This *ontos* is an explanatory and guiding principle for epistemology and moral conduct. The objective truth of this world is with Kant posited by the transcendental activity of the understanding. This truth is thought to be truth in-itself.

But Hegel's philosophy does ultimately not treat truth *itself* but truth *in-and-for-itself*.[19] Truth does not refer to an ahistorical correspondence of concepts with experiential phenomena. Truth does not lie in the concept of life. It is the notion of life with its historical relations. Hence it is not we who determine what truth is. Truth determines itself through internal self-movement. In this sense, reason does not apply a method from without.[20] Since reason is method itself it applies itself from within to itself. Thus, while a concept refers to the posited concept of a theoretical doctrine of method, the dialectical logic of the notion is the 'philosophical doctrine of method'.[21] Dialectic cannot be ontologically explicated in the traditional language of rationality.[22] On the contrary, dialectic is the historical ground for the understanding whose activity is directed towards the explication of whatever it chooses to explain. Yet this striving always falls short of establishing an actual truth correspondence.

If logic is internal self-formation, then it is constructive if it does not presuppose a 'meta-theory (ontology)',[23] so to speak, over and above rationality. Meta-physics, or a meta-theory, thinks the absolute (solus) separated from (ab) and beyond phenomenal finitude. But in that case the presumed absolute is not absolute at all because it excludes its phenomenal becoming, that is, its necessary history. In this case, metaphysics misses its own thought.[24] Therefore, Hegel says, 'the main point is to distinguish the genuine Notion of infinity from spurious infinity, the infinite of reason from the infinite of the understanding; yet the latter is the *finitized* infinite, and it will be found that in the very act of keeping the infinite pure and aloof from the finite, the infinite is only made finite'.[25] Conceptual objects are merely hypothesised absolutes and infinites. Their ontological status is not the in-and-for-itself of the subject but an in-itself of subjectivity. It is posited by a historically finite and contingent rationality.

If logic is the *self-construing* method it is not only theoretical but practical, as well. And that it is practical is to say basically that formal logic is transformed into dialectical logic. History implies praxis. Logic is not being, but is being only in so far as it is its own becoming. Dialectical logic is the historically coherent 'identity of the theoretical and the practical Idea'.[26] Theory, understood here as philosophy or as theoria, is the level of every unified present whose transformations are the dialectical stages of becoming. This movement may be described in the illustrated cycle below in which the plus signs (+) stand for the practical and mediating transformations of past epochs (a,b,c, and so on) which lead to new historical moments and which, ultimately, relate to the present. The present is accordingly the unity of itself (a) with itself (a). As a result it becomes – (aa):

I (a) (a + b + c + d + . . .aa)

(b)

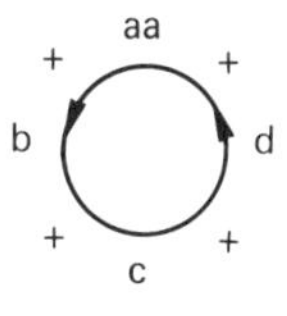

But this unity is fulfilled and actualised in the notion and not in the concept. Only that which is posited *in* a notion, says Hegel, 'belongs in the dialectical development of that Notion to its content'.[27] It is unity, the dialectically pure notion as 'self-consciousness'.[28] The interrelatedness of theory and practice, of posited present form and its developed historical content, constitutes the subject matter of philosophy. Philosophy is with Hegel the reflection upon historical praxis. And this reflection is necessary because only with it can the praxis of the thinking subject be related to its need for self-knowledge and the fully coherent identity with itself.

Ontology is the theoretical logic of being. Hegel's philosophy practically *logicises* being.[29] It penetrates and permeates it, and thereby renders it historically fluid. The world is thus not comprehensively constructed by the understanding, but as reason is self-constructed. The world is a living world;[30] it is historical life. It is the *active* subject that appears within itself to itself. This principle of the self-manifestation of dialectical logic is, because of its holism, methodologically superior to formal logic.

In Hegel's philosophical system the subject is treated after the object, the result of being after its becoming. The object is the subject's history or 'genetic exposition'.[31] The 'science of logic ... constitutes metaphysics proper or purely speculative philosophy'.[32] In it the 'objective logic ... takes the place rather of the former *metaphysics* which was intended to be the scientific construction of the world in terms of *thoughts* alone'.[33] In Hegel's dialectic the traditional view of ontology is critically examined by his 'objective logic'.[34]

The objective logic is the logic of the understanding and its notionalised concepts. And taken in the broader context of Hegel's system we can say generally that the *Phenomenology of Spirit* is to the *Science of Logic* what the 'objective logic' is to its 'subjective logic', or to the logic of the subject, in the *Science of Logic*. For Hegel concepts are objective, the notion is subjective. 'The subjective logic', he says, 'is the logic of the *Notion*'; it is 'free, self-subsistent and self-determining, or rather it is the subject itself'.[35]

Hegel's dialectic describes the method that thinks itself through, that reflects upon itself without referring itself to an external originator or cause of its reflection. Hence his logic is a critique of traditional ontology.[36] It is not, however, as in Kant, a rational critique of distant reason, but is reason's critique of its inner rationality.

The movement (Geschehen) of being dissolves traditional ontology into the history (Geschichte) of being.[37] History is the objective essence (Wesen) of being. The essence of being is that it has been (ge-wesen). And in this sense essence is the successor of being.[38] Essence links and binds presentness historically and hence essentially to its past. Thus, while traditional being is the object in its ontological givenness, Hegel considers essence to be the subject in its dialectical enfolding. Essence is historical coherence. Subject and object are not separated, they are unity. They belong together, and in their actualisation they are comprehended as notion (begriffen als Begriff).

To conclude: the nuclear age cannot, it seems, be ontologically understood. It can be meaningfully grasped only by means of the relational logic of Hegel's dialectic. The present is historically holistic unity. This unity, which we interpret as the self of mankind, is not deductively determinable with reference to an *ontos*. It is active in and through itself, and its determination is self-produced. Mankind is predicated only upon itself and not upon that which it is not. Hegel's dialectical method and its language allow us to fathom the depth of this truth.

SUBSTANCE AND SUBJECT

In the section on Negative and Positive Reason above (p. 97ff) we have introduced the relationship between substance and subject. This issue, however, merits some further explication. It is of interest both from the point of view of the history of philosophic thought and with respect to Hegel's own development of reflection as it is shown in the composition of his writings. And, besides, it represents an essential idea in our book because it is instrumental for describing *mankind* as a dialectically self-organising *subject* and not as an empty substance from which we derive a conceptual meaning for mankind.

Hegel's sublation of subjectivity into the subject is mediated through his discussion of Spinoza's self-caused *substance*. In this section we describe the critical connection between substance and subject since the former is the fullest formation of Hegel's rational or *objective logic*. It is the moment where he begins to think the philosophical *turning point* within the *Science of Logic*. This turning point involves the conversion of the objective logic into the logic of the subject.

Spinoza, in a first definition, declares that self-causation is that of which the 'essence involves existence'.[1] And, similarly, 'substance cannot be produced by anything external, . . . it must, therefore, be its own cause'.[2] Hegel takes issue with Spinoza's concept of substance or *causa sui* because it is a rational definition only. It does not refer to the self-conscious development of substance; that is, it is not the subject that externalises itself and reflectively returns to itself. For Spinoza the understanding posits a substance whose essence it then defines ascriptively. But, Hegel argues, 'no beginning of philosophy can look worse than the beginning with a definition'.[3] If philosophy is to do with the question of identity, then its total comprehension must be placed at the end of the dialectical development and not at its beginning.[4] Identity is concrete, not formal identity. It is the historically and coherently unified consciousness with itself, or is developed self-consciousness.

In order to substantiate this analysis, Hegel considers Spinoza's system to be a 'defective philosophy because in it reflection and its manifold determining is an *external thinking*'.[5] It is the understanding that ascribes particular attributes and modi to substance. This external positedness or determinateness is negation.[6] Thus rational negation implies that its posited object or substantive reason is not itself a 'determinative and formative activity, nor . . . a movement which returns into and begins from itself'.[7] Only the subject is such an activity which creates itself historically.

Another critical remark Hegel makes about Spinoza's absolute substance is that, though the rational 'exposition of the absolute is *complete* in so far as it starts from the absolute', its posited and externally attributed movements 'are only enumerated *one after the other*, without any inner sequence of development'.[8] The movement of substance, he says, 'is not negation *as* negation, not the negatively self-related negation which would be *in its own self* the return into the first identity, so that this identity would then be veritable identity'.[9] In other words, Spinoza's conception of negation refers only to the one externalising though continuous negation. It does not involve a second negation. And, therefore, since it is not the negation of the negation, it is not dialectical and coherent immanence, either. It is merely an endless string of theoretical variables whose togetherness, however, is devoid of any inner organic logic. But such an emanation remains in Spinoza unreflected.

Thus we conclude that, while predicative objects are ascribed to substance, there cannot be a dialectical substance/object identity. Substance as hypothesised self-emanation loses itself in its emanating definitional objects without finding and recognising itself in them. Substance, though it has objective existence or reality, is not yet actuality. Only the life of the subject is actuality, because only as life does the subject produce itself and reflectively wins itself in continuous reproduction. But when referring to substance, Hegel says of it that 'the process of emanation is taken only as a *happening*, the becoming only as a progressive loss. Thus being increasingly obscures itself and night, the negative, is the final term of the series [Linie, H.K.], which does not first return into the primal light'.[10] The line of substance is the infinite straight regress. Like a light it vanishes into the irretrievable dimness of distance. The line does not reflect itself within itself as does the life-line of the subject within the spiral of its non-finite cyclical self-development.

The subject alone can negate its negation, and again become positively itself. Therein lies its dialectical essence. It sublates its self-own becoming which it attributes to itself. In that it negates its negation it returns to itself. Unlike the subject that acts, and intentionally acts reflectively and, therefore, is manifestation, 'substance lacks the principle of *personality*'.[11] It is nothing but the emanation into abstract objectivity. But understood this way it is one-sided and dialectically incomplete. It is in need of being philosophically transformed into the subject which alone is capable of concretising itself into its historical objectivity.[12] This concretisation is the self-producing activity of the subject. It is because substance is abstract that its object is its external and separated difference, whose formal identity can never be rationally ascertained but only hypothesised. But the concrete subject relates to its self-own historical objectivity as to an inner 'perfectly transparent difference',[13] whose own inner self-sublating activity always yields the identity of presentness.

While abstract substance is believed to be known by another, or while the cognition of substance 'is not an immanent cognition',[14] the subject knows itself in its full historical concreteness. Put differently: while rational subjectivity is conscious of substance, the subject as reason is conscious of itself. Substance is 'being, and nothing else, without any further specification and filling' ('Erfüllung' = fulfilment, H.K.).[15] Fulfilment expresses the satisfaction of need and desire. And in dialectic it is the social accomplishment of re-cognition. It expresses the reflective result of the cyclical activity of the subject towards mediated self-conscious knowledge. Filling, on the other hand, means the definitional and unmediated content of substance.

Thus the subject is the fulfilled knowledge of itself. And 'this Knowing', Hegel writes, 'is the inbreathing of the Spirit, whereby Substance becomes Subject, by which its abstraction and lifelessness have died, and Substance therefore has become *actual* and simple and universal Self-consciousness'.[16] Spiritualisation is the actual life of the subject. Only the subject lives, and without the subject substance is dead.

Substantive life is only a posited rational idea. It is a conception that in philosophical reflection has not yet developed into its fulfilment. It is defined being which knows no becoming, and which is devoid of the notion of itself. But as a concept life is without the necessity of actuality and, hence, is in itself meaningless. The values of life are subjected to the internal contradictions of the understanding. Life understood independently of its historical reason is not life in-and-for-itself. It is a posited in-itself and conceptually in no way different from any other rational hypothesisation. To judge life conceptually is to say that it *has* only contingent and antinomial meaning. But life as reason, which judges (ur-teilt) or manifests itself reflectively into its becoming, *is* necessary because self-produced meaning. Meaning is development; it is not a definition. Life is actuality, and 'what is actual *can act* [wirken, H.K.]; something manifests its actuality through that which it produces'.[17]

The actuality (Wirklichkeit) of reason is not a rational reality (Wirklichkeit) of which one has theoretical consciousness. It is organic actuality and, philosophically speaking, reflected self-consciousness. *Act*-uality is the fulfilled act of the subject; it is the result of its effective and purposeful work. It is in and through historical work alone that the subject develops its relational self-consciousness and becomes identical with itself.

The absolute, to repeat an earlier quotation from Hegel, is not only as substance but *equally* as subject.[18] In their unity they are not externally but internally interrelated. Identity is thus not an expectational and formal correspondence but actual and dialectical coherence. Expressed otherwise: while the reality of substance stands in the context of a theoretical and finite understanding of it, the actuality of the subject stands in the context of historical continuity which finds its sublation through spiritual work. In philosophical dialectic it is the subject that comprehends substantive theory and historical praxis. The subject alone comprehends itself, and in this, Hegel says, it is 'actuality, and ... it gives this actuality to itself'.[19]

This is its philosophically organic *context* or *Zusammenhang* in which the parts, or rather members and developing formations, *hang together* historically in their coherent unity. The actual and always present subject along with its method are inner contextual reason. And about this Hegel writes the famous yet so often misunderstood and, therefore, misinterpreted words: 'what is rational [vernünftig, H.K.] is actual [wirklich, H.K.] and what is actual is rational'.[20] These lines do not mean that reality corresponds to or is to be equated with the conceptual ought of an arbitrarily positing understanding. It does not mean that reality is judged as being epistemologically correct or axiologically good in the way it is perceived. This sort of translation leads to an utterly wrong and damaging view of Hegel's intentions. In philosphical dialectic, *Vernunft* and *Wirklichkeit, reason* and *actuality*, mean the historical life of the subject only. No value judgment is ascribed to this life, because no such formal judgment carries with it the status of necessity. As the result of sublation life simply is actuality. But within dialectical development the result is a logical necessity. History is the context in which life constantly enfolds itself. But history, in turn, is through the becoming of a plurality of phenomenal subjects which relate to one another. Hence the individual person as subject, for instance, is 'actual only in its context with others',[21] that is, in the context of its history which is also the history of others. The subject stands in the context of its historical object which is its own otherness. Understood this way, the subject is in the end relational subject and, moreover, is communal subject.

This is the real significance of Hegel's philosophical turning point with which he thinks the dialectical method through to its ultimate conclusion. If there is no autonomous, particular subjectivity and, therefore, only a contingent and emanating substance, necessity must be thought to reside in the manifesting, individual subject.[22] The subject subsumes under and methodically sublates into its system all formations of rational developments. The subject is in the highest form of development the notion, and as the notion it is, as we shall elaborate in the next chapter, the unconditioned logic of mankind which defies any substantive definition, but which comprehends them all in their rational form.

To sum up: one of the greatest, though for some also rather irritating and uncomfortable, lessons Hegel teaches us is that every definition is itself historically contingent and, hence, is never necessary and of universal validity. A still more significant insight is that the subject, in the accomplishment of its reflections, describes a notion of community that dialectically unifies its particular internal differentiated members into the self-identical whole. We may not yet have reached this level of awareness in a time where our human existence is globally threatened. But the nuclear age has certainly returned us to Hegel. He has thought through the philosophical tool of dialectical reflection with the help of which humanity today may gain in spiritual strength and become conscious of itself as of its own sublated history.

METHOD AND SYSTEM

We have approached Hegel with a discussion of a few pairs of terms which are pivotal to his philosophy. In their terminological variations these pairs reveal the nature of the relationship between the parts and the whole, between the means and their end. Most importantly, the relationship is to be understood in the organic and not in a formalistic sense. In the last of these pairs we shall once more expound the way Hegel thinks relations by analysing the methodical development of self-consciousness into the free reflection of its life.

If we regard the Hegelian logic of reason not as a formal and abstract but as a dialectical and concrete logic, then its method is not one that is superimposed upon something external to it. Therefore, it is not to be associated with the rationally posited meta-theory either. Method is the immanent manifestation of its autonomous system. And it is in this sense alone that there exists a historically coherent identity between method and system. The development of history is, accordingly, the method, and the comprehended totality of its epochal moments is the system as actualised life. The system is history sublated in its present existence. The system is synonymous with the subject which continuously becomes and sustains itself through the reflection upon the method. Method and system exist interrelationally in and through all the stages of the historical and transformative development towards absolute self-consciousness. What in formal and particularising logic is abstract theory becomes in dialectical logic concrete and holistic philosophy. Hegelian dialectic is therefore the historical concretisation of a posited abstract life. It is the 'manifestation of its content', or 'living manifestation'.[1]

We have seen how the understanding employs methods by means of which it seeks to rationalise the phenomenal world conceptually. But even though the employment of method may be systematic, it is nonetheless applied only to the finite domains of the individual sciences and does not and cannot encompass them comprehensively as a historical totality. For the understanding method can never become its system. It can never fully conceptualise the factual and phenomenal world. That is to say, in rationality method and system do not correspond to one another, and they cannot develop into an identity with one another.

In Hegel, by contrast, the system of reason implies a historically completed and actively idealised totality, because reason thinks the relations between particulars. The way in which this becoming being of the present is preserved is determined by the dialectical method. Only if we regard reason in this relationship can we say that the method is the system, and that the system is the method. Both are identical. As presently preserved life history is coherently identical with itself. The becoming of history, and the development therefore of its intended present, are always a becoming as and towards totality. In the dialectical philosophy of history, Hegel says that 'method is nothing but the structure ['Bau des Ganzen' = the formation of the whole, H.K.] set forth in its pure essentiality'.[2] The term *essentiality* must be understood as the historically active comprehension of all antecedent stages of becoming. Essence is notional history. Life, in order to become sublated and self-conscious life, needs its history as means out of which it actualises and comprehends itself intentionally as end. But in order to become reflected history, it must make a willed effort. Life in its present has to work through its past. History is thus the 'strenuous effort of the Notion'.[3] The possibility of a self-conscious present is developed in that the subject becomes conscious of its becoming. The notion is not a passive label. It is active labour. The notion, says Hegel, is 'creative power' ('Schaffen' = work, H.K.).[4] Only in that the notion enters into its history, in that it absolutely negates itself, is it the 'shaper and creator'.[5] And since the notion is the subject, it shapes and creates itself. The self-understanding of the subject is mediated through its historical work.

Here is not the place to discuss specifically Hegel's reflections on work as such.[6] At the same time, however, it is important to point out that the *act*-ivity and the *act*-uality of the notion are its spiritual work. And the result of this work of reflection is the present coherence of the system with its method. Hegel's understanding of the notion that works through its manifestations is indeed a theme that makes the adoption of a wholly new philosophical attitude towards thinking necessary.[7] It is with Hegel that thinking is for the first time recognised as an activity whose intention is to understand self-consciously the history of its deeds.

Prior to Hegel thinking was never identified with work.[8] And after Hegel attempts of relational reflections were again suppressed by the dogmatic positivisms in the sciences and by the struggle for ideological righteousness in political life and the humanities. Today, however, at the nuclear crossroad of man's existence, historical and perspectival thinking must once more be recovered and become the guide for and guardian of our actions.

That which workingly thinks is the subject. What the subject thinks about and hence works on are the historical relations which form its method. The subject is history, and every history of the subject ends in a present. Hegel can be correctly followed only if it is granted that for him the subject becomes self-conscious as it appears in and is mediated through its own history. The appearance of history is the spirit, and its completion in a present is its work. It is through the continuous and non-finite self-sublation of history that the spirit returns to itself in the form of self-consciousness. Accordingly, Hegel writes: 'As Spirit that knows what it is, it does not exist before, and nowhere at all, till after the completion of its work'; only then is there a coherent relation of '*self-consciousness* with its *consciousness*', or is there a 'knowing that is *for itself*'.[9] The self-conscious present has developed itself through its consciousness of the past. The subject in all its historical transformations develops only towards and for itself and not towards and for another.

It is, finally, through this completed work of mediated self-relation that the subject becomes conscious of its freedom. It is the recognition of freedom to develop for its own sake, for its self-consciousness, and not for the sake of filling an alienating ought. Hegel's idea of freedom, interpreted as self-consciousness, and dialectically comprehending itself through its history, is the 'world-historical turning point'.[10] It initiates a fundamental change in philosophical thinking generally. Unlike the Aristotelian idea of individual happiness, for instance, which implies a contemplative, that is, static and passive state of being, Hegel's reflection on freedom involves the historical becoming of selfhood which is mediated through the dynamic and active work of a whole community.

To return to the issue of method and system. Hegel says at one point that 'hitherto philosophy had not found its method; it regarded with envy the systematic structure of mathematics and . . . borrowed it or had recourse to the method of sciences which are only amalgams of given material, empirical propositions and thoughts – or even resorted to a crude rejection of all method'.[11]

It seems as if today we have lost again the once found meaning of method. Philosophical reflection upon the historical whole has been reduced to scientific reflections upon dominating phenomenal and fragmented research areas. The reductionist and diremptive analysis of parts is mostly undertaken without the concomitant effort to reflect upon its implications, or to view it in its historical composition and holistic interrelatedness. Hegel's remark is therefore a comment on, even a shattering critique of, such contemporary intelligence.

The subjective and theoretical search for positivistic and paradigmatic results obstructs the philosophical task of the subject to remain its self-own positive result. Philosophy cannot be academically learned, but only existentially experienced. It is education, not instruction. It is the guide out of rigid and separating rationalities, out of the narrow confines of dogmatic group-think, and into the thinking of social convictions. It is not a path into the mere consciousness of contradictory theories. But this philosophical experience of existence is the experience of the subject that knows itself as methodical system. Hegel reflects upon existence as the relational totality of historical life which cannot be theoretically reduced to and particularised into empirical and abstract propositions. It can only be philosophically reflected upon in its universal and spiritual manifestations.

Hegel's own reaction to the rational efforts at methodologisation is in part directed against Kant. Hegel comprehends historically the analytical sciences and their scattered and manifold methods into the holistic system of reason, that is, into *one* philosophical science. But for Kant this is impossible to do because his objective is to methodologise the theoretical sciences through the hypothesisation of a transcendent rational reason. Kant's interest lies in furthering 'so far as in us lies, the growth of the [individual, H.K.] sciences' (Den Wachstum der Wissenschaften an seinem Teile befördern, H.K.).[12] Kant's 'critique of pure speculative reason' can therefore only be a 'treatise on the method, not a system of the science itself' (Sie ist ein Traktat von der Methode, nicht ein System der Wissenschaft selbst, H.K.).[13]

Hegel distinguishes in the *objective logic* theoretical communality (Gemein-schaft) from philosophical science (Wissen-schaft) in the *subjective logic*. The science of the subject is the consciousness of itself through its concrete and historical essence. In its philosophical reflection, therefore, science pervades its essential communality. About the latter Hegel writes: 'Essence is at first only the inner, and it, too, is for this reason taken as a wholly *external*, unsystematized, common element [Gemein-schaftlichkeit, H.K.]'; it is 'something common formed by an external aggregation of existing objects lacking any essential connexion or organization'; it is something 'immediate', something '*passive*, a *prey to otherness*'.[14]

That which is common and, from a historical point of view, unsystematised is only theoretically common. Communality implies a unity which is deduced from a posited and formal concept. And since it has no mediating and historical content, it is for this reason also empty and meaningless. The rational idea, for instance, of a *common good* therefore turns out to be a mere sham because it is nothing but the hoped-for, arbitrary collection of facts and fictions. As a reductionist concept it is not explained, but simply assumed and taken for granted. And because it is an amalgam, the conceptual idea of a *common good* is a prey to otherness, that is, it is subject to rational contradiction. The ontology of such a redeeming essence cannot hold itself. It is without any historical ground, and hence is lifeless.

Feyerabend, as we have shown, radically dissolves the Kantian mode of reflection into irrational activities for theoretical purposes. He not only denies, like Kant, the possibility of a rational system of science, but, unlike Kant, even rejects all attempts to establish rational methods for pursuing specialised scientific inquiries. Yet, in both cases, historical life and its reason are not thematised because scientific research presupposes them. Since Feyerabend himself takes reason for granted, he feels protected by it and therefore can afford to cultivate his dictum: *anything goes*. But this extreme doubt in rational system ontology and the sceptical dismissal of any form of methodical thinking also leads to such an increase in subjective sublimation that it only impedes the philosophical effort to reflect upon their historical reason.

In the theory of the understanding objects are rational representations which are allegedly unified by a posited reason. From its own limited vantage point the understanding seeks to reconstruct the world conceptually. But in so doing it can venture no further than to an abstract formalism to which it is unable to give any meaningful content, let alone a justification for its beginning and purpose. This kind of formalism, Hegel says, is the 'shallow ineptitude and barrenness of modern philosophic "construction" so-called, that consists in nothing but fastening this schema on to everything without Notion and immanent determination and employing it for an external arrangement'.[15]

Feyerabend, too, is critical of the rational variety of formalism when he writes that 'logicians . . . take it for granted that constructing formal systems and playing with them is the only legitimate way of understanding scientific change'.[16] At the same time he advocates a 'new formalism',[17] his own structureless dialectic which in its mere negativity collapses upon itself.

Over against the formalism of an analytical understanding, Hegel thinks the organically concrete reason which notionalises itself. As such, reason entails all the notionally determinate concepts of rationality. 'Philosophy', he says, 'as a totality of knowledge produced by reflection, becomes a system, an organic whole of Notions [the notionalised concepts, H.K.] whose highest law is not the understanding but reason'.[18] Reason is the 'germ of the living being' (Keim des Lebendigen, H.K.) it has 'urges' which are directed towards the fulfilment of its 'subjective end'.[19] It is this end itself as self-conscious subject; it is life and absolute truth. Reason is the 'urge towards totality',[20] towards its own self-same historical and holistic comprehension. Reason is developmental formation, it is not a sort of dogmatic formalism.

'The true shape in which truth exists can only be the scientific system of such truth.'[21] Or, as Hegel also says, 'knowledge is only actual and can only be expounded, as Science or as *system*'.[22] This shape is philosophy itself which must be brought 'closer to the form of Science', to the 'system of Science'.[23] Philosophy must be developed into the reflection upon the unity of the science of self-knowledge, and it must not be left to content itself with a spurious system of the plurality of theoretical sciences. Philosophy and theory, although related to one another, are not the same; they refer to different modes of thinking. Hegel warns that actual 'wholes . . . cease to exist when the unity of their Notion and their reality is dissolved; man, the living being, is dead when soul and body are parted in him'.[24] Life is a dead, conceptual idea if it is not the power to reflect historically upon its self and thereby to sublate its being into continuous actuality.

Reason is self-producing unity. It grasps or notionalises itself because as subject it has notionalised itself in its self-own historical object. The activity of notionalising becomes thus the absolute method. It is absolute because within history method develops only into a system that is dialectically determined through its past and into the present. It is absolute because system and method relate to one another in immanence. Only in such a system, that enfolds itself into mediated self-consciousness, is it possible for the subject to know itself.

Thus Hegel says, the method 'has emerged as the *self-knowing Notion that has itself*, as the absolute, both subjective and objective, *for its subject matter*'.[25] The 'method is only the movement of the Notion itself', and it is because the notion is notionalised history that 'anything whatever is comprehended and known in its truth only when it is *completely subjugated to the method*'.[26] Philosophical knowledge of the subject is actualised within its historically developed system. Only in the present is philosophy identical with self-consciousness, and have both become the notion. The present recognises itself as present only in and through its history. This *recognition*, according to Hegel, is in the end also 'the one single aim, action, and goal of philosophy – to arrive at the Notion of its Notion, and thus secure its return and its satisfaction'.[27] It is the return from the reflection about history, and it is the satisfaction about the developed and fulfilled self-consciousness.

Furthermore, it is also because reason comprehends the understanding that the latter is both analytic and synthetic. Writes Hegel: 'But though the method of truth which comprehends the subject matter is . . . itself analytic, for it remains entirely within the Notion, yet it is equally synthetic, for through the Notion the subject matter is determined dialectically and as an other'.[28] The analytic and synthetic are substance and subject, and together they are the notion as comprehended history and therefore as life. Hence synthesis is a formal concept, but is to be understood in terms of organic and historical sublation. What is dialectical is the movement of the notion which is 'the innermost source of all activity, of all animate and spiritual self-movement, the dialectical soul that everything true possesses and through which alone it is true'.[29] The living in its shapes or epochs develops to ever higher realisations of itself until it is actualised in its self-consciousness. Every stage has formed itself into a 'circle of circles' which is teleologically 'ensouled by the method'.[30]

Life in the present is fulfilled teleology, it is *entelechy* within which the method 'expands itself into a *system*'.[31] As a system entelechy is fully reflected reason, it is reason that has returned to itself. It is not an inadequate concept to which no phenomena correspond. Entelechy is the 'adequate Notion'[32] that has methodically notionalised itself in that it coheres with its history. History is only *one* history, *one* method relating itself to *one* system. In consequence, Hegel says, 'there can be but one method in all science, since the method is the self-unfolding Notion and nothing else, and this latter is only one'.[33] The historical development of the subject is 'being-for-itself, actuality'.[34] It is 'going forth', 'separation' and 'coming to itself' (Herausgehen, Sichauseinanderlegen, Zusichkommen, H.K.).[35] 'The act is thus really one, and it is just this unity of differences which is the concrete.'[36] The method is the concretised system.

The circle can also be said to be the cyclical spiral of thinking itself.[37] Life, which thinks itself historically, is thus the 'system of logic'.[38] It is the self-construing logic. The development is guided from rational consciousness (Be → wusst → sein) to the self-consciousness of reason (Selbst ⇔ be ⇔ wusst ⇔ sein), from phenomenology to logic. The latter reflects itself immanently in the former, that is, in its own self-positedness and self-production.

The transformative turning point which Hegel reflects upon[39] is the absolute subject or personality. 'The richest', he says,

> is therefore the most concrete and most *subjective*, and that which withdraws itself into the simplest depth is the mightiest ['mächtigste' = most powerful, H.K.] and most all-embracing. The highest, most concentrated point is the *pure personality* which, solely through the absolute dialectic which is its nature, no less *embraces and holds everything within itself*, because it makes itself the supremely free.[40]

Thus Hegel transforms the Kantian idea of pure though passive and impersonal reason into the idea of pure and active historical reason of personality. While the former is subjectively posited, the latter is self-produced as subject. With Hegel the ahistorical idea idealises itself in the self-realising act. The fulfilled awareness of the personality *qua* subject is the science of the actual notion. It is the notion that knows itself in its historical objectivity. 'Science', according to Hegel, 'dare only organize itself by the life of the Notion itself'.[41] And he says:

> scientific cognition . . . demands surrender to the life of the object [that is, to history, H.K.], or, what amounts to the same thing, confronting and expressing its inner necessity. Thus, absorbed in its object, scientific cognition forgets about that general survey, which is merely the reflection of the cognitive process away from the content and back into itself. Yet, immersed in the material, and

> advancing with its movement, scientific cognition does come back to itself, but not before its filling ['Erfüllung' = fulfilment, H.K.] or content is taken back into itself.[42]

What Hegel wants to point out is that the dialectical logic of the notion requires that the subject reflects upon its subjectively posited concepts in order to come to the awareness that they are not mere meta-objects, but that these can be grasped only and fully if their historical development is recognised. In other words, a concept is scientific only in that it is treated as a historical notion.

The activity of overcoming external and subjective reflection through the self-movement of the dialectical method is not an arbitrary thinking of the subject. Rather, the historical method immanently demands that the whole potential of reflection be comprehended in order to give it thereby the teleological movement towards its necessary system. 'The absolute method ... does not behave like external reflection.'[43] As a rational and subjective form of argumentation the latter is only 'freedom from all content, and a sense of vanity towards it'.[44] Conceptual thinking is not only ahistorical, but it even misunderstands and hence rejects historical reflection as an imposing yet unjustified historicism. It does not realise, however, that freedom from all historical and relational content means the elimination of all possibilities to reflect upon oneself as subject, to recognise oneself in and through mediation. History is not historicism. While the former belongs necessarily to the subject, and is productive, the latter is an arbitrary interpretation of a future historical content of law-like expectations, and is therefore positivistic. It trusts that the present, free from its past, is also free for the future.

But Hegel argues that this kind of rational freedom as

> self-subsistence pushed to the point of the one as a being-for-self is abstract, formal, and destroys itself. It is the supreme, most stubborn error, which takes itself for the highest truth, manifesting in more concrete forms as abstract freedom, pure ego and, further, as Evil. It is that freedom which so misapprehends itself as to place its essence in this abstraction, and flatters itself that in thus being with itself it possesses itself in its purity. More specifically, this self-subsistence is the error of regarding as negative that which is its own essence [its own history, H.K.], and of adopting a negative attitude towards it.[45]

Abstract freedom is the freedom of an arbitrarily positing rational method. Absolute freedom, however, is the freedom of reason, of the system as sublated life which bears itself and concretises itself into rationality. Historical reason demands from the vanity of rationality that it makes the effort:

> to give up this freedom, and, instead of being the arbitrarily moving principle of the content, to sink this freedom in the content, letting it move spontaneously of its own nature, by the self as its own self, and then to contemplate this movement. This refusal to intrude into the immanent rhythm of the Notion, either arbitrarily or with wisdom obtained from elsewhere, constitutes a restraint which is itself an essential moment of the Notion.[46]

Thus, unlike the finite and rational method, the non-finite method of reason 'takes the determinate element from its own subject matter, since it is itself that subject matters's immanent principle and soul'.[47] Dialectical reason refuses to eliminate its history. On the contrary, in order to reflect upon itself it needs history because it is its subject matter through which alone it is able to determine itself.

And Hegel clarifies further that:

> it is in this nature [of the historical method, H.K.] of what is to be in its being its own Notion, that *logical necessity* in general consists. This alone is the rational ['vernünftige' = reasonable, H.K.] element and the rhythm of the organic whole; it is as much *knowledge* of the content, as the content is the Notion and essence – in other words, it alone is *speculative philosophy* . . . This nature of scientific method, which consists partly in not being separate from the content, and partly in spontaneously determining the rhythm of its movement, has . . . its proper exposition in speculative philosophy.[48]

The Hegelian method of dialectic, which describes the necessary movement of historical life as system, is the 'course of the subject matter itself' (der Gang der Sache selbst, H.K.).[49] It is the 'immanent development of the Notion'; hence, it is what Hegel calls the *autonomous* 'self-construing method' (der sich selbst konstruierende Weg, H.K.).[50] The earlier dialectic of the understanding was 'contingent'[51] because it moved only between concepts. Rational dialectic is the dialectic of 'error, confusion, opinion, endeavour, caprice and transitoriness' (Vergänglichkeit, H.K.).[52] In the dialectic of reason, however, these concepts are comprehended as spiritualised historical notions and developed further into and by the '*necessity* of the Notion'.[53] Absolute reason is the self-related infinite, it is the self-sublated present which has developed itself out of its non-finite history. And because life is reason that notionalises itself, it is for Hegel ultimately 'imperishable *life [unvergängliches Leben*, H.K.*]*, *self-knowing truth*, and is *all truth*'.[54]

Therefore, 'the method is not merely an aggregate of certain determinations, but the Notion that is determined in and for itself' as system.[55] The subject as historical life is '*fulfilled being*, the *Notion that comprehends* itself [erfülltes Sein, der sich begreifende Begriff, H.K.]'.[56]

The life of the subject is *invisible* because it is transparent. And it is because of this transparence that it can see its true nature which is its relational and spiritual history. In that the subject pervades itself it gains insight, or it sees into its historical content. Insight is the insight into its concreteness, or into the concretisation of itself as subject. To have insight is to think in terms of relations. And when fulfilled, it is the insightful reason into itself. The subject matter is thus reason and logical ground. That is to say, the logic of life is its dialectical history. Only when life is history can it develop into self-consciousness.

The one subject is life, the all-encompassing universal individual. About this *one* life Hegel says that it

> even when it posits itself in a determination [that is, in a historical formation, H.K.], *remains* therein what it is. It is the soul of the concrete which it indwells, unimpeded and equal to itself in the manifoldness and diversity of the concrete. It is not dragged into the process of becoming, but *continues* itself through that process undisturbed and possesses the power of unalterable, undying self-preservation.[57]

Let us bring this section to a close. The dialectical system of reason is the self-preserving power of life over the dividing forces of its rational methods. As such it is the positive of the double negative. The system, however, is this power only in that it, first, freely resolves itself, in order, then, to penetrate the creative methods, and finally, in order to comprehend or to notionalise its methods as its developed self-conscious self.

It is within the light of transparent historical reason that the understanding moves. But, unaware of its other forces, the methods of rationality may drag the developmental power of life into its destructive process and thereby darken the systemic ground of its developing and living history. The nuclear age, more than any other period during the spiritual evolution of mankind, entails the paradoxical and tragic relationship between the beginning of holistic self-consciousness and the consciousness of the possibility of its self-inflicted global death. But even in these troubled times thinking is not without philosophical guidance. For even in today's menaced world Hegel quite suredly provides us with the dialectical means to see our life in its historical perspective. It is only on the basis of such Hegelian comprehension that reasoned action can again be envisaged.

THE APPLICATION OF LOGIC

Every method stands in a determinate relationship to the object to which it is applied.[1] Now, if dialectic is to be thought through to its ultimate conclusion, that is, if dialectic is to become autonomous, reason as the notion must give itself its own method and may not obtain it from somewhere else.[2] It will be our concern in this last section of the present chapter to describe the nature of self-application, and to explicate the term in its dialectical meaning.

We have stated throughout that for Hegel the historical method is the development of the subject. That the subject develops means that it is the immanent and therefore autonomous method. Rational subjectivity applies theories from without to a conceptual object. Its method makes it into an epistemological science. Reason as subject, on the other hand, applies itself to itself. It is this methodological self-application that transforms the logic of a theoretical science into its philosophical science.[3] Dialectic is the historical ground which makes possible any though always finite theoretical episteme. 'This dialectic', Hegel writes,

> is not an activity of subjective thinking applied to some matter externally, but is rather the matter's very soul putting forth its branches and fruit organically . . . To consider a thing rationally [vernünftig, H.K.] means not to bring reason to bear on the object from outside and so to tamper with it, but to find that the object is rational [vernünftig, H.K.] on its own account [für sich selbst vernünftig, H.K.]; here it is mind [historical spirit, H.K.] in its freedom, the culmination of self-conscious reason, which gives itself actuality and engenders itself as an existing world.[4]

The question as to how to interpret the logico-dialectical method and its application is a highly debated one among Hegel commentators. Does it relate to the object of religious contemplation or to the subject of humanity? One view holds, for instance, that Hegel sees religion in the service of humanity, not humanity in the service of God.[5] This general conclusion is accepted by us in the sense that our own reading of Hegel strongly leads us to believe that his philosophy describes the dialectic of a self-responsible and communal humanism. Yet, another and for us more controversial opinion about this matter maintains that man is the vehicle of cosmic spirit, and that man will come to himself in the end when he sees himself as the vehicle of a larger spirit.[6] This analysis, according to our understanding of it, is questionable in so far as it conjures up too much the rational forms of alienation which are precisely Hegel's task to overcome. We do not intend here to delve into the literature about this dispute, or participate critically in the attempt to resolve the issue.

However, although we shall in the following chapter see in the subject the genus mankind, at this point we wish to take a more detached view. There is, for example, the argument that we should not only take the subject to be the full concrete I of life, the *whole human nature*, the *totality of our essence*.[7] Instead, we must note that the logical category *subject* does not designate a particular form of subjectivity (such as man) but a general structure that might best be characterised by the concept *mind*,[8] or, more appropriately, by the spirit. Thus the subject is to be regarded as being not only human,[9] not as a human subject alone, but primarily as an ontologically universal type of being Being.[10]

In a still less committed way one can accept Hegel's logic even if one is of the opinion that its content is neither the 'exposition of God as he is in his eternal essence before the creation of nature and a finite mind',[11] nor that God is conscious of Himself at the end of the world development. In other words, the logic is *neutral* irrespective of which world view one may hold.[12]

In the light of these differing attitudes we shall adopt for the moment the more neutral understanding of the problem of the application of method, and refer to Hegel himself. Generally speaking, in formal logic the understanding posits a concept *in-itself* and *for-us*, that is, for particular subjectivity. Yet in dialectical logic reason produces the notion in-and-for-itself, that is, for the mediated individual subject.[13] How is this logic to be treated?

Hegel writes that:

> now, if we inquire into the truth of knowledge, it seems that we are asking what knowledge is *in itself*. Yet in this inquiry knowledge is *our* object, something that exists *for us*; and the *in-itself* that would supposedly result from it would rather be the being of knowledge *for us*. What we asserted to be its essence [that is, its traditional ontology, H.K.] would be not so much its truth but rather just our knowledge of it.[14]

However, this distinction between *for us* and *for it* is not made by us but 'falls within it',[15] that is, within the historical spirit itself. Human 'consciousness knows *something*; this object is the essence or the *in-itself*; but it is also for consciousness the in-itself'.[16] It is being-for-consciousness of this in-itself. The in-itself 'ceases to be the in-itself, and becomes something that is the *in-itself* only *for consciousness*. And this then is the True: the being-for-consciousness of this in-itself'.[17]

Therefore, the in-itself of the understanding is also the in-itself of historical reason. But while the rational in-itself is *for us* and finite, this same in-itself is *for it* and is continuous or infinite, that is, it is for reason. The *for us* is essentially *for it*, for history. And history is, from the dialectical point of view, not the history of a particular individual person but of the holistic individuality of the subject mankind. The understanding is for reason, and the application of the dialectical method refers to the object/subject relationship or to the in-and-for-itself. Reason as the dialectical subject applies the subjective understanding to itself in such a way that it, in the course of its historical formations, achieves ever higher levels of comprehension and self-consciousness. This movement is shown in the dialectical form in which the individual understanding hypothesises transcendent objects for its rationality. These objects, however, are dissolved by reason and sublated in and for its holistic history. Hence, rationality in itself becomes and is reason for itself.

I (a) Object ← Understanding ⇔ Reason → Subject

(b) For us → For it

(c) In-itself *and* For-itself

It is important to realise that Hegel's thinking does not content itself with a theoretical reflection of what history is conceptually. It changes the knowledge of a hypothesised conceptual object. Hegel philosophically reflects upon the subject and its historically mediated efforts so that it may come to terms with itself from within. He does not ponder the question what man is, but what it socially means to be human. The subject appropriates itself in its practised relational history in order to become self-conscious and hence communally free. In this sense, Hegel's method has little to do with the empty idealism of rationality, but everything to do with idealising and fully concretising reason. Hegel is not a romantic dreamer but, as we have argued elsewhere, a realist who carefully works out the logical relations as they are expressed in the developing becoming of the subject.[18] In Hegel's dialectic the subject applies itself methodically to itself. This self-application constitutes its historical task.

If the dialectic should discontinue, the history of the subject would discontinue, as well. Mediation and self-sublation would then come to an end. The present would become meaningless, and an imagined future would be deprived of its historical logic. It is with this speculation in mind that we can say that unlike the analytical understanding, reflecting reason produces the subject in its holistic science as self-awareness. If subjectivity is to respond to its need to become the subject, we may also agree with Hegel and require that logical thinking 'in future must always be based on this [that is, on historical reason, H.K.], the only true standpoint'.[19] Rationality must always reflect upon its reason that as life manifests itself historically.

Hegel's philosophy is the philosophy of immanence. It describes the subject as it reflects upon its historical becoming by applying the objective method of dialectical thinking to itself. The subject thus responds to itself. And in that the subject responds to itself, it recognises itself in the responsibility to its life. This as well, then, is what Hegel teaches us, namely, to acknowledge that mankind is responsible ultimately only to itself, for its becoming conscious of itself and for its own continuous self-sublation.

SUMMARY

In the preceding sections we thematised various conceptual and notional movements as they manifest themselves and relate to one another within Hegel's dialectic. At the heart of this study lay the concern with Hegel's language and its philosophical exposition. What has become quite obvious in these discussions is the idea that the unity of the subject's self-consciousness is comprehended only in and through its objective history. Hegel therefore transforms the formal part-whole relationship, which is devoid of correspondence, and expresses it in terms of the concrete and coherent object/subject relation and identity. This identity is historically fulfilled in the present, while the former theoretical concept of equation is not only transcendent and future-oriented but therefore also without philosophical content.

Hegel's reflections are of the deepest insight into the philosophical nature of the subject and the spiritually organic growth of its self-consciousness. It is also this intellectual perception which throws light upon the question of what it is in the subject that allows it to preserve itself. It is because of what is at stake in the nuclear age that Hegel's philosophy is invaluable for comprehending the idea of mankind and its historical relations. How the subject mankind logically differentiates itself, and what the dialectical implication of this is, will be the theme of the following chapter.

4 Hegel's Phenomenon of Logic

The essence of logic is its activity. That which acts is a subject, and only a subject is history. History itself is the phenomenon of dialectical logic. In Hegel's philosophy history is the equivalent of method. Since to speak about method is meaningful only in relation to its application, we shall direct the issue of method to the question of how mankind dirempts itself into the state and how it mediates itself through the states-system. In other words, the aim of the sections in this chapter is to bring to bear dialectic on that which is ultimately threatened in the nuclear era – life itself.

We begin our inquiry with some comments about the philosophically interpreted relationship between mankind and God, and a preliminary description of the spiritually organic differentiation of mankind itself. In these first two sections the issue of self-determining agency will be addressed. As will emerge from this discussion, we place the locus of agency not in a transcendent God but in mankind. This will set the stage for the subsequent terminologically more technical parts of the chapter.

We shall then proceed by employing Hegel's logic of *judgment* and by giving an extensive textual account of its internal dialectical progression. Although the idea of dialectic is always demonstrated in the same way, whatever the developmental stages within the overall system of Hegel's reflections, the articulation of the notion of judgment is perhaps more suitable to our purpose to explicate the part-whole relationship than other examples might be.

The analysis of the judgment will allow us to follow the various mediative steps towards the theoretical conceptualisation of the state and the system of states. And it will provide us with a method to see these phenomena actually advancing towards the *syllogism*, that is, towards their logical comprehension within the notion of mankind. The relationship between the *states* and *mankind* is that between the *parts* and the *whole*.

This intimation of the relevance of the judgment may here suffice to indicate that we are not so much concerned with giving an explanatory or definitional answer to the question: 'what is this or that object?'. The point of interest is to do with the description of the answer to the question: 'how and why do we have to think dialectically about the logical differentiation between the parts and the whole, or between life and its history?' In order to facilitate the reading and application of Hegel's intricate language we shall accompany the syllogistic forms of mediation with illustrative graphs and dialectical *relations*. The directional movements of mediation are drawn by arrows. One arrow symbolises a one-sided determination, while a double arrow stands for the mutuality of determinations. In this way of exposition we hope to preserve the nature of an exegesis and to complement it with a clarifying interpretive style to deal with a rather complex text. And, as in the case of judgment, by syllogism we do not mean a formal process of ratiocination in which, in Aristotelian fashion, a particular conclusion is deduced from a dialogically arrived at universal premise. In its Hegelian version syllogism will signify the organic mediation of historical moments into an actualised result which is always considered in terms of the present.

In this chapter we endeavour to convey the meaning of dialectic when this mode of reflection is taken to be the expression of mankind itself. The account presented, however, is not a description of the contingent histories of individual states at particular times, or of the evolution of the system they have come to form in our contemporary epoch. We are not telling a story in the manner of historians and social empiricists. Instead, we are raising phenomenal facts to the level of their logical notion, thereby rendering the relations between them dialectically necessary. Yet this transformation is in need of a philosophical standpoint from which alone arguments about the purpose of history can be put forward. Reason in history is that of its self-consciousness whose actualisation in mankind is mediated in and through the real history of states. But if reason is self-consciousness, then the problem which the idea of nuclear war, for instance, poses for reflection can find a solution only if mankind freely recognises itself in its history and therefore learns to be responsible for creating the possibility for its self-comprehension and continuous sublation.

THE IDEA OF MANKIND AS LIFE

In the Hegelian system of subjective logic the notion notionalises itself towards and comprehends itself as the non-transcending, absolute idea. That is to say, the subject is in its final cognition idea. The idea itself, however, is life, and the result of the logical activity of its historical relations is with Hegel *imperishable life*.[1] And the corollary of imperishable life is the idea of *infinite freedom*. Freedom, of course, is a term which we have encountered already during our discussion of Plato's dialogic dialectic. But there it could manifest itself only in its finite form.

Ideas describe the thinking about relations, and for this reason are subject to philosophical, not empirical, scrutiny. It is because life as freedom is idea that it is therefore equally open to philosophical, and that is in its Hegelian reading, dialectical inquiry. According to our interpretation of Hegel, and in the context of this book, the notion of free idea is manifested in the subject mankind. And of this mankind we say that nothing stands over and above it. By this is meant that mankind is not governed by the determining acts of a God who is conceived of in a leap of faith. Instead, mankind is determined in and through its own activity. And we think of the idea of mankind as being the subject which relates to its history as to its own object. The principle of this possibility of self-development is the principle of immanence. The philosophical assignment for us, therefore, is to elucidate the internal relationship between mankind and history.

The freedom of the subject mankind is, further, the realm of spiritual life within which it determines self-referringly the historical moments of its unfolding. The reflected unity of this internal dialectic of history is the necessary condition of life in its freedom. In other words, reflection is the necessary condition of self-consciousness. Life is not without its relation to reflection, and the goal of reflection is to achieve self-consciousness as the manifestation of absolute freedom. This absolute freedom is that of the idea.[2] And since for us the idea of life is mankind, the idea is therefore also the '*adequate Notion*, that which is objectively *true*, or the *true as such*', because 'when anything whatever possesses truth, it possesses it through its Idea', or 'something possesses truth only in so far as it is idea'.[3] The idea is the adequate notion, and only that is adequate which has completely notionalised itself. The idea of freedom is for Hegel the highest principle to be actualised in and for mankind. And what we recognise in Hegel's idea of freedom is its necessarily immanent relation to the historical actualisation of self-comprehension.

Now, if Hegelian logic is the logic of development and historical becoming, freedom itself is, as we have said, freedom as immanent activity. But because it is not a grace of God, it is for that reason also a spontaneous activity. Its development can be described more specifically as the self-construing method, whose telos is to sublate and preserve itself in its self-consciousness. What the dialectical activity of the idea of freedom implies is the ability to create this freedom by making the decision to become at first conscious of its nature, and then to reflect upon its history as it develops out of nature. Through the dialectical movement the subject not only comes to think of freedom, but has actually fulfilled it in the self-consciousness of its present. Hence freedom is true freedom only after the completion of an activity. It requires a Hegelian task, namely, the task to externalise, or to judge (ur-teilen) itself. Life as self-conscious freedom is this freedom only after it has consciously judged itself into the moments of its dialectical becoming.

The first step involves the consciousness of nature. Freedom 'in its own absolute truth ... resolves [entschliesst sich, H.K.] to ... go forth freely as Nature'.[4] The freedom of mankind in its idea is the decision to reflect itself within and through the world as its natural phenomenon. To judge is for Hegel to negate what is merely believed to be identity. And to re-establish identity, but this time as true knowledge of it, the act of judging must be negated in turn so as to bring about the idea of positive union. The positive of the double negative can also be expressed as the historically arrived at syllogism. Accordingly, nature is the first negation of the notion. But, in order to become positive, the notion must make a second step. It must negate nature and sublate itself within spirit, that is, within itself as historical phenomenon. Man is not confined to the determinations of natural processes. He exists only in the recognition of the possibility of his spiritual self-development. Man concretises himself because he relates past particular moments of his spiritual formation to one another, and unifies them into the present self-consciousness of his holistic history. It is only because he is history that man is man. And by the same token, it is only because mankind is history that it is mankind. Mankind is one, and as such is individuality. The term individuality comprises the universalised form of man, that is, the totality of all individual persons.

Freedom can be obtained and reflected upon as a philosophical idea only in a present. The past is not, and the future is not yet. Free activity is the infinite or better non-finite movement of dialectical logic. The freedom of the idea is the freedom of the subject. And Hegel elaborates that the:

> Idea exists *in* the self-subsistent subject, for which, as organ of the Notion, everything is ideal and fluid; that is, the subject *thinks*,

> makes everything in space and time its own and in this way has universality; i.e. its own self, present within it. Since in this way the universal is now *for* the universal, therefore the Notion is *for itself*; this is first manifested in spirit in which the Notion makes itself objective to itself.[5]

Absolute freedom is freedom through the sublation of its internal contradictions, that is, its manifested immanent natural and historical differentiations. The freedom of mankind, in other words, is its freedom to sublate itself as its life-world. And this world is therefore only as long as mankind preserves itself.

To sum up: by dialectical progression we mean with Hegel that 'the logical principle turns to Nature and Nature to Mind [spirit = history, H.K.]', and the 'syllogism is *in the Idea*'.[6] This principle is visualised in the following figure:

I

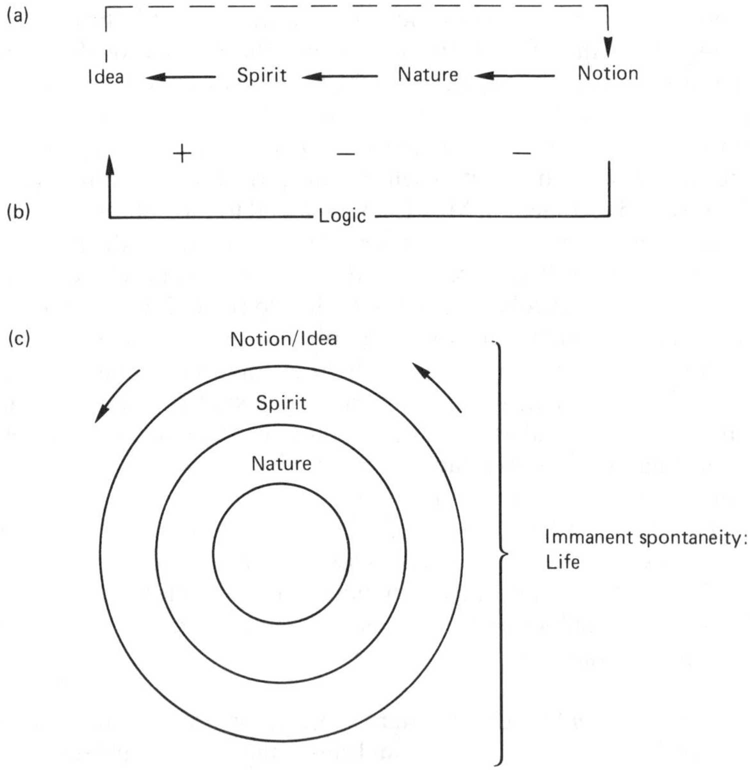

In this figure, (a) shows the positive of the double negative, whereby the second negation indicates the mediating moment towards spirit, that is, towards man's historical formations. The dotted line symbolises the first part of the full circle, which with (b) refers to the syllogised adequacy between the idea and the notion. The sublation of nature and spirit is the sublation of man through himself. It is self-sublated historical life. And, finally, (c) describes the same in the form of the Hegelian syllogistic cycle within which man appropriates nature and the rational concepts which he posits in his spiritual history in order to become self-conscious. It likewise says that dialectical logic is the principle of immanent spontaneity. It is spontaneity which turns an abstract thought of posited life into the concrete and producing life of thinking. The free activity of the self-thinking subject is the historical production of its self-consciousness. This is the true meaning of the Hegelian notion of the absolute, namely, that it does not refer to a fact as an external mental construct one can think of. It refers to life which thinks itself in relation to itself. But the turning point of reflection, of the second negation, is the mediating *medius terminus* which is manifested in the spirit, that is, in history, and which stands between nature and the idea of the present. Therefore, Hegel substantiates, the:

> syllogism is the standpoint of the Mind [spirit, H.K.] itself, which – as the mediating agent in the process – presupposes Nature and couples it with the logical principle. It is the syllogism where Mind [spirit, H.K.] reflects on itself in the Idea: philosophy appears as a subjective cognition, of which liberty is the aim, and which is itself the way to produce it.[7]

Absolute freedom, however, freedom in its fulfilled aim, is the idea as imperishable life. It is the ground of and reason for everything of which it is cognisant within itself. But the idea is not to be regarded as a posited noumenal idea. Unlike the subjective and external concept of the Kantian idea, for instance, which is static and rationally hypothesised, the Hegelian notion of the idea is dynamic because it is historical reason internally producing itself towards itself as the self-conscious subject. And again, unlike the posited external idea which does not require the mediation out of nature, the self-producing immanent idea mediates itself out of nature and through the spirit of mankind. Let us below show this difference in another graph.

In subjectivity (a), the rational spirit of individual man posits a transcendent idea which refers back to transcendental rationality

II (a) Subjectivity (Kant)

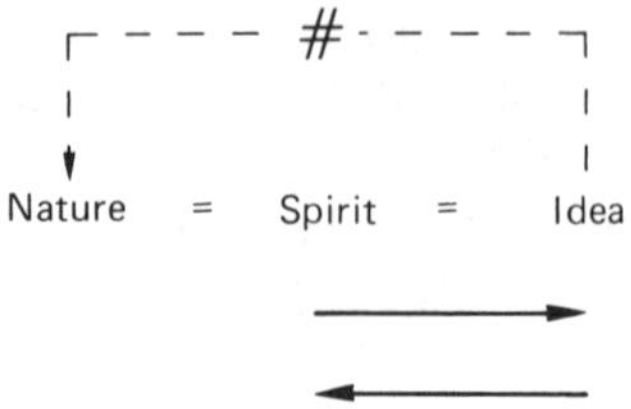

(b) Subject (Hegel)

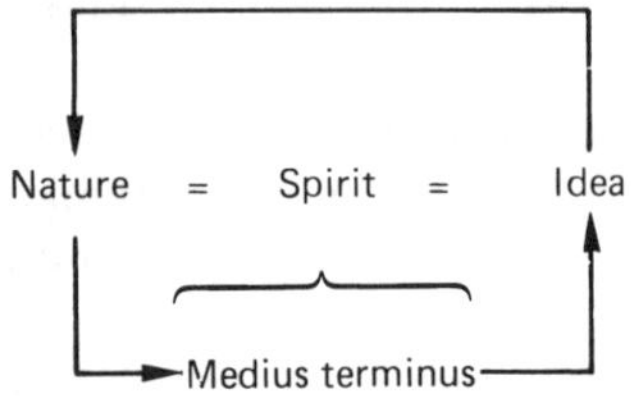

alone. The Kantian idea merely unifies hypothetically the categories of the understanding without relating to the phenomenal experiences of natural consciousness. In the subject (b), however, the Hegelian idea of reason posits itself in nature and produces itself self-referringly through the historical and rational spirit of universal man. In other words, while the former is to explain a dialectical ontology or a teleology, the latter describes the manifestation of dialectic which, in its actualisation, is entelechy. Entelechy here is not the posited conceptual filling of Being (Sein) but the absolute activity in its fulfilment, or it is the end in-and-for-itself. And the fulfilment is the absolute self-conscious freedom to act as life.

The idea as adequate notion is the subject matter (die Sache selbst) of logic in this fulfilled and sublated activity. It is, therefore, says Hegel, the 'nature of the fact [Sache, H.K.], the Notion, which causes the movement and development, yet this same movement is equally the action of cognition. The eternal Idea, in full fruition of its essence [an und für sich, H.K.] eternally sets itself to work, engenders and enjoys itself as absolute Mind [Spirit, H.K.]'.[8] It is because the idea as mankind is infinite spirit and history that individual man in his ideas has only a finite spirit. Of what significance is this conclusion? We shall interpret this religious dimension in illustration III by considering the relationship between man, God and spirit.

In (a) it is man's finite, that is, subjective spirit that posits God. Individual rationality hypothesises the idea of God as a conceptual

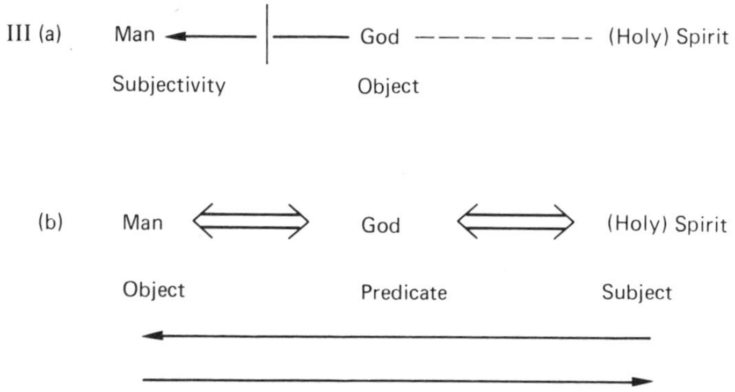

object. This object, however, transcends rationality and is said to be separated from it. As such it is invoked as a one-sidedly determining redeemer.[9] The movement of determination is indicated by the arrow. Finite historical rationality posits an infinite rational reason. The God of the understanding is the yonder world which is separated from and alien to man. But it is also because he only *has* an idea of God that man at the same time takes for granted the spiritual history that comprehends man and God. And similarly, the thought of the *holy spirit* (dotted line) remains a contentless leap of faith that is dialectically defective in so far as its mediating role is one of hope and not of actuality.

It is, therefore, in (b) that the infinite spirit as the subject mankind posits man, and produces itself through man's finite spiritual object. This object is rendered historically transparent in the sense of being spiritualised into a mediating means. In other words, the subject is dialectically predicated upon an object. Unlike in (a), the holy spirit is here the actualised cyclical syllogism of mankind. It is the mutually determining, historically developed '*circle* returning upon itself'.[10] And this movement is shown by the double arrows.

The word *holy* (heilig or heil) means to appropriate or to claim something as one's own.[11] It equally denotes health, invulnerability, security and completeness.[12] The holy spirit is the absolute and holistic idea as imperishable life. It alone is the self-sublated, because self-relating, *in-and-for-itself*. It does not stand for the life to which we rationally ascribe contradictory values of, for instance, good or bad. Rather is it the historical life of reason which not only permeates the existence of man and his subjective activities, but which needs man in order to produce itself, as is shown in figure III (b). Thus the absolute subject mankind, in its work to return to itself as historically developed self-consciousness, must step into its own world of dialectical mediation as its phenomenal object. In this self-externalisation the absolute manifests itself as being present in the world. To become self-conscious present signifies further that man cognises the absolute. The absolute as self-sublated presentness therefore needs the history of man. Man's historical spirit is the mediating agent and a necessary organic member of the concretisation of the absolute.[13] This absolute is the life of mankind.

If the absolute is life, and if life needs man, then historical man is the mediating means between nature and mankind. It is through the appropriation of man that mankind transforms itself into actualised and imperishable life. That man in his universality is finite does not mean that he is mortal. In his self-knowledge he realises that he is mortal, and thus temporally limited as an individual instance of mankind. Finitude means that man with his purposeful activities achieves a reflectively intended historical result, namely, the preservation of mankind. The finitude of man is thus sublated into the infinite life of mankind. The finite is the in-itself but *for* another, for that which is larger than itself. It is for mankind. But if mankind has preserved within itself its historical activities, it has thereby sublated itself.

If man is the mediating means, then man is, in his universality, the absolute individual subject as mankind. That is to say, absolute life is in man himself. Individual mankind is in universal man. It is the fulfilled dialectical principle of *one in all* and *all in one*. Put differently, if the logic is the notion notionalising itself into the absolute idea, man is the notion in its dialectical becoming. The becoming is the logic as eternally self-creating life. This mediating syllogism is thus:

IV

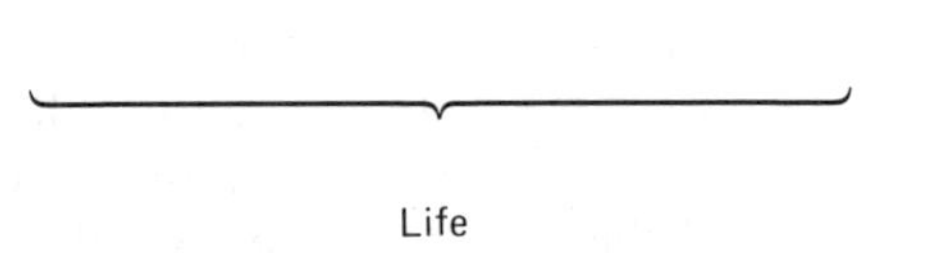

In his spirituality, man creates the history of life. History is the essence of the notion, and in this it is akin to Hegel's division of dialectical thinking. The absolute is internalised history as spiritual activity. Hence the absolute is not external to man but immanent in his becoming. Present being is historicality. The history of finite being is not a process towards a rationally determined goal. It is not a history of transitions from one stage of being to another and different level of being. It is dialectical history purely and indifferently within itself as sameness. It is the ever-present immanent self-development and organic transformation of historical moments. Finite man never has a history, but always *is* history. And apart from nature, as we have seen, the spiritual history of man is only one mode of universal history which, holistically speaking, is comprehended as *one*, or as being syllogised with nature.[14] The infinite is not beyond the finite, a point of reference from where the finite in its being would have to be deductively determined. The finite bears within itself its own non-finite and in this sense alone infinite history. The infinite *is*, is there and present.[15]

The history of man is the spirit within his life. Life appears as the history of man. And the non-finite continuity of life is man's immanent progress. The meaning of progress is its development. It is cyclical progress without having a fixed rational and linear telos. And progress without telos is possible if telos is regarded as an inner measure of dialectical transformations and not as a measure of rational transitions which are ascribed to the epistemological processes of external objects. What the idea of the cycle refers to is the mediated progress man makes from being conscious of external objects to becoming conscious of himself as mankind. Progress cannot be measured from outside; it is the mode of internal movement itself.[16] Progress is the sublation and hence the continuity of life, whereby life is understood as the developing self-consciousness of mankind. Life progresses within itself and towards itself and not towards something other than itself.

The history of universal man is the history of spirit or of imperishable life. Man is the historically mediating fulfilment of life. He is its continuous entelechy. But life is therewith actual and is the true God. God is not the hypothesised, external and conceptual creator, but the internal and notional God. God is therefore not a personalised *He*, but should be reflected upon as the indifferent but differentiating notion of *It*. As self-creating life *It* is immanent in man. And, therefore, the spiritual history of man is the history of God. Man posits a rational God. But it is because this movement is, from the point of view of mutuality, in fact non-reflective that both, man and his rational God, are themselves truly comprehended by the idea of

V

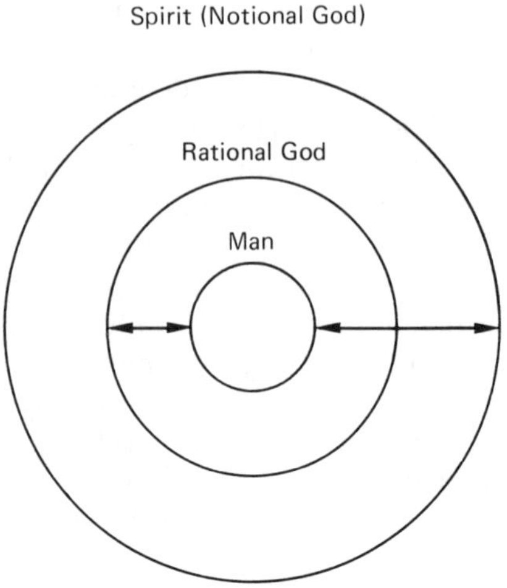

the notional God. Notional God is life itself. Yet because life is actualised history, it is the veritable spirit and coherent identity with man. These comments are translated into the drawing above.

To the effort of spiritual life to become self-conscious, Hegel adds: the 'Spirit is only to what it makes itself. For this reason it is necessary that it presupposes itself [as its own history, H.K.]. Only insight can reconcile Spirit with the history of the world – viz., that what has happened and is happening every day, is not only without God, but is essentially [that is, historically, H.K.] His work'.[17]

In the trinity of man-God-spirit the term God is merely a rational idea of man, and is one among a possible multitude of ideas representing divine or secular forces. The rational God is God in reality. Spirit, on the other hand, is God in the actuality of reason. And that the true God is actual means that *It* is the power of spiritual life which comprehends the nature of man and his finite fictions. The nature of man is his being, while his spiritual activity is his essence as becoming history.

The work of God is the work of life which concretises itself in the history of man. God's presence in man is his absolute actuality. 'Only the Present *is*, that Before and After are not.'[18] But imperishable life is in its continuity the freedom to resolve or externalise itself into its imperishable history. And although only the present is, it is in its eternity 'pregnant with the future'.[19] The present therefore bears within itself the future as its continuity. But the hypothesised future is future in form and theory that still lacks its historical content and practical realisation. It does not yet make possible the philosophy of actuality, for there is no relation between a future present and its past. The dialectical unity of form and content is still not presentness. Only the historically developed present manifests this actualisation. Its notional aim is to be the result as the fulfilment of absolute cyclical activity or of the dialectical mediation towards self-consciousness. And therewith the present of living human history bears within itself its future as the future of God. Man as history, therefore, is the presupposition of God as life.

This is the ultimate *cunning of reason*, namely, that absolute spirit is the result of the historical work of finite spirits which it has posited in and for itself. 'Only from the chalice of this realm of spirits foams forth for Him his own infinitude.'[20] It is this notional syllogism, that is, the nurturing of God through the mediating historical deeds of man, which for Hegel is the *good*.

The *good* (das Gute) for man is the farm (das Gut). The two terms are etymologically related. Both involve necessary mediation.[21] The good is the farm, and it refers to the means which man applies to the land and with the help of which he transforms and appropriates this land in such a way that he can concretely fulfil his necessary needs. These needs are satisfied by nature. But – and this is reminiscent of Aristotle – apart from appropriating nature, man seeks to recognise himself in nature through the theoretical articulation of it. It is through this spiritual activity directed to nature that man sublates and actualises himself. Hence he is not only conscious of a passive nature, but also mediates himself out of nature. This activity is his essential history that always results in the present. Yet at the same time the life of man is never achieved or posited once and for all. It must be continuously produced because the end, natural and historical, is always consumed and in this sense, as Hegel would say, contradicted. The present must continuously sublate and preserve itself. More to the point: life, as the history of self-consciousness, is not finitude; it is not a *given* (Gegebenes) as nature is. In its possibility it is a *task* (Aufgegebenes) and hence in need of actualising itself in and for itself. Life is not finite; it is infinite.

The end is therefore contingent upon its necessary means. Says Hegel in an analogy: 'the *means* is *superior* to the *finite* ends of *external* purposiveness: the *plough* is more honourable than are immediately the enjoyments procured by it and which are ends. The *tool* lasts, while the immediate enjoyments pass away and are forgotten. In his tool man possesses power over external nature, even though in this respect of his ends he is, on the contrary, subject to it',[22] that is, to the forces of nature.

The idea of man is his life which mediates and fulfils itself in that man, with his creating finite spirit, must apply a tool to nature in order to preserve himself and thus to re-establish the identity with himself. This syllogism reads:

VI

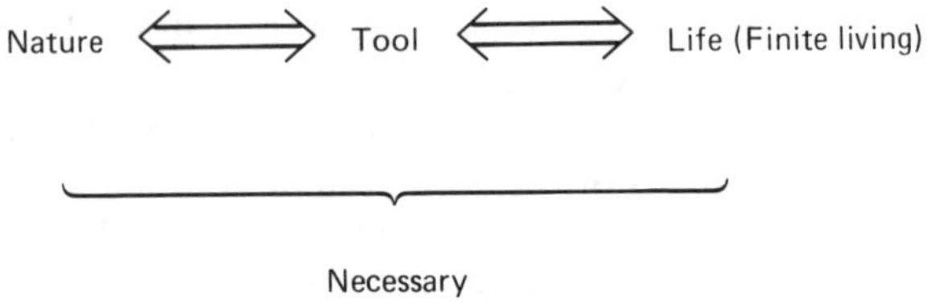

And upon this necessary syllogism depends the other extreme of spiritual creation, namely, man's rational God:

VII

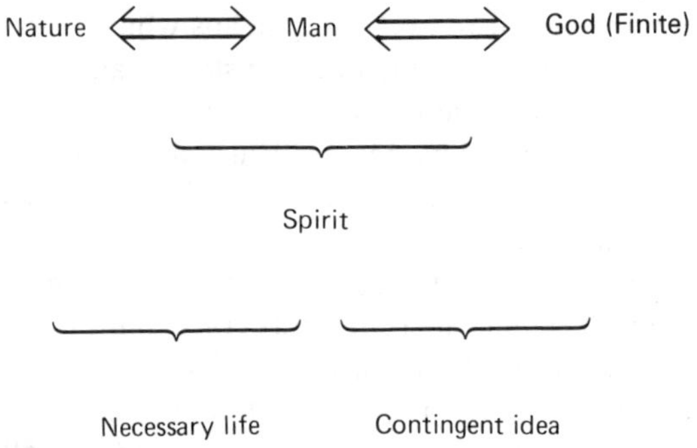

The God of reason, however, creates himself out of nature and through the history of universal man as infinite individual mankind. And 'we have to give ear to its urgency [life, H.K.]', writes Hegel, ' – when the mole [mankind, H.K.] that is within forces its way on – and we have to make it a reality ['Wirklichkeit' = actuality, H.K.]'.[23] Actuality is the produced and mediated present of life. Mankind thus becomes the ploughing tool of God as life. And mankind, which as means syllogises God with nature, is the continuous history of imperishable life as is shown in figure VIII opposite.

Since God as absolute life is immanent in man, man's life depends upon himself as his self-own tool. If mankind sustains its history as activity, so will be its life. But if mankind dies, God will perish with it,

VIII

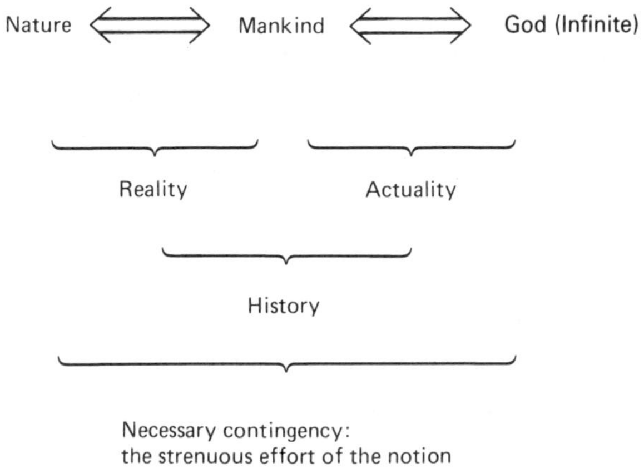

because outside the self-knowledge of mankind there is nothing we can know or be conscious of. Whatever we say of God, we say of a rational concept God. Without subject there is no object. Hence the meaning of God is and is only mediated through the concept which is nothing but a hypothesis of the human understanding. Only within actual life is there real knowledge. Absolute knowledge is therefore not the rational knowledge of a conceptual reality. It refers to the self-knowledge of notional reason which is mankind in its present and dialectical actuality.

Absolute knowledge is the actuality of mankind as absolute life. But life knows itself truly in that it spiritually experiences itself through its sublating history. And this experience is mankind that unfolds and enfolds itself within itself. Mankind is historical experience of itself. The notion notionalising itself, therefore, implies that universal man, that the mediating middle in the syllogism of life, grasps or comprehends himself as individual mankind. Mankind is in and for itself absolute subject. Mankind is sublated life.

In concluding this section let us add a few words about the relevance of rethinking the relationship between mankind and its history for a comprehension of the nuclear age. According to historical dialectic the destiny of mankind is not determined by any divine providence. The consequence of our discussion is therefore the insight that whatever threat mankind inflicts upon itself cannot be redeemed from without, either. Unlike in the tradition, where man could still uncritically believe in the saving graces of God, it is humanity today which must reflectively respond to the self-threat from within. And its need to respond is the need also to acknowledge the responsibility for the actuality of its own life and not for the fictitious reality of man's conceptual God. Mankind alone is responsible for its history. The philosophical task that we are confronted with in our time is the dialectical articulation of the relationship between mankind and its history. And this means ultimately that we must attempt to think through the relationship between present and past and raise its reason to the level of self-consciousness, because it is in this relationship that responsibility first manifests itself.

THE DIFFERENTIATIONS OF MANKIND

After having described the dialectical relationship between the idea of mankind and its history, we shall in this section study further the Hegelian meaning of history. The appearance of history will be recognised as what we call the *differentiation* of mankind. But it refers also to the differentiation of history itself into the interrelatedness of its developmental stages.

We have learned that the rational spirit is the object of the notion as subject. Within the framework of Hegelian dialectic it can likewise be distinguished as the historical phenomenon of the logic. Hence the freedom of notional logic is manifested in its spirit which is its historical essence. The spirit is man, and man, in his undifferentiated universality, is only manifested and not yet the actualised freedom of mankind. But implied in this manifestation is the freedom of spiritual man to become conscious of himself. This becoming is the spirit's activity. Spirit, Hegel explains:

> is by nature active, and activity is its essence; it is its own product, and is therefore its own beginning and its own end. Its freedom does not consist in static being, but in a constant negation of all that threatens to destroy freedom. The business of spirit is to produce itself, to make itself its own object, and to gain knowledge of itself; in this way, it exists for itself.[1]

The freedom both of man and mankind can thus in either case be seen as the idea of the positive of the double negative. But while the freedom of the logical idea of mankind is the 'real Notion' in the sense of 'realer Begriff',[2] of actuality or of present holistic life, the freedom of the phenomenal spirit or of man is 'real Notion', but this time in the sense of 'reeller Begriff',[3] that is, of reality or the becoming of mankind through the communal histories of man. The translation of the two German words *real* and *reell* with the one English term *real* is incorrect and does not convey the philosophical differentiation that ought to be made between the two meanings of the notion. For only if differentiation is recognised is it possible to reflect upon relation and the dialectical syllogism of the historical moments that immanently relate to one another.

With reference to this understanding of differentiation the reality of man, however, is accordingly finite actuality; that is, it is the reality of man to have a finite life. It is finite and purposefully finite because there is the absolute and actual life of mankind. While the absolute freedom of mankind is not itself teleologically sublated by and into something else, the finite freedom of man is posited by the absolute freedom of mankind which sublates it into itself as the infinite continuity of life.

The idea is actuality, its spirit is reality. Dialectically expressed: while the logic *is* present, its phenomenon *ought* to be the present, and that is historically reflected present. The real *ought* of the spirit is to respond to the actual *is* of the absolute idea whose 'supreme and sole *urge* [is] to find and cognize *itself by means of itself in everything*'.[4] Hence, from the point of view of the idea, Hegel says that 'what man is in reality, he *must* also be in ideality'.[5] The reality of man is embedded and grounded in the actuality of mankind. History is the differentiated notion only in that there is life.

Since the phenomenon is the manifestation of its notional logic, man strives towards his own notionalisation. Only that which is differentiated history can be dialectically notionalised (be-griffen). Thus man achieves his self-consciousness in that he mediates himself through the whole of his historical essence. And this tells Hegel that:

> as a spirit, man does not have an immediate existence but is essentially turned in upon himself. This function of mediation is an essential moment of the spirit. Its activity consists in transcending and negating its immediate existence so as to turn in again upon itself; it has therefore made itself what it is by means of its own activity. Only if it is turned in upon itself can a subject have true reality ['Wirklichkeit' = actuality, H.K.]. Spirit exists only as its own product.[6]

The idea is the actual, absolute subject. The manifestation of the idea is finite spirit as its essential appearance. Hence the spirit is likewise subject though only as reality. But as reality it is, in accordance with our previous discussion, better expressed as subjectivity. Bearing this qualification in mind, it is evident that man is a finite subject in relation to mankind which is the infinite subject. But in being manifested, man can also be said to be the finite historical object of the infinite life of mankind. Manifestation, however, presupposes itself as notional coherence which, in the language of dialectic, is subject/object identity. Yet, furthermore, coherent identity is notionally mediated identity. That is to say, the subject mediates and thereby produces itself out of its posited object by means of or *through* (*dia*-lectic) a middle term. This middle term we call the predicate. Its dialectical role will be explained in the section on the Historical Judgment (p. 158ff) below. It may suffice here to state that the predicate is the *medius terminus* and constitutes the differentiations of the extremes in the notional syllogism, that is, of the logic and its phenomenon, or of individual mankind and universal man. How is this to be understood?

We have previously characterised the phenomenon as the finite spirit of man and the logic as the infinite spirit of mankind. Yet, in the context of this section we shall speak of the object man as a universal, and of the subject mankind as the true individual. The philosophical reading of this is that the consciousness of the subject mankind, in order to become conscious of itself, posits itself into its object. This object is man. And because man is at first undifferentiated, he is a posited universality only. Individuality is then the dialectically mediated result of a universality which differentiated itself into history.

Let us illustrate what we have just said with a simple relation, and develop the argument further into its triplistic form. The direction of the arrow indicates the relationship between the whole and the part, which the whole posits not only in and through but also for itself. Thus we have:

I

Part ← Whole

Man ← Mankind

Object ← Subject

Universal ← Individual

Now, as mentioned earlier, coherent subject/object identity is mediated through a predicate. This predicate describes the historical differentiation or particularisation of man into the state. In other words, mankind is historically predicated upon the state. The state is the first moment of the differentiation of man. What the deeper philosophical significance of this dialectical predicate is we shall discuss in the later parts of the present chapter. Here we only make some preliminary remarks.

We regard the universality of man as historically differentiating itself into the state, whereby the development of differentiation here and in general must not simply be understood literally and as an empirical fact, but, more importantly, in its comprehending historical idea. The principle of production is in this case shown by the arrow from left to right. The first reflected historical moment of differentiation is therefore:

II Man ⟶ State

But just as man particularises and enhances himself dialectically into the state, or into a wider circle of historical experience, so does the state, in turn, differentiate itself, and is logically produced, into the quantitatively expanded states-system. Accordingly, we have a second moment of differentiation, and mankind is now predicated upon the states-system:

III State ⟶ States-system

And the third and final moment of differentiation is qualitatively produced when the system itself is notionally comprehended by that which permeates it, that is, by mankind. This last moment is individuality as it is dialectically mediated into the present and through the historical differentiation of universal man:

IV System ⟶ Mankind

These three movements, which are the differentiations of the simple relation in figure I, can now be restated and written into syllogisms:

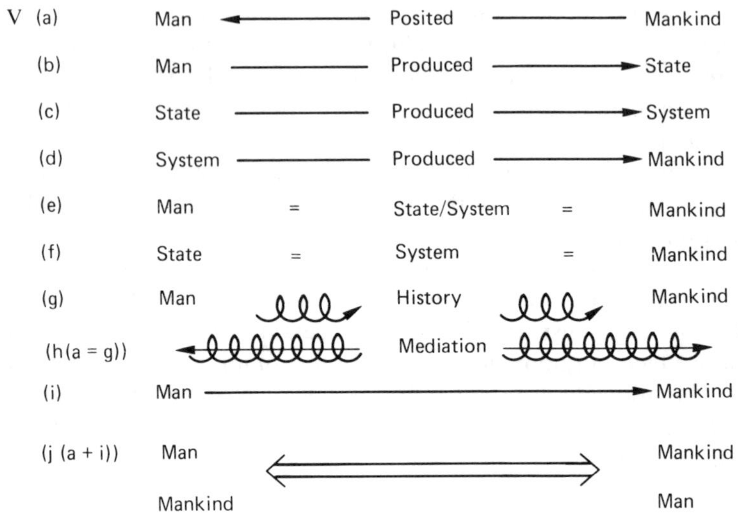

We can also articulate these historical syllogisms in the following philosophical expressions, some of which have already been explained, while the remainder will be elaborated as we go along in our exposé. These relations, which correspond to Hegel's own usage of them, are the terminological tools we employ to describe the meaning of dialectic.

VI (a)	In-itself	=	And	=	For-itself
(b)	Object	=	Predicate	=	Subject
(c)	Universal	=	Particular	=	Individual
(d)	Species	=	Differentiation	=	Genus
(e)	Being	=	Essence	=	Notion
(f)	Nature	=	Spirit	=	Idea
(g)	Reality	=	Mediation	=	Actuality
(h)	Phenomenon	=	Dialectic	=	Logic

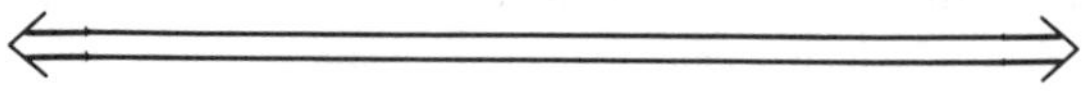

The various syllogisms in figures V and VI state generally that mankind syllogises and thus creates itself out of man, into whom it has judged and particularised itself. But the syllogism is ultimately effected through man's reflected historical differentiation into the state and the system of states. History as the activity of this system constitutes the total history of man's spiritual world. 'The whole history of the world', Hegel writes, 'is nothing but the realization of spirit and therewith the development of the Notion of freedom'.[7] Therefore, if the system is dialectical and predicative ground, then this *medius terminus* is the absolute reason for both man and mankind, for neither extreme can subsist without the other. They are meaningful only in relation to one another, and together they are the notion. Thus the system is the *praedictum*, the principle of an implicitly dialectical order that mediates the object man into the explicitness of the subject mankind.

Let us at this stage of our discussion dwell for a moment on the direction of the arrows in the above syllogisms. We recall that the dialectical syllogism constitutes historically the positive of the double negative, and that in Chapter 3 in the section on Negative and Positive Reason (p. 104) we wrote it in two different ways:

VII

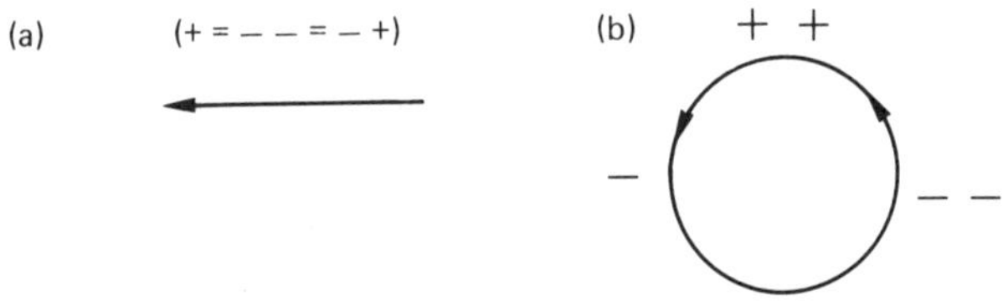

But notice: the direction of these movements must be read as leading from East to West. This agrees with Hegel's own account of the development of spiritual world history. Because of the beauty and concreteness of the description of this development, we wish to quote him in full:

> The sun rises in the Orient. The sun is light, and light is universal and simple self-relatedness, i.e. universality in itself. This light, though universal in itself, exists in the sun as an individual or subject. We often imagine someone watching the moment of daybreak, the spreading of the light, and the rise of the sun in all its majesty. Descriptions of this kind tend to emphasise the rapture,

> astonishment, and infinite self-oblivion which accompany this moment of clarity. [This is antiquity, H.K.] But when the sun has ascended further, the astonishment diminishes, and the eye is constrained to turn instead to nature and to the self; it will see by its own light, become conscious of itself, and progress from its original state of astonishment and passive contemplation to activity, to independent creation [namely, the historical formation of spiritual culture, H.K.]. And by evening, man has constructed a building [the state of modernity, H.K.], an inner sun, the sun of his own consciousness, which he has produced by his own efforts [Arbeit, H.K.]; and he will value it more highly than the actual sun outside him. As a result of his activity, he now stands in the same relationship to the spirit as he originally stood to the external sun, except that this new relationship is a free one: for his second object is his own spirit. Here, in a nutshell, [Hegel then concludes], is the course of the whole historical process [Weltgeschichte, H.K.], the great day of the spirit and the day's work it accomplishes in world history.[8]

The building that Hegel talks about is the state which man constructed through himself and for himself alone. And because the state is the spiritual work and the only true object of man,[9] it is in and through this work that he truly finds himself reconciled with himself. As the philosopher puts it in another though similar context: 'Man is at home in it, and that only passes for truth in which he finds himself at home.'[10]

What Hegel is saying in passages such as these is that man creates and mediates his identity only within a form of differentiation, the form of differentiation being of a secular kind. But, in a general way, he is saying more still, namely, that man, in his communal realisation, relates to something larger than himself, and that this relation is even necessary for his own actualisation in self-consciousness. That which he relates to is a protecting whole, a true home, in which alone man is not only secure but free and hence himself.

Our concern in this chapter, however, does not revolve about the state *per se* and man's relationship to it. We do not propose to formulate a theory of the state as an empirical phenomenon, or to comment critically on its already existing thematisations. Rather shall we describe the dialectical relationship between the state as *a*, and hence epistemologically indefinite,[11] form of the necessary historical differentiation of man/mankind and its system, on the one hand, and the mediation between the equally necessary system and mankind, on the other. Our building, then, is principally the system as the predicate between the object state and the subject mankind (cf. figure V f).

Yet, here again, we shall not try to determine what the system is in its conceptual articulation and as a historical occurrence. Ultimately, however, we wish to narrow it down to the nuclear states and the dialectical relationship between the two superpowers. By system, in general, we simply have in mind a philosophical and heuristic principle of order which in the experience of man expresses a complex form of phenomenal differentiation. As a mediating predicate the system comes to stand within the syllogism and between the state and mankind.

But what is for us the significance of this middle term? Hegel may have taken the perpetual historical life of mankind for granted. There was then perhaps also no need to conceive another actor in history other than and beyond the state as the manifestation of mankind. Today, however, this very mankind is struggling to survive the nuclear threat. Yet the menace to its life does not only come from the internal constitution of individual states. More importantly, it may be the dialectically sharpened resultant of the immanently contradictory and differentiated formation of the system, and particularly of the system of nuclear states. This system is constituted as *one*, and it acts as a phenomenal subject. In other words, if mankind is predicated upon the system, then it contains within itself the threat to its sublation.

In Hegel's view, though a state could throughout the history of its consolidation and expansion overcome another state, it thereby did not jeopardise, however, the survival of other states in the system. Neither was it in a military and technological position to eliminate the system itself. The system in its predicative role and, therefore, the life of mankind which it mediated were at no historical moment seriously at stake. Yet in our case there is the system beyond the state. But what distinguishes this system is that, in the historical experience of the present, there is no further actor beyond it. Within the scheme of historical dialectic the system has therefore replaced the state as the true object of man.

The consequence of this is that, although there is a plurality of states, there is only *one* system. In other words, the system cannot destroy another system and preserve, at the same time, other remaining systems or a still higher historically organising notion. The system can only destroy itself. But once it has destroyed itself, it has done away with itself as the mediating reason and historical ground not only of its states, but also of that in which it is dialectically embedded, namely, mankind. In that it will have broken its absolute historical continuity it will have killed the life of mankind, as well. It is because there is no superior finite and therefore mediating spirit between mankind and the nuclear system that the syllogism (states = system = mankind) collapses upon itself. The subject mankind will have committed suicide through the states-system which is its historical object. The end of history must then be seen as the self-inflicted finality of a humanity that has lost sight of its holistic life. The power of life will have succumbed to its manifested historical forces, the result being that with the death of mankind the infinite will not have sublated the finite, but the finite will have annihilated the infinite.

In our syllogism we regard mankind in its historical life as the highest form of individuality to which the state can relate itself, because the state is mankind's necessary mediating predicative judgment. Dialectically speaking, the finite state has no other philosophical meaning than to sublate itself into historically non-finite and continuous mankind. That mankind is *highest* does not mean that it *has* a conceptual value ascribed to it by our understanding. What it does imply, however, is that, in whatever way one judges it conceptually, it *is* the ultimate reason for everything which it comprises within itself.

Hegel could still maintain in his time that:

> the particular has its own interest in world history; it is of a finite nature, and as such, it must perish. Particular interests contend with one another, and some are destroyed in the process. But it is from this very conflict and destruction of particular things that the universal emerges, and it remains unscathed itself. For it is not the universal Idea [in our case: actualised mankind, H.K.] which enters into opposition, conflict, and danger; it keeps itself in the background, untouched and unharmed, and sends forth the particular interests of passion to fight and wear themselves out in its stead. It is what we may call the *cunning of reason* that it sets the passions to work in its service, so that the agents by which it gives itself existence must pay the penalty and suffer the loss.[12]

Consequently, 'the particular interests of passion cannot therefore be separated from the realisation [Be-tätigung' = activity, H.K.] of the universal'.[13] These lines, read in the light of our still to be educated nuclear consciousness, need no further comment. For the moment they are already interpreted through themselves.

We bring this section to a conclusion by identifying, in the syllogistic relation below, the judgmental differentiations of the notion and by stating how we intend to proceed during subsequent deliberations.

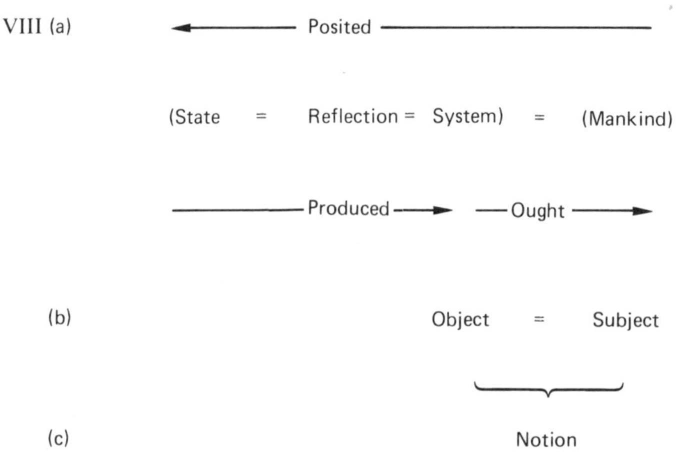

The logical subject mankind is itself its own posited object. This object is the historically produced phenomenal states-system which, in turn, is the reflective result of the development of the state. If we were to consider it independently of the notion, the states-system would be a subjective and rational concept awaiting definition and empirical investigation. But since it is here regarded as the object of mankind, the system with its differentiations has notional character and hence functions as phenomenal subject. In other words, real and empirical subjectivity has been notionalised and converted into higher forms of phenomenal subject actualisation.

Furthermore, although the object is immanently posited, its systemic formation, however, contains an *ought* towards its logical subject. That is to say, the subject mankind *is*, but it produces itself through its systemic and historical *ought*. Mankind syllogises itself with itself in and through its system. The juncture where the past *ought* coheres reflectively with the present *is* is the rose in the cross:

IX

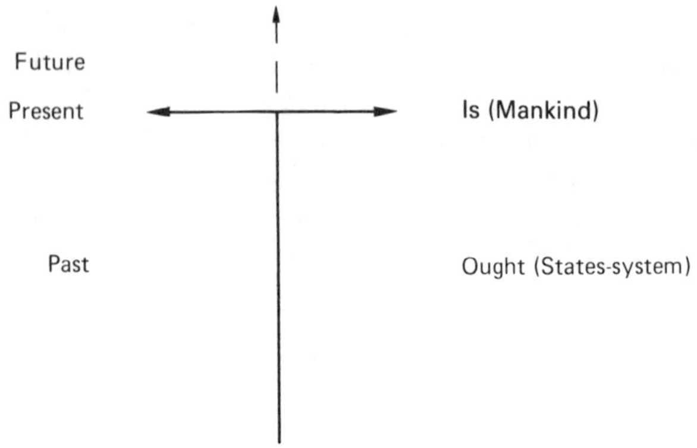

How the judgment differentiates itself into its notional formations, and why these are reflectively sublated will be the theme of the next and subsequent sections. We first analyse, however, the term judgment itself. Following this, we shall describe each one of the formative stages of the syllogism depicted in figure VIII: (state = reflection = system), and then treat the dialectical development of the *ought* from the phenomenal system to the *is* of logical mankind. As our inquiry will show towards the end of this procedure the existence of mankind is comprehended as being mediated through the constitutional organisation of the relationships that prevail within the system of states.

THE HISTORICAL JUDGMENT

In the preceding two sections we discussed the idea of mankind as life. And we also have outlined the dialectical forms into which mankind historically differentiates itself. In the philosophical description that will occupy us throughout the remainder of this chapter we shall substitute the technical term *judgment* for differentiation in order better to analyse the spiritually organic relationship between subject and object, or between mankind and states. These considerations will offer us an insight into the historicality of the judgment and its application.

We already had occasion to clarify the difference between reason and rationality and to introduce the dialectical (object = predicate = subject) syllogism. Yet before continuing with the more detailed statement of historical logic, we should perhaps first recapitulate what we said so far and relate it directly to the very important but also difficult Hegelian logic of judgment. We consider this restatement worthwhile in that the subsequent discussion will be expressed in the judgmental form of the above syllogism. This section, therefore, aims at analysing a particular terminological problem in Hegel's philosophical language. It will at the same time provide us with a guide for reading the textual references we shall make subsequently.

If the notion notionalises itself, it implies that the notion is not simply a given concept but a complex and developed notion. The nature of the notion, Hegel says, 'can no more be stated offhand' (die 'Natur des Begriffes' kann nicht 'unmittelbar angegeben werden', H. K.).[1] Accordingly, the notion is not a rationally defined or posited ahistorical kind of immediacy (Unmittelbarkeit) or universal, either. It mediates itself into a syllogistic expression in the form of a historically sublated and determinate immediacy. In other words, to notionalise is to transform immediacy into mediated immediacy.

The graph below may depict this. Conceptual immediacy 'a' is historically mediated to conceptual immediacy 'b'. The two concepts are two varying ways of understanding any one posited term. Both together, however, are through mediation transformed into a notion, which is to say that the concept contains within itself the notion in universalised form. Consequently, the notion itself can be grasped only in its historicality. In that it is in this sense holistic the notion comprehends the immediacy of concepts which function as its parts or as its historical moments.

I

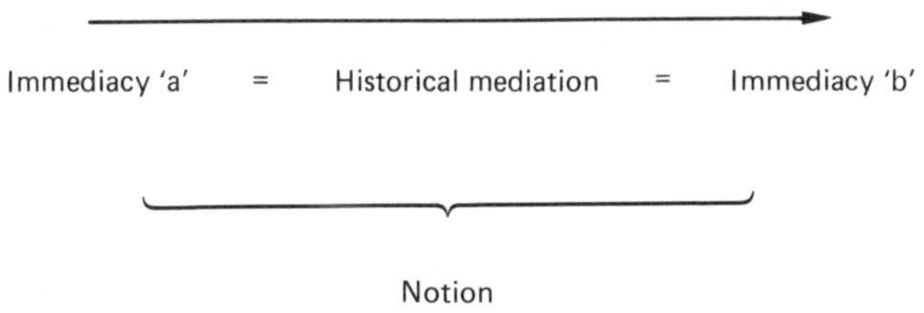

In addition we can say more specifically that the notion is subject in-and-for-itself and that it is accordingly the 'free subjective Notion'.[2] The first immediate being and the mediating essence of the notion are therefore the nature and history of its second and sublated immediacy. This second immediacy is the present. Together they are the particularistic object of the holistic subject. That is to say, the logical subject judges itself reflectively into its phenomenal object. The object is the subject's dialectical presupposition. The object itself, however, is specified and described with Hegel as being essentially the 'genetic exposition of the Notion'.[3] Stated otherwise, the notion in its actual signification is subject in that it manifests itself into its object nature and into the mediating history upon which it is spiritually predicated:

II (a)	Being	=	Essence	=	Notion
(b)	Object			=	Subject
(c)	Object	=	Predicate	=	Subject
(d)	Nature	=	History	=	Present

Without the predicate the object of the subject is the first judgment of the notion. The immediacy of the notion divides itself immanently or organically into or posits itself into its judgment in order then to produce and to syllogise itself through the historical predicate into mediated immediacy. At first, therefore, the 'judgment is the *determinateness* of the Notion *posited* in the *Notion* itself'.[4] Hegel calls this judgment the 'proximate "realization" of the Notion, inasmuch as reality denotes in general entry into *existence* as a *determinate* being'.[5] The judgment is the as yet undifferentiated object of the subject. It is the universal reality of all individual actuality. The coherent relationship between the holistic present (right side) and its historical particularisation (left side) is written in the following forms of dialectical coherence (see figure III opposite).

Since the actual notion is only as mediated syllogism, 'its return into itself is therefore the absolute, original *partition of itself* (ursprüngliche Teilung seiner, H. K.), or, in other words, it is posited as *judgment* (Ur-teil, H. K.)'.[6] But this positing, let us remember, does not refer to a rational subjectivity that hypothesises over and above

III	(a)	Judgment	=	Notion
	(b)	Phenomenon	=	Logic
	(c)	Object	=	Subject
	(d)	Reality	=	Actuality
	(e)	Universality	=	Individuality

←

itself a conceptual object, or that judges an object by ascribing to it indeterminate values or predicates. Neither is it a subjectivity that posits a rational object, calls it the subject and then values it predicatively. In this case we would have a defective situation:

IV (External) Object or Subject } = Predicate ↑

Subjectivity

Unlike one-sided subjectivity, it is the notional subject's own activity to judge itself organically within its holistic self into its own object, of which subjectivity itself is but a part. Subjectivity cannot determine itself in the form of a transcendent definition, as it were. It itself is determined, namely, historically. Subjectivity only experiences what the *cunning of reason* does with it without, however, rationally knowing the meaning of this experience. It is objectively subjected to the subject and is not the true subject itself. The immanent movement of the true subject reads instead:

V (Internal) Object ← Subject

Therefore, Hegel observes: 'the Notion is not indeterminate but is in its own self determinate; this division, however, expresses this its determinateness as *developed*; it is the judgement of the Notion, not a judgement *about* some object or rather picked up from outside, but the *judging*, that is, *determining*, of the Notion in its own self'.[7] To be *in its own self* is for the subject to be within its own historically or objectively developed circle of the present:

VI

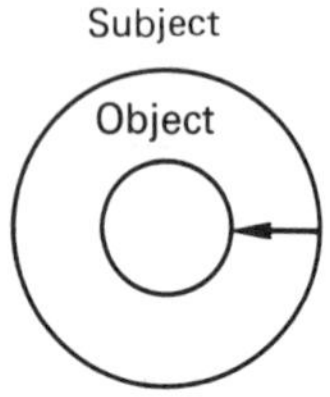

Contrary to the subject the understanding as rational subjectivity hypothesises universal conceptual objects by retaining those features of them which are merely 'common to them all',[8] without taking into account their organically differentiating aspects. In other words, they are not holistic. But therewith, Hegel remarks, the concepts 'just miss the Notion'.[9] They do not dialectically cohere with it. But what is only common is deprived of the possibility of its predicative historical fulfilment. Concepts are only abstractions lacking vital concretisation, which is to say, they lack the vital and reflected relationship to one another. They are transcendent, 'hollow and empty' concepts:[10]

VII

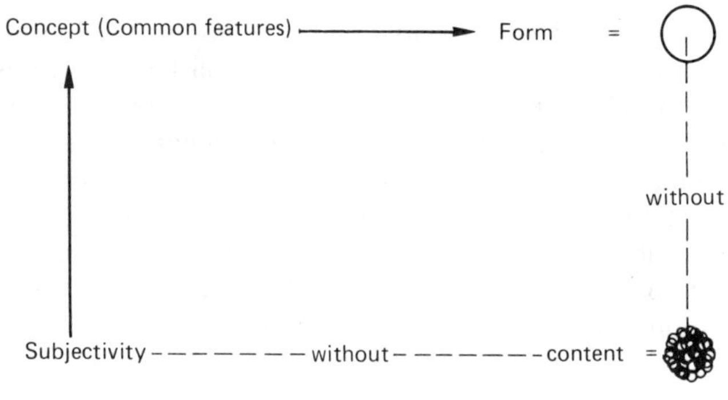

The notion of historical reason, however, is not something posited over against and is not separated from itself. It posits itself into its own content. It is, says Hegel, 'self-particularizing or self-specifying, and with undimmed clearness finds itself at home in its antithesis (bei sich selbst bleibende, H. K.)'.[11] The term *antithesis* is a very misleading and confusing rendering of the German text. It denotes a formal and separating contradiction and not the dialectical and historical differentiation within the holistic notion. The expression *bei sich selbst bleibende*, on the other hand, refers to the subject that, in its intentional and internal teleological activities, is always historically itself; it is in unity with itself. Hegel nowhere speaks of the notional syllogism in terms of a formal triad (thesis – antithesis – synthesis). The subject in its actualised formation, or in its form together with its historical content, is represented in the next figure:

VIII

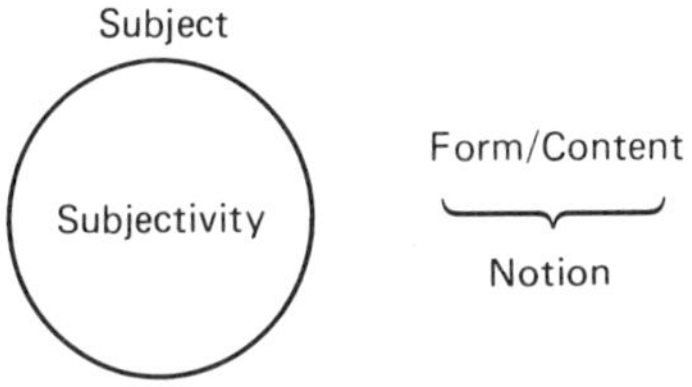

It is then also because the notion is not a formal concept that it is not formed by the understanding either. It is not an arbitrary, rational construct but notional or historical self-construction. Hegel argues that 'it is not *we* who frame the Notions . . . it involves mediation, but the mediation lies in itself. In other words, the Notion is what is mediated through itself and with itself'.[12] And further: 'we are not performing a subjective act', but instead are 'observing the object in the specific character imposed by its Notion'.[13] But since the object is the relational subjectivity of the subject, we are observing and describing ourselves in our past conceptual determinateness. This determinateness is in the end historical life, which is the dialectical ground of our existence. In order to clarify this point we can write:

IX (a) Not: Subjectivity ⟶ Subject as Object

(b) But: Object ⟵ Subject

(c) [Object = Predicate] = [Subject]

(d) Subjectivity = Specific historical character = Subject

Let us elaborate this a little bit further. We have said that in the judgment the notion steps outside of its universality and into the reality of historical existence. It is in the historical judgment that the notion begins to concretise itself, because there it begins to relate historical experiences to one another and to itself. Now, common sense thinks of the abstract subject as being the posited conceptional object of rational subjectivity. And it also thinks of the copulative judgment as being the subject's predicate. The first and rational understanding of the judgment is expressed in the posited *equation* of correspondence:

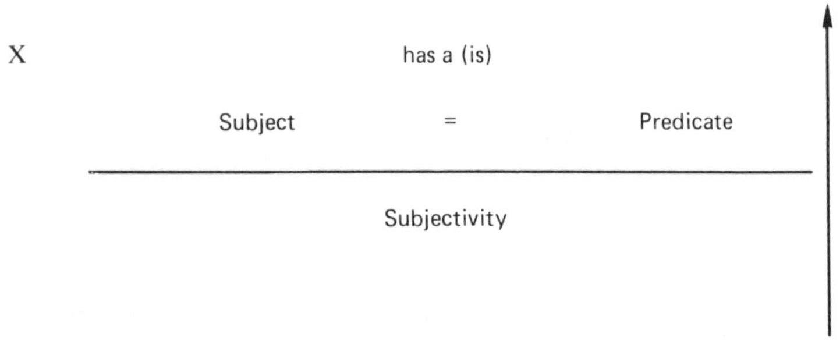

A rational judgment is then a judgment of presupposed formal correspondence. It contains, so Hegel maintains, the 'independence of the two extremes, the subject and the predicate', whereby the former is a conceptual object and the latter a 'general term outside the said subject and somewhere in our heads'.[14] It is in this sense of subjectivity that it ascribes and attaches to the object attributes. What combines the non-identical extremes in this judgment is the copula *has*. This copula, however, can function only as an externally posited and hence illusory relation. It symbolises a false copula expressing a false consciousness.

Yet in the movement of notional dialectic the copula *is* manifests itself in a different mode. What it exhibits is the historical and concrete coherence relationship between the subject and its logical predicate. Here the present subject is predicated upon its historical past through which, upon reflection, its self-consciousness is mediated. We therefore have in the notation below a second judgment, that of reason, which contains the real copula as *relation*. This copula expresses organic coherence:

XI

is

Predicate = Subject

←

The copula *is* of this judgment develops qualitatively, that is, historically out of nature. The dialectical transformation constitutes the turning point between *to have* and *to be*, between ascription and existence. It 'springs from the nature of the Notion, to be self-identical even in parting [Entäusserung, H.K.] with its own'.[15] This parting is historical externalisation or differentiation, an activity of reflection which is subject-immanent. Only a subject *kann sich äussern*, that is literally: express itself or speak. Speaking is an activity. Only a subject which is historically notionalised can rationally work and therefore engage in purposeful and holistic *activity*. It can act towards itself through itself and is no longer merely subject to the static law of natural events. Its circle of consciousness has widened so as to include the transformations of nature into history. The latter is the *medium* of speaking subjects, and it alone relates them to one another. Thus the activities of speaking and working are notionally understood only if they manifest themselves in and through a medium. In history, however, the subject, though it parts with itself in the developmental sense, does for that reason not separate itself from itself. The copula *is* is the subject's self-own spontaneous activity, an activity which is directed towards itself but through another. What is concrete is the subject's historical spirit, is its appearance in becoming itself. The philosophy of the subject describes its reflectively mediating activity towards its self-conscious actuality.

Unlike notional dialectic, the copula in conceptual dialectic signifies a contingent *having* rather than the necessary *being*.[16] While in the latter case the notional subject *is* the objective predicate, in the former example the conceptional object merely *has* a subjective predicate. It is a judgmental predicate which the understanding ascribes to what it hypothesises. Yet, from the point of view of the notion, this external view is false and, according to Hegel, even 'contradicted by the copula *is*' itself.[17] Not only is it 'not we who from outside attach' a predicate to a subject, but it is also, and precisely because the subject is in fact a conceptual object, posited by a finite understanding that 'makes the judgement look as if it were something merely contingent'.[18] And the subject itself, being only a posited conceptual object, is for that reason also static. It cannot act on its own accord. And since it is static, it lacks the dynamic spontaneity of active historical life. There is therefore, Hegel argues, no 'advance'[19] from the conceptual to the notional judgment.

And Hegel continues saying that the notion:

> does not, as understanding supposes, stand still in its own immobility. It is rather an infinite form, of boundless activity, as it were the *punctum saliens* of all vitality [Lebendigkeit, H.K.], and thereby self-differentiating. This disruption [Selbst-unterscheidung, H.K.] of the Notion into the difference of its constituent functions – a disruption imposed by the native act of the Notion – is the judgement.[20]

What the notional subject differentiates itself into are the developmental formations of its historical life upon whose dialectical relations it reflects with philosophical insight. Hegel considers life in its infinite or non-finite form. It is life which, in its attempt to become conscious of itself, actively, that is, thinkingly gives itself the historical content. Life is incomprehensible without its differentiated and reflected history.

Thus the notion is the originating principle of reflection from which everything else springs and develops into historical moments. It is the 'genuine first'; and, insists Hegel: 'things are what they are through the action of the Notion'.[21] The notion is not a dead representation posited by the understanding, but the re-production of itself as historical reason. It is the 'infinite form, or the free creative activity, which can realize [actualise, H.K.] itself without the help of a matter that exists outside it'.[22] The notion is not posited but positive life, which is only in and through its historically sublated double negative. It is form and content whose coherent identity is dialectically syllogised. 'The Notion', Hegel writes therefore, 'is concrete out and out: because the negative unity with itself, as characterization pure and entire, which is individuality [subject, H.K.], is just what constitutes its self-relation ['An-und-Für-sich-Bestimmtsein' = self-actualisation, H.K.], its universality'.[23] Only in individuality is universality first and truly fulfilled.

The notion is not an in-itself; it is the in-and-for-itself. That is to say, the dialectical reason of the subject is for itself. As the for-itself it is historically mediated by the in-themselves of subjectively posited rational concepts and their mediated relations. And accordingly Hegel makes the statement that the dialectical identity of reason and understanding is 'indissoluble' (der Verstand kann von der Vernunft 'nicht abgesondert werden', H.K.).[24] The present cannot be separated from its past, either cognitively or existentially. And so mankind cannot be separated from its spiritual history.

To sum up: Hegel's idea of judgment is notional, not conceptual. It is dynamic, not static; it is concrete, not abstract – in short: it is not to do with posited equations but with historical and hence developing relations. And because Hegel's judgment describes the reality of relations and not the ideality of facts separated one from the other, it cannot be confounded with the subjective claim of a historicist positivism either. Hegel's idea of judgment treats the subject as it thinkingly negates itself into and becomes conscious of its history, and reflectively re-establishes itself in positive or present self-conscious identity. This interpretation of the judgment allows us to apply it to our philosophical considerations, for it describes adequately the dialectical syllogism of mankind as it historically develops itself through the phenomenal medium of the states and their system. We shall now turn to the thematisation proper of this syllogism.

THE STATE

The analysis of the historical reflection of the present has shown how individual mankind posits universal man. We have also spoken of the dialectical production of the state, the states and the system out of universality. Two further points follow from this. The first is that in dialectic the posited concept *universal* makes sense only when it is historically differentiated into what Hegel calls *particularity*, and when this particularity is, in turn, sublated and unified into *individuality*, that is, into mankind. In more abstract terms, the individual subject mankind notionalises its conceptual antecedents. The second point we wish to make is that the subject mankind, in that it posits man, subjectivises man. And subjective man uses his rationality in order to conceptualise or theorise mankind's first judgmental differentiation, which is the state.

In this section, then, we shall be interested in unravelling the *concept* state. But lest we lose sight of what we have just said, let us illustrate the above arguments in the relations below:

I	(a)	Universality	=	Particularity	=	Individuality
	(b)	Man	=	State/States/System	=	Mankind
	(c)	Subjectivity	=	Concepts/Notions	=	Subject

We have stated before that we shall discuss the judgment in terms of subject, predicate and object. Accordingly, we can say that the state is the object of the subject mankind. But in being subjectivised the object state is turned into the universal or immediate subject. This situation is the logic whose elements are shown in (a) of the following figure. But, further, since the immediate subject state is a posited concept, its descriptive clarification is a predicate, and it corresponds to figure IV in the last section. This we call the phenomenal judgment as indicated in (b) below:

II (a)

←

Object	=	Subject	Logic
State	=	Mankind	
Immediate subject	=	Mediated subject	

(b)

→

Subject	=	Predicate	Phenomenon
State	=	Predicate	

Since the state is a historical phenomenon, its truth is to be established subjectively, that is, as a theoretical in-itself. And being at first still unmediated within reality, the state is, for epistemological purposes, merely a universal concept, though, from the point of view of the notion mankind, a notionalised one.

It is now the task of the judgment to establish within itself a corresponding truth relationship between its constituent elements, that is, between the subject and its predicate. The 'judgement is *truth*', Hegel says, if there is the 'agreement of the Notion [concept, H. K.] and reality',[1] or if a rational correspondence can be established between the subject and its predicate. 'But this is not the nature of the judgement *at first*'.[2] In the beginning the subject is not yet reflectively mediated with and through itself. It is merely 'immediate' and universal, and as such is in Hegelian terms the 'judgement of existence'.[3] In this judgment the phenomenal subject is given a predicate in the form of existence. Yet this existence is not subject-immanent and concrete, but is ascribed to it. Being posited the subject has thus only a conceptually abstract existence.

This is expressed in the formal relation: the state has (is) a predicate. Or, put differently: the abstract individuality is described and defined through an abstract universality which the understanding predicates of it:

III	(a)	Subject	=	Predicate
	(b)	Abstract individuality	=	Abstract universality

Both forms are abstract because the relations refer only to an external and simple judgment without yet having developed the internal syllogism. The copula *is* itself, 'which as yet contains no mediation or negation', is therefore only 'an immediate, abstract *being*'.[4] That is to say, the copula does not give the predicate a filled and comprehensively determinate content. The reality of the immediate subject is neither rationally exhausted, nor is it in its notion actual and self-coherent identity.

What are we to make of a phrase such as: the individual is universal? Let us take as an example the judgment: *the state is democratic*, and clarify the equation in terms of its variations:

IV	(a)	State	=	Democratic
	(b)	Subject	=	Predicate
	(c)	Individual	=	Universal

To begin with, here the *state* refers to the individual subject, while *democratic* is the universal predicate which is subjectively attached to it. That the predicate is universal is to say that the subject is not concretely determined. We do not know what it means conceptually to say of the state that it is democratic because, being abstract, the predication allows for a plurality of interpretations which only history can dialectically sublate into determinateness. Rational predication is unable to establish a direct one-to-one correspondence between a concept and its definitional content. The meaning of predication is thus indeterminate, as well. In other words, the judgment *the state is democratic* is an incorrect equation.

But more needs to be said about it. This judgment is incorrect also because, as Hegel puts it, it 'floats before the mind'[5] among many possible and similar formal judgments. And it is because we are dealing with only one particular judgment that the latter's content is in fact much less interesting[6] than if it were the content of the conceptually filled form of judgment. Hegel maintains that every rationally posited subject contains a potentially infinite number of descriptive objects. One definition alone is one-sided and therefore negative; it yields at most an incomplete understanding of the subject.

The predicative universal has a further and more objective signification. To say that the individual is universal is also to refer, on the one hand, to the 'perishableness of individual things' and, on the other, to 'their positive subsistence in the Notion as such. The Notion itself is imperishable, but that which comes forth from it in its partition is subject to alteration and to return into its *universal* nature'.[7] The universal notion *democratic* is imperishable because the dialectic of historical formations makes it clear that such a universal cannot be separated from them. As any other rational predicate it is an intrinsic part of spiritual development. At the same time, the predicative ascription of *democratic* to an individual state changes that universal because, as we have argued earlier, the predicate is not subject-immanent or does not of necessity belong to the state. The state is only contingently predicated upon being democratic.

Secondly, logical coherence demands that if the individual has a universal, the universal must have an individual. This relation means that the universal 'resolves' itself into or gives itself a 'determinate being'.[8] The determinate being is the existence of the state. The universal *democratic*, therefore, concretises itself into a particular moment, that is, into the individual state. Thus the state as 'the subject, which in the first instance is the *immediate individual*, is related in the judgement itself to its *other*, namely the universal; consequently it is posited as the *concrete*'.[9]

The universal as a particular predication, however, is only one among many possible characteristics of the phenomenal subject state:

V	(a)	Subject	=	Predicates
	(b)	State	=	a + b + c, and so on

About the aggregate of such predicates Hegel writes in general: 'These manifold determinations . . . belong to the subject' which '*continues* itself through them, maintaining itself in them and equally them in itself. The positedness or determinateness belongs to the being-in-and-for-self. The subject is, therefore, in its own self the *universal*'.[10] The subject is the universal because it contains within itself the universality of all possible ascriptions.

But in our example, *the state is democratic*, the singular predicate democratic expresses only a part and not the whole of possible predications. In the language of Hegel it 'contains only *one moment* of the subject's totality to the exclusion of the others'.[11] That is to say that the state cannot only be democratic, whatever our determinate interpretation of this predicate may be. Apart from this description it can also be socialist, big or small, rich or poor, strong or weak and so forth. In other words, it has multiple determinations each of which is 'not implied in the predicate' democratic.[12] And, besides, since these predicative objects are rationally posited as concepts, they are infinite in number. All abstract descriptions fall under this category. The other determinations, however, are also, like the predicate democratic, not necessarily implied in the immediate subject. These logical observations lead us to the conclusion that enumerative and collected predicative descriptions alone do not render the concept state notionally concrete. For this reason it remains epistemologically formal and abstract and, from a dialectical point of view, its meaning is empty because historically unmediated.

Conversely, the predicate democratic can be ascribed not only to the state but to other forms of historical differentiations, as well. Organisations, parties or ideologies, may be democratic. Here again, then, the predicate as an abstract universal does not exclusively and of necessity belong to one individual phenomenal subject or to the state alone.[13] But this is also to say that the predicate has become one individual, while now 'the subject is the universal'[14] in that the predicate democratic has a broader and more varied application.

The consequence of this 'reciprocal determination',[15] however, is that 'the subject and predicate in the immediate judgement touch, as it were, only in a single point, but do not cover each other'.[16] And Hegel argues that 'what is predicated of the subject is a *single contingent* content' only.[17] In the immediate judgment, then, there is only one subject and one predicate, only the state and its characteristic of being democratic, while in conceptual reality there can be a manifold of historical manifestations and their descriptions.

Hence, though it may be 'correct' to say, for instance, that the state is democratic, this conceptual judgment, expressing only a 'limited circle of perception', remains with Hegel nevertheless 'untrue'.[18] Yet truth, as opposed to merely opined and conceptual correctness, is the non-limited dialectically developed cycle not of finite singular perceptions but of non-finite notional cognition. And this cycle is not a conceptual but the historical state; it is the sublated judgment within the syllogism (state = states-system = mankind). The truth of a particular depends on the relationship to its universal. It 'depends solely on the form, viz. on the Notion as it is put and the reality corresponding to it'.[19] Conceptional reality, whose thought content is to be identity in terms of correspondence, yields ultimate truth only within the notional and coherent truth of historically actualised mankind. Mankind is the only notionally fulfilled subject which contains all its conceptually filled judgmental predicates. Mankind relates these predications to itself syllogistically. And it is because of this immanent dialectic alone that the immediate judgment gains any purposeful meaning at all. But, because of the cunning of historical reason, rationality is usually not aware of this. It claims to know, where in fact it only opines.

The state in the judgment of existence, however, is immediacy. It is conceptually abstract and not yet notionally concrete. And because it is devoid of historical mediation it is finite and not infinite. In its immediacy the state is unrelated and, in dialectical terms, unknown to itself. Being as yet unmediated the inner one-sided and defective universal of the concept state nevertheless urges forward and towards its particularisation and the notional sublation of its finitude. And that which resolves or consciously decides to accomplish this mediation is the notional and reflective power of the idea of mankind. Philosophically speaking, mankind posits the state and produces out of the beginning of phenomenal history its own self-conscious reflection. It is through this reflectively active history that mankind mediates and syllogises itself into sublated life.

To sum up: from the point of view of mankind the state is the notion, but when considered by man it is merely a concept. A concept is dialectically defective since it lacks historical mediation. This limitedness, however, cannot be overcome rationally, and so philosophical thinking changes the singular concept state into a historical notion that seeks to become conscious of itself. This activity involves the dialectical mediation of itself to itself but through another state subject. The conclusion is, of course, reminiscent of our discussion of the Platonic dialogue within whose reflection alone the truth of a subject matter could be discussed and, if not fully ascertained, then at least approximated. And so it is with the state, as well, whose idea of selfhood is contingent upon its reflected relation to another state. An example of such notional reflection will be given in the next section.

THE REFLECTION OF THE STATE

In applying Hegel's language of dialectic we have so far interpreted the differentiation of mankind as the immediate and phenomenal subject state. The state has the signification of historical individuality to which is rationally ascribed a contingent conceptual predicate. Such a predicate, however, is not subject-immanent. It is, as we have concluded, 'an *abstract* universality, or a *single property*'.[1]

But even if we said of the concept state that it is predicated upon a multitude of characteristics, its essential nature could not be grasped adequately. The rationally posited noumenal idea of the infinity of properties is a hypothesis to which no phenomenon corresponds. Although we may be conscious of the concept state, we can never obtain full theoretical knowledge of it. Conceptual infinity cannot be cognitively demonstrated, no matter how many descriptive variables we may wish to include in a series of them. But since the unity-seeking mind cannot bear such a dilemma, it has to approach the subject-matter from a different, from a philosophical point of view. Hegel's method of reflection overcomes the epistemological dichotomy. It enables us to begin to thematise the dialectical relationship between one state to another state, and thereby to develop the concept state into the historical notion of the essential relation between states. It is in and through the idea of relation alone that the true nature of a state is manifested. And the problem is then not merely to do with the explanatory question of how much knowledge of the universal state can be accumulated. Instead, the issue at hand is the description of the dialectical mediation of the consciousness of self. And the self is self only *qua* reflection. This self is in our case the historical subject state. In consequence, we now come to the second form of judgmental differentiation, that is, to that of reflection.

Unlike in the previous judgment, where a predicate was subjectively attached to an object, in the present judgment of reflection the universal predicate is posited by the subject itself.[2] In this case the predicate is subject-immanent; it belongs to it intrinsically. Reflection means that whatever else the subject may be abstractly predicated upon, the concrete or relational determination of reflection sublates and therefore comprehends all predicates historically. It is through the subject that the predicative content determination of the universal has gathered itself into a unity. In other words, concludes Hegel, 'it is in the judgement of reflection that we first have, strictly speaking, a *determinate content*'.[3] What was only alluded to in the first judgment of existence, or of the conceptual existence of the state, is now further developed and concretised in a higher moment of dialectical logic. The existence of one subject is comprehended in relation to the existence of another subject, and both have in philosophical reflection become objects for one another.

Accordingly, the content we are now speaking about is another thing, as it were, but not another thing in the sense of a descriptive external predicate rationally and hence only contingently attached to the posited subject. The other thing is in the judgment of reflection a predicate referred to as the immanent and that is necessary nature of the subject. It is therefore internally posited by the subject itself as its own manifested objective nature. It exhibits 'the subject as in relation to something else'.[4] That is to say, the determinate content is the determining predicate of the subject, a predicate in which, according to Hegel, the subject is 'reflected into identity'.[5] This identity is notional in so far as it manifests a historical determination. The dialectical logic of the self-conscious identity of the subject with itself inevitably involves its conscious relation to its opposite or to another subject which historically mediates the first subject to itself. Hence necessity is the principle of internal relation which, in turn, describes the notional essence of the historical subject and never the conceptual essence of a factual object.

The following two examples which Hegel gives himself may illustrate the notional judgment of reflection. One is: 'man is *mortal*, things are *perishable*'.[6] And the second says that 'this punishment has a deterrent influence'.[7] In analysing these judgments we find that 'the subject . . . [is] standing in connection with something else . . . by means of its predicate'.[8] Unlike in the previous judgment of immediacy, in which the property was only contingent for the subject, the predicate in the judgment of reflection is rather an 'essential determination'.[9] As such it necessarily constitutes the essence of the subject. But this essence is not a hypothesised identity; it is the historically mediated finitude of the subject. It 'constitutes the *basis* [es macht das "zugrunde" liegende aus, H. K.] by which, and in accordance with which, the subject is to be measured and determined'.[10]

It is the predicative finitude which underlies (liegt zugrunde) the phenomenal historical subject. The term *zu-grunde* can be interpreted in different though related ways. At first, it refers to that which immanently underlies or is the nourishing ground of the subject. That which underlies is a ground to which the subject reflectively must return in order to sublate itself historically. And this ground is another subject. That is to say, the reason of the sustained being of one subject is historically grounded in the existence of another subject, or: the being of one subject is its mediated becoming through another subject. But *zu-grunde* also means that, because of the phenomenal subject's finitude, it must of equal necessity return to the ground and go under. As an individual instance in phenomenal history it must perish, or *es geht zu-grunde*. The life lived towards the natural death of the individual is the individual's historical telos. That the phenomenal subject is finite is to say, thirdly, that it not only does not notionally develop into a higher historical stage of selfhood, but also that it comes to depend necessarily for its identity upon something which at first it thinks is not itself.

This explanation we elaborate by looking at our two examples given above. The first, *man is mortal*, or, translated into our context, *individual states are mortal*, is a rather evident judgment. The predicate determines the universalised individual subject. And conversely, the subject goes under in its own internal and predicative ground. The reflection in this judgment is through the copula directly and immanently 'self-related', but at the same time is also 'related to something else'.[11] The subject is both positive, namely, itself, and negative, that is, its otherness. Its positive existence is determined by the pre-knowledge of its death which is its negative. This relationship is shown below.

I

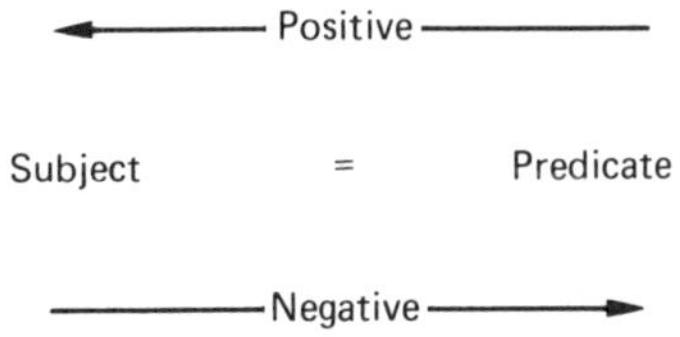

That in the judgment of reflection the negative underlies the positive means that the subject, even though it develops notionally and historically, is nevertheless conditioned by its own determinate finitude. The individual human being must nourish itself out of the objective ground of nature in order to sublate itself, or in order to establish notional identity within the difference of the historical moments of social development. But being finite the individual must also return to the same ground. It perishes and dies in its necessary negativity. This negativity, however, determines the positive history of the individual throughout its life.

And with respect to the state we may argue that it, too, has similarly developed out of its historical and spiritual ground and has dialectically formed itself into various shapes. It likewise is identity within historical, although higher developed, differentiations. Furthermore, being an individual instance and therefore equally contingent, the state also perishes and goes under. The logical principle of historical finitude precludes the eternality of the phenomenal state. That there are some states that have existed for a very long time makes for no logical urgency to conclude that they will last forever. That other states have indeed perished already modifies the principle. In this context it is interesting to point out also that the Augustinian *Eternal City* is only a hypothesised ascription to a phenomenal entity. No historical state corresponds rationally to the conceptual description *eternal*. Merely to believe (credere) is not the same as to know or to understand (intellegere). These observations we can bring into a more general form and say that it is too bad for the facts that they cannot hold out against the truth of their historical dialectic.

Let us now go over our second example and state: *this punishment has a deterrent influence*. What we see here is that the predicate itself involves an additional determination which expands the simple (subject = predicate) relation we discussed previously. In this judgment, writes Hegel, the predicate does not directly refer back to the subject, but does this only through the mediation of another subject, that is, it is 'related to something else'.[12]

The appearance of another historical subject is an indication that the logical subject mankind differentiates itself not only into the phenomenal immediacy of the singular state. There is no historical phenomenon as *the* universal state. Another immanently posited subject means more concretely that mankind is dialectical in that it is mankind only in so far as it sublates this immediacy into the relation of states. In other words, mankind not only posits itself into immediacy, but with the judgment of reflection begins to produce or to mediate itself through the medium of historical state plurality or particularisation. It is because the activities of the states are finite that they are dialectically sublated into the unity of mankind which comprehends them in its actuality.

The finitude of the individual elements in this judgment lies in the awareness that a state, in being related to another state, has only a limited or circumscribed identity with itself. Its identity is not based on being posited and asserted. It is mediated identity and therefore dialectically produced and accomplished. In the context of subject plurality the identity of the phenomenal subject is then defective and illusory because the subjects are objects for one another. What determines a subject dialectically is not an adjectival description of the form we have looked at before. Instead, at the level of judgmental reflection the subject is predicatively mediated to and sublated through another subject. This is to say also that the status of universal immediacy never becomes for the theoretical concept state a philosophically notional object of reflection. Such a reflection is possible after it has particularised itself, that is, only after it has come to stand in a dialectically determinate relationship to another state or to other states. The notional essence of a subject is then its necessary relation to another subject.

Although the mediating predicate exhibits a transformative advance beyond the one we have analysed in the judgment of existence, it still does not go so far as to indicate the adequate notion.[13] With the expansion of the phenomenal and historical predicate alone the logic of mankind or the notion is not exhausted,[14] just as the enlargement of ascriptive predicates did not exhaust the conceptual immediacy of the state. Even the relational essence of the subject remains therefore a 'universal', albeit a dialectically more developed, predicate,[15] a predicate whose own concreteness and constitution is rationally unknown. The subject state is not fully determined in and through its predicate and, therefore, does not completely identify itself in the copula either. It is because the subject does not and cannot know rationally how and why deterrence affects another state subject that it of necessity must remain indeterminate and uncertain about itself. This dialectical necessity is its finitude. And because subjects depend upon one another, it renders the becoming of their self-consciousness contingent upon the content of their mutual relations:

II

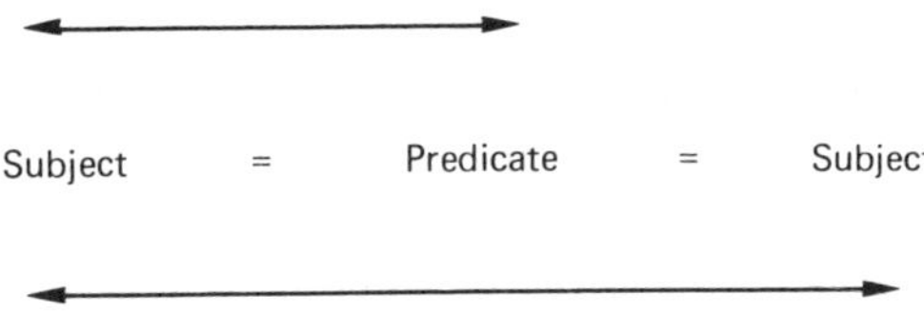

In order to work this out, let us take our contemporary historical situation and assume the following judgment: *the United States' threat of nuclear retaliation is a predicative deterrent:*

III	(a)	United States	=	Deterrent
	(b)	Subject	=	Predicate

As it stands this judgment is meaningless unless it is expanded into the implied and intended object of the predicate. The reference to another object is dialectically necessary because it logically inheres in the predicate. And it belongs to the predicate because, denoting an activity, it is intrinsically intentional and refers for this very reason to a subject, and only to a subject. Thus we have:

IV	(a)	Deterrent	⟶	Soviet Union
	(b)	Predicate	⟶	Object

But the predicative object is at first another historical subject. This transforms the above movement into the following relation:

V	(a)	Deterrent	⟶	Soviet Union
	(b)	Predicate	⟶	Subject

Thus the predicate relates back to the original subject, the United States, only through the mediation of the dialectically inherent link between deterrence and the Soviet Union, that is, between the predicative activity and its intentional object which is another historical subject. The true object of the subject is then not its simple conceptual objectification into the predicate but the mediated object of this predicate itself. The relationship of the terms in this form of the reflective judgment can therefore be read like this:

VI (a) ←——————→

Subject = Predicate ——→ Subject

←——————————————

This becomes:

(b) Subject = Predicate = Object

In this syllogism the subject is the United States, its object is the Soviet Union, and the latter is mediated to the former through the interpolation of the predicate deterrent. The predicate functions as the dialectical copula between the two states. The copula, unlike in the judgment of immediacy, in which it was abstract, is now concrete because it implies a historical mediation. However, since both extremes of the relation are external to one another, that is, since they do not cover one another, the relationship is one of reciprocity:

VII (a) Subject = Predicate = Object

United States = Deterrent = Soviet Union

——————————————→

(b) Object = Predicate = Subject

United States = Deterrent = Soviet Union

←——————————————

The particularised judgment determination is also a further notional development of the previous one of immediacy in that its reflection is a predicative reflection into another subject. The dialectical result is that both subjects are with respect to one another necessarily finite phenomenal individualities. Their historical identities are mutually circumscribed. The identity of the one is conditioned by and hence contingent upon the identity of the other. Both are mediated through the predicate deterrent which describes a subject-immanent activity. Therefore, the notion of identity is at this stage also only defective and illusory. It is, in fact, conceptual and based upon rational belief only. The true objectivity of assertive though subjective expectations is the predicative relation between subjects; it does not reside in the subjects themselves. 'By means of particularity', Hegel says therefore, 'the immediate individual comes to lose its independence, and enters into an interconnection [Zusammen-hang, H. K.] with something else'.[16] Only in that the subject reflects itself into another subject as into its object and dialectically mediates itself through it does it become identical with itself. Thus, here again, the notion of identity is concretised through its manifested differentiation or through the activity of historical relations.

That the subjects are interconnected and hence hang together (hängen zusammen) has in the context of this book an appropriate though also daunting double meaning. With some linguistic licence we may argue that in the nuclear age the United States and the Soviet Union are either politically prepared to accept the dialectical truth of conditioned independence, and therefore to allow for the workings of deterrence, or else this predicate which unites them in difference collapses with the possible final historical result that both will hang together and perish.

THE DEVELOPMENT OF STATE-REFLECTION

In order for a state to become conscious of itself it must dialectically reflect itself in the existence of another state. Since both states are subjects the mediating relation between them turns out to be a reciprocal one. Although both states *qua* subjects attempt to become self-conscious, this aim, however, is never truly fulfilled because of the necessary mutual dependency that prevails in any relationship between subjects. On the other hand, such contingency implies differentiation which for rationality is antinomial and which, therefore, the dialectic of historical reason must sublate and notionalise into a higher form of philosophical comprehension. What this essentially involves is the development of state reflection into the system which comprises the totality of states and their reciprocal relations.

Now, analogous to the logical differentiation of mankind we have the phenomenal differentiation of the state which, in its Hegelian dialectical description, develops into the idea of *allness*. The term allness, however, is mediated through its judgmental parts. These are determined as: *this* state and *some* states, or *singularity* and *particularity*. Before proceeding let us refresh our memory and recall figure VIII (a) in the section on the Differentiations of Mankind (p. 157). We can then write:

I ←————————————————————————

(State ——→ Reflection ——→ System) = (Mankind)

————————————————————→ ——————→

The relations left to the copula develop themselves out of the dialectical movements as they are shown in (a) and (b) below. Their function is after that clarified in (c), (d) and (e) with reference to the logical status they hold:

II	(a)	This state	→	Some states	→	All states
	(b)	State	→	Reflection	→	System
	(c)	Singularity	→	Particularity	→	Universality
	(d)	Subject	→	Predicate	→	Object
	(e)	Immediacy	→	Mediation	→	Mediated immediacy

As at every level of dialectical syllogism, the original and unmediated judgment in the present case accords also with the relation: the individual is universal. We interpret this notation demonstratively and say that *this* individual state is universal, or that *this* state entails the idea of all states. That a singular subject bears within itself its universal is a logical determination that manifests itself within historical dialectic. That is to say that spiritual development realises itself according to the principle of organic formation. And organic formation signifies that, reflectively speaking, a beginning develops itself towards its end through the mediation of its historical means. It is in this sense that the subject state is immanently predicated upon all states:

III	(a)	Individual	=	Universal
	(b)	This state	=	All states
	(c)	Subject	=	Predicate

In general dialectical terms there is no immediacy without resolution, or without an opening-up for further intrinsically teleological development. And there is no resolution without it syllogising itself into mediated immediacy or into its completed purpose. In dialectic there is only internally reflected immediacy. With respect to our example this means that universal allness is only through its mediating essence. It is not conceptually posited but notionally produced. The totality of states is not a historically given fact but a dialectically developed historical moment. Put differently: the essence of the existence of all states is the historical becoming of their totality. With this anticipation in mind let us look first, however, at the state in the form of its singularity.

Individuality is, according to Hegel, determinate and it can be referred to demonstratively as: 'this' individuality is 'essential universality'.[1] Every activity of a subject points demonstratively at its self-consciousness. In other words, every demonstrative act requires mediation. And, moreover, the intentional and teleological development of the formations of the subject implies the realisation of totality and of the fulfilled notion of actual self-consciousness. The existence of the individual is thus meaningful only in and through its universal essence which is its reflected resultant communal history.

But *this* state does at first not yet constitute the universality of states. It is not yet the universal individuality of totality as fully developed reflection. It is simple and immediate universality only, without the developmental mediation towards its true allness. At the level of immediacy the state and its allness are still separated one from the other. And the state in its allness is realised only when it has mediated itself historically to this level.

Thus the positivity of singularity implies its otherness as developmental negativity or as that which it is not. Hence, says Hegel, the 'positive' must be taken 'negatively'.[2] In dialectical logic a sublated and positive historical moment dissolves itself into the resolution of further development. In this movement the positive negates itself. To develop, therefore, implies negation. But because it is a subject the positive then negates its own negation and reaches the result of its inner determination. What singularity is to be after the dialectical negation of negation is its universality or its allness. Thus, again, the positive as historical immediacy is not static. Because of its vitality it inherently externalises itself; it is 'alterable and awaits determination'.[3] The conceptual idea of the state is in and of itself not complete. Since it is a phenomenal appearance it has meaning only in that it realises itself in historically mediated and manifested allness, that is, in the reflected relation to other state subjects.

Dialectic is history within which every notion develops logically towards the complete notionalisation of a particular epoch. Development refers to the immanent transformation of the determinate moments of the self which is the original state. Thus the individual mediates itself to its universal expression in that it judges or partitions itself (ur-teilen) into a plurality of historical formations. One subject implies the existence of another subject to which it stands in a mutually reflective relationship. It is in this essential plurality that the individual comes to approximate its universal comprehension.

From the dialectical standpoint, then, the second form of judgment reads: 'the singular judgement has its proximate truth in the *particular* judgement'.[4] This judgment states that the immediacy of the subject or of the individual is 'divided in itself'.[5] It expresses the philosophically organic division of *this* state to *some* states. The result of this development is now that 'some individuals are a universal'.[6] Translated into our situation we write: a plurality of states, or some states, are *all* states.

But, unlike in the former case of singularity, Hegel says now that in this present situation 'the positive and the negative judgements no longer fall apart, but the particular judgement immediately contains both at the same time, just because it is a judgement of reflection'.[7] On the one hand, the particular includes and contains the singular. On the other, the particular, in its turn and according to the principle of intentionality, points already at its true universal form. However, while the movement from the singular to the universal needs the mediation of the particular, the movement of the particular to the universal is a direct one. In that form the universal will be filled with both, with the singular and the particular. Historical mediation, therefore, manifests itself only through the appearance of a plurality of developmental stages. True dialectical mediation requires the medium of history. At the moment, however, where the particular simply bears within itself the universal, the universal is only 'anticipated' in it.[8]

This relation can be explained with the following observation when comparing *this* state with *some* states. *This state* is a form whose content we want to describe as being, let us say, *this United States*. But the movement from the singular to the particular judgment no longer allows us to say *some United States* but only *some other states*. Hence *this* is not this single United States alone. The United States stand beside other states and become one in the crowd, as it were.

Just by this means, however, it belongs to its universal allness, and is consequently 'raised' (gehoben, H. K.).[9] What it is raised to is its higher philosophical, and that is with Hegel, notional comprehensibility.

This is only, and can be referred to as *this* only, because there is *that*, or because there are others. The meaning of *this* is related to and mediated through another which is not *this*. Dialectically speaking, *that* is the negation of *this*. But that the particular is *raised* (gehoben) is to say also that it is not yet *sublated* (auf-gehoben). It is not yet raised to a still higher notional form that not only contains it but preserves it and, therefore, itself. This higher form is universal allness or the system of states. Yet its highest and truly notional formation is actually mankind as life and as that which permeates and sublates all the particular phenomena which it contains in its history.

At this stage of phenomenal particularity, however, notional differentiation is neither filled nor fulfilled, although it is 'already posited as the totality of the determinations of the Notion'.[10] But this positing indicates only phenomenal or external reflection because the extension of *this* to particularity is a generalisation which is not adequate to the *this*. The true *this* is individual universality. As all states it is, unlike the *this* of universal individuality or of this state, something historically and in its present 'completely determined', while *some* is in its historical meaning still 'indeterminate'.[11] The extension 'must be ["soll" = ought to be, H. K.] appropriate to the "this"'.[12] But that which is totality is at the same time mediated universality as the developed historical individual which is reflected in its first individuality as simple or immediate universality. The *this* of singularity *becomes* the *real this* in universality.

Thirdly, then, Hegel explains further, 'universality, as it appears in the subject of the universal judgement, is the external universality of reflection, *allness; "all"* means all *individuals* and in it the *individual* remains unchanged. This universality is, therefore, only a *taking together* of independently existing individuals'.[13] This external collection is, from a rational point of view, 'only a subjective action'.[14] Its universal is merely a 'community'.[15] But the community as *all states* within the development of reflection is the mediating essence of the phenomenal notion. It is the middle term in the relation:

IV State = All states (Community) = System

Essence in this relation is 'only the inner, and it . . . is for this reason taken as a wholly *external*, unsystematized, common element';

it is an 'external aggregation of existing objects lacking any essential connection or organization', and hence is merely 'passive'.[16] But if universality is pictured as allness, an abstract universality which is supposed to be exhausted in the individuals as individuals that compose it, then this is a relapse into spurious infinity. Sometimes even 'mere *plurality* is taken for allness', which is also only a 'vague awareness of the true universality of the Notion'.[17] Thus the rational '*method* or *rule* . . . gains nothing in universality through the increased number of the term'.[18] The habit of collecting items into a mere plurality or even communal allness is notionally vacuous.

The truly phenomenal universal is not obtained by simply adding states to the singular state and thereby going numerically beyond the finite. This does not only lead to spurious infinity. It is also absurd when we compare the finite list of states to the very concept of infinity. Notional infinity is instead that which pervades allness. It is a historical connectedness, which is dialectically necessary in order for allness to develop coherently and non-finitely into the system. The contingency of allness bears within itself the *task* to develop beyond itself. It is something which 'ought to be done'.[19] It is the activity of history guided towards and by its sublating life. This task, which is not an imposed but an immanent *ought*, relates itself to allness. Allness is the universal, and Hegel describes it as 'the ground and foundation, the root and substance of the individual'.[20]

Similar to the Greeks' understanding of true dialectic, so for Hegel universal allness manifests itself as the organic *genus*. The subject which first 'contains the true universality as *presupposed*, now also contains it as *posited* in it'.[21] The term *all states*, for instance, expresses first the *genus* state. Secondly, this genus is sundered into individual states in such a way that 'the individuals are at the same time extended to the universality of the genus; conversely, the universality through this connection with individuality is just as completely determined as the individuality; thus the *posited* universality has been equated with the *presupposed*'.[22]

Therefore, the expression *all states* reveals a generic structure because the notion is historically or essentially effective. Without the generic universal 'individuals would not be at all',[23] just as there would be no individual without its historically organic universal. It is as generic becoming that the universal 'permeates and includes'[24] the particular and its singularity. It is in this sense, writes Hegel, that the genus as subject is through its mediation 'in its own self concrete'.[25]

This state of affairs of dialectic has significance for the role of the copula. The connection between the individual and the universal is the relation:

V (a)	Subject	=	Predicate
(b)	Individual	=	Universal

This is the original judgment of singularity. Yet within the dialectical movement the singular:

> subject, in raising itself to universality has, in this determination become equated with [come to be related to, H. K.] the predicate, which as reflected universality also contains particularity within itself; subject and predicate are therefore identical, that is, they have coalesced into the copula. This identity is the genus or absolute nature of a thing.[26]

Generic identity as the intrinsic and explicit connection, or as the connection in-and-for-itself, manifests a relation of necessity. This relation says that '*what belongs to all the individuals of a genus belongs to the genus by its nature*'.[27] Instead of saying *all states*, for instance, we say *the state* because, from the point of view of philosophical description, the essence of all states is the logic of dialectic. 'Whatever appertains to all, appertains to the species, and is therefore necessary'.[28] The relational identity is the historical copula as the real and dialectically mediating predicate of the subject. Both subject and predicate are thus sublated in the copula. But if the copula *some states* is the predicate, then the predicate *all states* becomes the dialectical object of the state as subject. This syllogism expresses a necessity which sublates the unmediated allness into its universality. Phenomenal universality is the generic and historical system of states. And in its logic it is the fulfilled genus as the life of mankind.

To conclude: it was the purpose of this section to treat the dialectical principle of particularity or, when applied to our theme, of *some states*. With the notion of reflection we have transformed the conceptual universality of the state into the idea of self-consciousness as it is mediated between two state subjects. However, in order to expand the idea of self-consciousness to that of true and free individuality, that is, to the unity of mankind, the state in its singularity must first be mediated to the notion of *all states* into which mankind is differentiated. This mediation is dialectically effected through particularity.

What our discussion has shown is that organic spirituality can be meaningfully spoken of only if all its essential moments are developed and dialectically related to one another. If mankind is predicated upon the historical state, then it must for logical reasons be predicated upon all states, as well. And *all states* connotes a pluralism which, in turn, is unified in the phenomenal system. As in organic nature, however, every historically completed system bears within itself the seed of its own destruction. It is therefore also no coincidence that the nuclear age is the time in which the states-system has been most fully developed, and that the greatest threat to mankind appears at the moment of greatest system unity. This threat comes from within and, as we shall see, is determinate. But whether humankind can avoid the extinction of its life will depend upon its ability to transform the awareness of this turning point into the higher level of generic self-consciousness. Without this effort nuclear peace is nothing but illusory, while the atom wind, which will then awaken us from slumber, is all the more reality.

THE FORMATION OF THE STATES-SYSTEM

Following the discussion of judgmental differentiation in the form of the state and its pluralistic reflection, we must now analyse the third and final stage of the historical judgment, namely, the system of states and its development.

As we remarked towards the end of the preceding section, the threat to mankind is effected from within and, moreover, is determinate. By this we mean that in the atomic age the spiritual decay of the system, and the danger this poses for the survival of mankind, originates ultimately in the two superpowers that, on a higher level of reflection, form the new medium between the system as all states and mankind. In accordance with this reading the possibility for the sublation of mankind is predicated upon the relationship between the United States and the Soviet Union. The aim of this section is, therefore, to follow the logical progression of the judgment, and to observe how the system of nuclear states has become the present objectification of mankind.

The universal judgment is dialectically necessary identity. It is because the universal is implied in the singular that the genus system is generically related to the state. This relation belongs to the notion whose '*difference* is immanent in it'; or, it is the 'principle within itself'.[1]

Immanent identity does not refer to a formal equation. It is to be understood in terms of its concrete dialectic which involves the historical relations between phenomenal subjects. Immanence is the manifestation of logic whose identity is historically coherent development and self-production. Identity is in the end the life of mankind. In this sense, and only in this sense, can we say, according to figure V(f), p. 152, that just as the state belongs immanently to the system, so does the system dialectically belong to mankind. All three elements of the syllogism are coherently identical with one another and thus constitute the notionalised notion. Before we come to the relationship between the system and mankind we wish first, however, to treat the judgmental necessity of the system itself.

If in dialectical diction the state and the system are generically related to one another, then the state itself is a genus, although, as we shall see below, the actual necessity of the genus is identified with the system. The genus state develops into the system through its state differentiations. According to Hegel, dialectical mediation here signifies that a '*genus* essentially sunders itself, or repels itself into *species*; it is genus only in so far as it comprehends species under itself; the species is species only in so far as on the one hand it exists in the individuals, and on the other hand is in the genus a higher universality'.[2]

When we say, for instance, the United States is democratic, the lower universal predicate, democratic, expresses only a contingent and specific feature of the individual subject, the United States:

I State = Democratic

A different predicate is expressed, however, when we write the relation:

II State = System

In this case the higher universal predicate, system, exhibits the necessary and generic nature of the subject. Hegel develops this judgment of necessity out of three subordinate judgments which make it up: the *categorical*, the *hypothetical* and the *disjunctive* judgment. In the following we shall apply these forms of judgment and discuss each in turn.

1. The Categorical Judgment

Let us look at the second relation above again. In this example the subject state is reflected in the predicate system into its being-in-and-for-itself. The copula in the relation has therefore the meaning of necessity which assumes the relational form of positive identity or of the 'categorical judgement'.[3] This is a judgment, however, whose 'objective universality' is here still only in its '*immediate* particularization',[4] that is, the active and mediating objectification is merely presupposed and not yet actually posited.

It may be necessary here to pause for a moment and reflect upon the notional turning point. In the relation just referred to the state is the subject whose predicates are, on the one hand, democratic and other universal ascriptions, and, on the other, the system. But in the light of the second identity, and in accordance with the reflective mode in which we treat the issue of notional judgments, it is the one system that is the phenomenal subject. For this subject the state comes to be the immediate, presuppositional and judgmental predicate:

III	(a)	System	=	State
	(b)	Explicit	=	Implicit

It is with this recollection in mind that we can now say that what is categorical is the dialectical awareness that whatever else the United States *qua* state may be in its contingent characteristics, the self-knowledge of the individual United States becomes meaningful only in relation to what it is an immanent part of, namely, the universal system of states. The system is the determining generic subject without which the predicative species United States 'would be unable to subsist'.[5] And Hegel generalises this by making the incisive comment that 'it is only when things are studied from the point of view of their kind ['Gattung' = genus, H.K.], and as with necessity determined by the kind, that the judgement first begins to be real'.[6]

However, even the categorical judgment is to a certain extent 'defective'.[7] If the genus is the subject then, in accordance with the dialectical requirement of differentiation, 'the subject is subject only as a *particular*'.[8] But the species as particularity is not one but a plurality. Not only are the United States a state and therefore belong to the system. The Soviet Union, the United Kingdom, France,

China, and so forth are also states and are individually a necessary generic member of the system. Yet the relationship between the genus and its species is in the categorical judgment not fully expressed. This is explained with the help of the following figure:

IV Species = Genus

In this relation the genus 'as such has no leanings ['verhält sich als gleichgültig' = indifferent, H.K.] to any of its particular species'.[9]

The consequence of generic necessity, therefore, is that the universal predicate must differentiate itself so as to include other specific state entities. The development of the genus is the development of its manifold species. Since the generic subject is the negative identity of its particularisation, the copulative function of the predicate is not only to specify the subject but to fill the subject with all its differentiations. With the further determination of the predicate the development of the notional judgment moves towards a more adequate and fuller relation.

2. The Hypothetical Judgment

The categorical statement is now raised to a higher, that is, to what Hegel calls the 'hypothetical judgement'.[10] This judgment states that: 'if A is, then B is; or, the being of A is not its own being, but the being of another, of B'.[11] And Hegel clarifies the hypothetical judgment by saying that in it 'the specific character of the content shows itself mediated and dependent on something else: and this is exactly the relation of cause and effect',[12] or of '*condition* and *conditioned*'.[13] This means that the notion of the particular emerges only in its 'negative identity'.[14] But, unlike in the categorical judgment, which expresses only a non-mediated presupposition, 'the *necessary connection* of immediate determinateness' is in the present judgment 'posited'.[15]

If, for instance, we consider the being of the United States to be a particular effect, then its universal cause is the system. The being *A* of the United States is not its own determination, but the determination of another, namely, of the universal *B*, or of the system. Or, we can write with Hegel more generally that 'the being of finite things is posited by the Notion in accordance with their formal truth, namely that the finite is its own being, but equally is not its *own* being, but that of another'.[16] The other is the non-finite system that posits the finitude of individual states.

The hypothetical judgment, Hegel says, 'expressly realizes the universal in its particularizing'.[17] This means that the universal system as cause *B* posits itself in the particular United States as its effect *A*. Or: if the effect *A* as particularity is posited, then cause *B* as the universal of particularity is also posited.

But this rendering of the hypothetical judgment is problematic. For example, the movement from the effect to its cause expresses a clear relationship between species and its genus. That is, the universal of the particular is determinate. In this case the system is the necessary genus of the specific United States. However, the development from the cause to its effect is indeterminate. Only in the specific mediation is the universal particularised and does it begin to realise itself.

But the particular, since it is the developmental species of the genus, is, dialectically formulated, not one but is itself differentiated and comprehends a plurality. Yet the hypothetical judgment does not manifest this. It only states that '*if* one is, *then* the other is', that is, 'only the connection of the extremes is posited as being, not the extremes themselves'.[18] And 'just as the particular judgement has an indeterminate content, so the hypothetical is indeterminate in form, since its content is not determined as a relationship of subject to predicate'.[19] In other words, if we have the relation *subject is predicate*, or *genus is species*, the copula is not yet exhausted.

It is for this reason that the hypothetical statement is, like the categorical judgment before, defective. It 'fails to give due place to the function or element of particularity',[20] or to the species predicate. We have said above that the particular is species development. But the further predicative determinations are in the hypothetical judgment merely presupposed and not yet fully posited.

Thus we state that: if the system is the United States, then it is also the Soviet Union. In general this can be expanded so that we have: the United States is a specific state, but so are the Soviet Union, the United Kingdom, France, China, and so forth. The being of the universal system as the United States is not its own being but is also as the Soviet Union *and* as all the other states. The system is therefore organically mediated through the dialectical connective *and*:

V	(a)	States	=	System
	(b)	US + SU + UK + FR + CH, and so on	=	States-system
	(c)	Species (1 + 2 + 3 + 4 + 5, and so on)	=	Genus

The Hegelian reading of this is as follows: 'Since the being is the being of another, for that very reason it is *in itself a unity of itself* and *its other*, and consequently *universality*'.[21] Thus, in order to employ Hegel's interpretation, we hold that both the states and the system are mutually one for the other, and that their relationship needs to be grasped as such. They are unity and phenomenal universality.

3. The Disjunctive Judgment

The result of the development we have sketched so far yields the further consequence that the systemic judgment determines itself as the 'disjunctive judgement'.[22] This judgment describes generally *both-and* and *either-or* relations. The generic system is now universal since it forms itself dialectically as the United States, the Soviet Union and other specific states.

Thus the copula in this judgment is filled because the differentiated 'objective universality', which was at first merely presupposed as the total predicative content of the systemic subject, is now also truly 'posited at the same time in union with the form',[23] that is, with the subject. What is objective, or what is the object, is the historically developed state specification of the universal systemic genus. The subject and its predicative objectification have become a unity in which the one is sublated in the other. The phenomenal genus and its specific developments have coalesced in the dialectical copula. The result is that the universal has fully particularised itself. Form is also its content, and content is then only because of its form. The variations of this relation may exemplify this:

VI	(a)	Object	=	Subject
	(b)	Species	=	Genus
	(c)	Particular	=	Universal
	(d)	Content	=	Form

In the disjunctive judgment the union is not a posited abstract universality but manifests the posited concrete universality as genus and hence as subject. The historical predicate, which is transformed into distinct determinations, has thus developed into and forms a generic and necessary 'totality'.[24] Here, says Hegel, the 'particularity in its development constitutes the *predicate*, for it is the *more universal* in so far as it embraces the entire universal sphere of the subject'.[25]

But why is the concrete universal as totality disjunctive? This question can be answered if we bear in mind that dialectic describes historically generic development within which the notion of totality assumes two fundamental characteristics.

At first it is the combining result of species differentiation, the result being mediated through the connective *and*. This is formulated as: 'the subject is . . . *both B and C*; this *both-and* denotes the *positive* identity of the particular with the universal; this objective universal completely maintains itself in its particularity'.[26] The manifold species are contrary to or separate from one another. In a dialectical sense it means that 'species are contrary in so far as they are merely *diverse*, that is to say in so far as they possess through the genus as their objective nature an existence that is in and for itself'.[27]

If we consider, for instance, the system to be the universal that has through its enfolding generic history concretised itself into a systemic totality, then the existence of all the particular or diverse states is an existence in-*and*-for-itself only because they as species developments belong to their universal genus. To give an example. Even if we are making a conceptual difference between the United States and the Soviet Union, that difference is actually a notional one in the sense that it is immanently sublated and historically preserved in the higher notional form of the universal system. The system comprehends generically the differentiated singular existences whose separation from one another is nothing but a conceptual assertion and hence an illusion.

The second characteristic of the dialectic under consideration is that it is necessarily also disjunctive in that the species 'mutually exclude one another: A is either B or C',[28] or the species are 'contradictory'.[29] Thus the positive identity of the universal and its particulars is at the same time expressed negatively, that is, the *either-or* of the particulars B, C, D, and so on is their '*negative* relation. Yet in this they are just as identical as in their positive relation: the genus is their *unity* as *determinate* particulars'.[30] But each of the contrary and contradictory 'determinations by itself is one-sided and lacks truth'.[31]

How are these Hegelian positions to be dealt with? In order to explicate them let us give two complementary interpretations. The first we shall call the *vertical* genus-species relationship and the second the *horizontal* genus-species relationship. The former is illustrated in the following figure:

VII

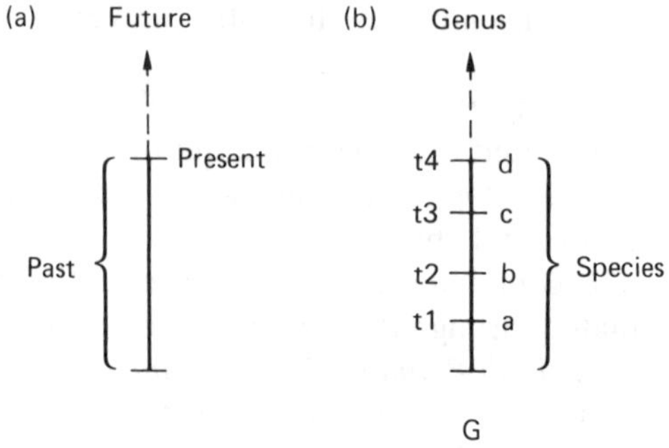

From the developmental side the genus dialectically unfolds itself and is at any particular point in time (t) the enfolded present species. Every present is an absolute historical result of antecedent developments. This means that at t4 the development of the genus (g) has reached a historical and reflected insight which embodies all previous species differentiations (sp) at their specific times:

VIII sp (a at t1) + (b at t2) + (c at t3) + (d at t4) = g

As this dialectical relation suggests every present is as a result the positive and coherent identity of the double negative. It is the way in which the system has historically formed itself. Species 'b' sublates the antecedent 'a', 'c' preserves within itself both 'b' and 'a', and so forth. And every resultant double negation is the present mediated positive genus. But the negative identity is the one in which the genus, at any particular point in time, can only be, for example, either (a at t1) or (b at t2). The disjunction in this example consists in the mutual exclusion of the mediated species determinations. In other words, it is the very essence of historical continuity to be disjunctive.

It is obvious from what we have said that neither the positive nor the negative alone can subsist. The former exists only as the result of past, negated and positively sublated developments, and only through the insight into the mediating historical ground. At the same time, however, the result can also only be *one*. It can only be either this or that total species universality and not both, let alone several. And this one result refers to the last species content at any particular historical present. The present is generically always an absolute.

Thus reason, as dialectical manifestation and taken as the logical unity of the positive and the negative, is necessarily historical, just as history is necessarily determined by reason. In the spiritual development of self-consciousness it is ultimately the life of mankind, comprehending notionally the system with its state differentiations, that lives through this mediated coherent identity. Its life is reflected in its historical medium. It is the concrete and actual universal, and as such is the absolute individual subject. It is concrete because it is historical. And it is precisely because it is historical that the form of mankind can give itself a further systemic content in the future as continuous actuality, although, philosophically speaking, it contains a universal only at any particular present. But present presentness does not preclude the development into a future presentness. In fact, since it refers to the activity of the subject, the present implies it intentionally. The activity of the subject bears within itself its own logical future. But for the subject in its presentness the future is as yet only, according to its form, a posited object to which no historical or phenomenal content is given. Dialectical identity can be spoken of only in the present in which subject and historical object already cohere in actuality. Only the present exists and, therefore, only the being of the present exists and, therefore, only the being of the present is in a position to reflect upon its becoming in a philosophical manner.

The disjunctive judgment permits also of another interpretation:

IX

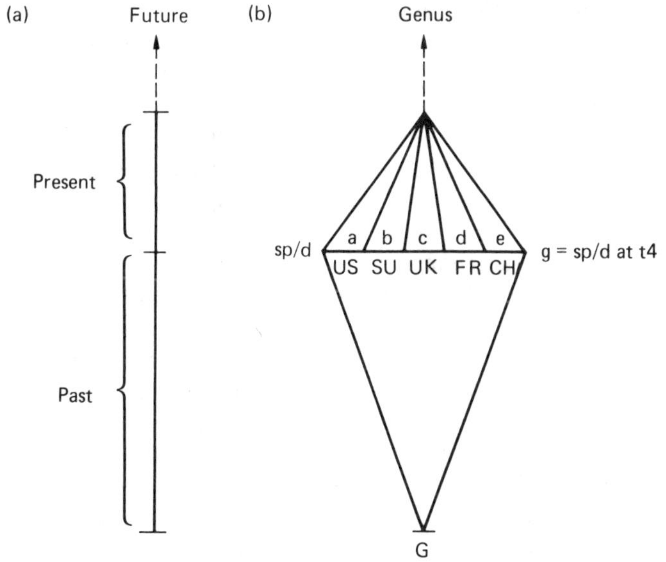

This viewpoint we call the horizontal genus-species relationship. What it shows is a close-up, as it were, of genus (g) at the present time (t4) of the species development (sp/d) as it is depicted in figure VII above. We are here not concerned, however, with the species point (d) which is one among others on the scale of historical becoming. What we shall discuss instead is its linear horizontal content, the differentiation of the present universal system.

X sp/d (a = US) + (b = SU) + (c = UK) + (d = FR) + (e = CH) = g at t4

To begin with, the species differentiations *a*, *b*, *c*, *d* and *e* mutually exclude one another because they represent state existences in-and-for-themselves. Secondly, in the course of the foregoing sections we have referred to the dialectical and generic identity between all states and the system. Now, the conjunctive identity poses no problem. All states together form the system, and the universality of the system assumes the genus form of one individual subject.

But what about the disjunctive judgment in this second example? On the one hand, it would make little empirical sense to equate the system with any one species differentiation, that is, for example, with either the United States or the Soviet Union, although we have said above that the universal system belongs to any particular individual state. But the individual state contains the universal system only implicitly. However, because of its dialectically organic nature, it must follow the principle of reflection and externalise and historically objectify itself in the explicit sense.

The difficulty with this judgment lies in the fact that single empirical species do not correspond to their universal genus. That is to say with Hegel, the 'empirical disjunctive judgement lacks necessity . . . because the species . . . have *already been given*; strictly speaking, this cannot give us an *either-or*'.[32]

This citation is a clarification of the non-necessity of empirical and theoretical judgments in general, and it refers in Hegel's text to a somewhat different treatment of the issue. However, for the purpose of a broad application of Hegel's system, his development of dialectical logic may serve us here to make another contextual point which will then also lead us to the judgment of the notion in the following section.

From an empirical point of view a purely disjunctive identity cannot be formulated. Such a judgment would describe a formal correspondence between the genus and one species only. In this case it would indicate a filled object relation. But since the historical world contains essential subject plurality, empiricism can never yield a true relation.

And yet, despite this illusion, dialectic requires that unity be established. Despite the conceptual defect it is nevertheless correct to say also that species are species because there is the generic system which implies them. A single species subsists because of its necessary historical relationship to other species differentiations and hence to the genus. The relationship between species and genus contains thus an *ought* which is required by the species if it is to subsist.

Apart from this general statement about how a species relates to its system, there are also particular species; let us take for instance 'a', which seeks to further the generic development of the system in such a way that the other differentiations 'b', 'c', 'd' and 'e' and, therefore, the genus itself correspond to the content of species 'a'. In other words, in the empirical world of religions and ideologies we observe the function of the rational *ought*. This ought is logically conditioned by the all-encompassing notion that employs it as its tool. The ought is thus the *cunning of reason*. We can put this less assertively and ask how operative the *ought* is in the geopolitical, ideological and other forms of spiritual aspiration which transcend the state, be it the Soviet Union, the United States, or any other subject?

About this example it is possible to say two things. First, the disjunctive exists between and among the predicative species. But, secondly, the disjunctive is apparent also, though in impure form, between the subject genus and its predicate, because the latter does not constitute a true species, perhaps 'a', but only a 'mixture'[33] of, let us say, 'a and b', or other mixtures of historical differentiations. Thus, says Hegel, 'the disjunctive judgement has the members of the disjunction in this predicate; but it is itself no less disjoined; its subject and predicate are the members of the disjunction'.[34]

So, irrespective of the, for instance, ideological drive of some specific state activities to unify conceptually the predicative disjunction, underneath remains the objective universality or the necessity of dialectical differentiation. If there were ever to be phenomenal and rational unity, it would amount to historical stasis. It would spell the discontinuity of dialectical and historical sublation. If mediation breaks up, the present will be without meaning since it could no longer bear within itself its continuity as future. The future as form, though logically presupposed within dialectical movement, is given a historical content only on the basis of essential differentiation. Only that which is organically differentiated develops into sublated and actualised unity. It is therefore the insight of the universal to pluralise and to spread its particularisation. The genus is genus only in and through the totality of its species, no matter how many forms of differentiation there may be. It is in this sense that the 'objective *universality* has completed itself *in its particularization*'.[35]

If universality is completed, the rational mosaic is filled with the totality of its specific but constituent elements. Complete universality contains all the historically developed states on a conceptual map. Complete universality is the system of states. However, this totality is notional necessity, and it is for this reason that differentiation exists.

But what is less clear is whether the particular form of differentiation, namely, the state is with respect to mankind necessary or whether it must not itself undergo mediative changes and therefore allow for other historically viable forms of spiritual developments. From the point of view of the past-present relationship the necessity of the state can be confirmed. But in reflecting on the possible further developments of historical species differentiation neither the future of the state nor its empirical content can be apodictically assumed.

The question also imposes itself for another reason. A filled map is like a completed conceptual puzzle whose individual elements or states are not only locked but are, therefore, also in their traditional historical movements blocked. Thus, while in earlier times states could physically expand outward, this is difficult to risk today. In the nuclear age territorial expansion is with some exceptions sublimated into ideological, economic, political and other state-transcending forms of expansion or externalisation. Hence, whatever transformation the present states-system may or may not undergo – because of the movement of dialectically existing ought-differentiations – history would still break through this other kind of inflexibility, destroy its conceptual uniformity and produce out of it another form of mediated universality.

We have interpreted universality as *all states* which as the system form the object of the subject mankind. But, partly answering the question put before and partly answering it more positively, history has interposed between the universality of *all* states and the individuality of *one* mankind the particularity of *some* states, that is some nuclear states. If nuclearisation were to proceed this, in turn, would lead to a conceptual allness, albeit one with a different content. That is, the problematic of proliferation would result in a new form of stasis similar to the map we made mention of above. But the present situation is such that the dialectical mediation is historically preserved and sublated in a higher form of system formation:

XI All states = Nuclear states = Mankind

Thus we can sharpen the historical contradiction between logic and phenomenon and narrow it down to those five states that have openly declared their nuclear weapons status. Since these nations themselves imply a present totality they are formed into notional universality. The five states, however, are hierarchically structured into an asymmetric system. This means they are further differentiated into the United States, the Soviet Union, on the one hand, and the United Kingdom, France and China, on the other. The originally universality is thus differentiated and has in our treatment undergone the dialectical transformation from *all states* to *five nuclear weapons states*, and from there to the *two superpowers*:

XII (a) Phenomenon = Logic
(b) 1. All states
2. 5 Nuclear states } System = Mankind
3. 2 Superpowers
(c) Object = Subject

The interconnectedness of states within the system is subject to the historical changes and re-arrangements. But even though this fluidity of the system may profoundly affect that totality itself, it does not alter the necessity of the dialectical relationship between the system and mankind. From the perspective of our question as to what is at stake in the nuclear age, it is therefore possible and justified to argue that, at present, it is the United States and the Soviet Union that not only fill the objective and concrete universality. They also form the true intra-phenomenal differentiation:

XIII All states = US/SU = Mankind

It is, furthermore, because of the reciprocal deterrence structure that a formal interrelatedness of the Soviet Union and the United

States is turned into the concrete individuality of the system. Hence the subject mankind has objectified itself into a predicate containing two states as the universal system:

XIV (a)	System	=	Subject
(b)	US/SU	=	Mankind

Both these states are the necessary generic differentiation of mankind. They are the phenomenal manifestation of logic. But, although we have said above that the nuclear states at present constitute a positive historical sublation, such a sublation can in the future no longer be taken for granted. It is far from certain that the logic will continue to mediate itself unimpededly through the activities of state differentiations. The turning point for philosophical reflection is therefore that it is rather the specific character of the systemic part that will decide the generic development of the whole of mankind. And this character is today such that the logic can either sublate or annihilate itself. Mankind may or may not negate and eliminate itself without sublating the possibility of future historical mediation. This possibility, however, is according to dialectic a necessity.

THE DETERMINATION OF THE STATES-SYSTEM

If we rightly argue that it is the relation between states and, in particular, between nuclear weapons states that pose a threat to the survival of mankind, then one might perhaps also be tempted to ask why it is that states ought to beware of the consequences of their relational activities. What are the dialectical reasons for supposing that the system of states is responsible for humankind. In order to address this very complex issue of the *ought* and from where we get it, we briefly introduce what we call the predicative constitution of the system, but shall consider it more expansively in the next section. By constitution is meant generally a notional determination which entails an *ought*. We interpret this *ought* in a way that describes it as the regulative politics of the states within the system. It is dialectically and, therefore, purposefully directed towards the sublation of that which it is the predicate of, namely, mankind.

We can specify this a little further. In our Hegelian reading of dialectic mediated mankind is the adequate notion as imperishable life. And life, in order to become conscious of itself, must dirempt itself into and reflect itself out of its historical differentiations. Mankind is accordingly the subject whose objectification leads to the manifestation of itself into its own total historical object. This object is the *filled* states-system. But the life of mankind is life only if it is the generative power to act as actuality. The immanent purpose of life is to sublate the particularising forces of its systemic reality in order to preserve itself self-consciously. Dialectic is the faculty to act self-referringly through the differentiating medium of history. Mankind acts in its being organic and spiritual. And it is only in that it acts that it preserves itself. It reproduces this end, this immanent dialectical continuity of its life, out of itself, out of its own historical means.

Now, the system itself has been described as the highest developed phenomenal subject. However, from the point of view of dialectic, the truly sublating activity is effected by the idea of mankind. Mankind, therefore, *fulfils* with Hegel the ultimate notion of 'individuality'.[1] The syllogistic movement of reflective sublation along with its terminological variations can be written thus:

I	(a)	Universality	=	Particularity	=	Individuality
	(b)	Object	=	Predicate	=	Subject
	(c)	System	=	Constitution	=	Mankind
	(d)	Phenomenon		=		Logic
	(e)	Implicit subject		=		Explicit subject

What this schema describes is this: it is the power of the subject to negate itself immanently into its self-own object and then to reproduce itself reflectively and hence positively out of that which the object posits conceptually in the middle term. This term functions as the mediating historical predicate. What the historically objective system of states rationally posits is the conceptual idea of a *constitution* in-itself. Yet in mankind the constitution itself is produced and sublated as an internal syllogistic for-itself, that is, for mankind. Mankind is mankind not as it is contingently posited in its conceptually ascribed-to nature, but only as it necessarily is in and through its reflected spiritual manifestations. It is these manifestations which, from the vantage point of the present, form the reason in history. In history itself, however, they are first expressed in rational terms. The relations below may illustrate this:

II (a) Object = Predicate = Subject

(b) In-itself *and* for-itself

(c) ← Posited ——

(d) Posited
→
Rationality

(e) Produced
→
Reason

We have on a number of occasions discussed the distinction between rationality and reason. Above this difference appears again. It says here that rationality is the posited object of reason as the self-producing subject. If we now combine figures I and II of the present section, we get:

III (a) Object ⇐ Subject

(b) Implicit subject ⇒ Explicit subject

And, according to the distinction mentioned, we can further state that what for the explicit subject *is* the historically reflected present and fulfilled reason, is for the implicit and past subject merely a rational and filling *ought*. It is an ought in the sense that the past ought to be mediated into every reflecting present. Thus the phenomenon, as it were, ought to be dialectically developed into the conclusion of its self-consciousness. The rational system bears within itself the *ought* as the as yet inadequate *is* of mankind. The idea of fulfilled self-consciousness requires the sublation of the whole of history and not of only a part of it. Accordingly, every formative period of the past contains a teleological *ought* towards the completed reflection of all historical moments into the present.

But note, unlike the East-West movement of reason, rationality is to move from West to East. This is explained by saying that the abstract *universal* but holistic thinking of the East has differentiated itself into the particularising rationalities of the West, out of which this thinking is again to be mediated into the concrete *individuality* of its reason. The externalisation from East to West, and the subsequent sublating development from West to East, is the manifestation of the dialectical principle which describes the positive of the double negative.

Thus, philosophically speaking, the true object of the implicit and conceptual subject is its explicitness as historically reflected notional reason:

IV (a)	Rationality	=	Reason
(b)	Implicit Subject	=	Explicit subject
(c)	Subject	=	Object
(d)	System	=	Mankind
(e)	Ought	=	Is

How are we to treat the *ought* in the above relations? Let us say again that the *is* is the activity of reflection and that it is in the logical subject the life of mankind as actuality. In reality, however, where we are dealing with the phenomenal subject, we have the historical and rational *ought*. This is directed at the spiritual *task* whose activity is directed towards the fulfilment of the life of mankind. But, although the *ought* is reflectively determined by the *is*, both are in dialectical terms the same in so far as they are mediated mankind. There is no separation between the present and its past, and none either between mankind and the system of states. Only a present subject, however, can engender its objective activity of reflecting itself in itself in order to become for itself. East and West are reason and rationality, and both are sublated in the idea of mankind.

Hence the system as 'objective universality' stands in 'relation to the Notion',[2] that is, to the individuality as mankind. But, according to rationality, this relation to the actuality of reason is for Hegel an '*ought-to-be*, to which the reality may or may not be adequate'[3]:

V	(a)	Rationality		=			Reason
	(b)	Subject		=			Object
	(c)	Subject	=	Predicate		=	Object
	(d)	Subject	=	Ought to be		=	Object
	(e)	System	=	Ought to be		=	Mankind

Thus whether or not the phenomenal subject sublates itself coherently into its logical object depends on the mediating predicate *ought*. And this *ought* constitutes or 'contains a true appreciation' ('wahrhafte Be-urteilung' = a truly determinate judgment, H.K.) whose predicative terms are, for instance, 'good, bad, true, beautiful, correct, etc.'.[4] The application of harmless concepts such as these have never affected the ability of mankind to sublate itself and, therefore, did not even have to be applied to it either. They were affixed to transcendent objects from which then was deduced our understanding of the universal conception of man. It was always possible to mediate reason through rationality irrespective of the latter's ascriptive nature. Partial conceptual objects never undermined the subject.

In the nuclear age, however, the employment of a conceptual ought makes a fundamental difference for philosophical reflection. Not only does the concept have another relational content – though we are not clear about what in fact it ought to be. Its meaning, as well, is qualitatively a different one. The question according to what rational principle the system of states ought to be regulated in order for mankind to survive requires in our time a determined answer. For otherwise what ought to secure the continuity of human life might sever it beyond even secular redemption. But only because there is this dialectical requirement this is not to say with certainty that we are also capable of formulating let alone of living up to such precepts.

THE DEVELOPMENT OF THE STATES-SYSTEM

In the disjunctive judgment (p. 192ff) the objective universality of the system was determined as phenomenon, both in its vertical and horizontal sense. The system, however, was not yet notionalised, because at this stage it is only the first negation of mankind. But mankind is actualised throughout the development of a second negation, or by means of the sublation of the reality of the system into actual self-consciousness.

Having specified the states-system as the *ought*, we shall now in this last part of the phenomenon of logic develop its determination further, but more in the context of its judgmental differentiations. This will involve a discussion of the way in which one negation is sublated by a second one and thereby is transformed into a positive moment or into the *syllogism*.

According to Hegel's dialectic, the disjunctive judgment shows a defect in the sense that 'although objective *universality* has completed itself *in its particularisation*, yet the negative unity of the latter merely returns *into the former* and has not yet determined itself to the third moment, that of *individuality*. Yet in so far as the result itself is *negative unity*, it is indeed already this *individuality*'.[1] It is already pregnant with the development into its actual determination, that is, into the *syllogism*. Let us convert this paragraph into relations and interpret it:

I (a) Universality = Individuality

(b) Object = Subject

(c) System = Mankind

— # +

No correspondence

(d) System = Mankind

— — +

Coherence

In the above relation (c) indicates that no formal correspondence is presupposed as given between the universality of the states-system and the individuality of mankind. The interconnection between these two extremes can only be mediated historically through the copulative constitution. The constitution operates as the conceptional and predicative link by means of which syllogistic coherence (d) is established as result.

We have characterised the system as the phenomenal subject. We shall now treat the constitutional mediation of this system to mankind or to its conceptual object. This involves, following Hegel's division, three dialectical stages, respectively described as the *assertoric*, the *problematic* and the *apodictic* judgments.

1. The Assertoric Judgment

As in all dialectical movements the judgment of the system is also at first only 'immediate', that is, at this level only 'assertoric'.[2] In this relation the subject in its immediacy is subject in-itself:

II (a)	Subject	=	Object
(b)	Subject in-itself	=	Subject for-itself
(c)	Immediacy	=	Mediated immediacy

These relations have the significance of reciprocal immanence. Since the notional subject for-itself is dialectically born within or is enclosed in the conceptual subject in-itself, the latter's immediacy is not yet itself produced into the mediated subject. Thus the immediate subject has itself as predicate:

III (a)	Subject in-itself	=	Subject for-itself
(b)	Subject	=	Predicate

We have said that mankind is logical individuality. Individuality, however, is in its immediacy universality. Besides, the result of the judgment of necessity was that the phenomenal identity of genus and species is concrete or objective universality which functions as phenomenal individuality. Thus, in accordance with what we have argued above, the genus and species are not only universality, but are in their identity the objective universality of subjective individuality or of the notion mankind. This we can state in more simple terms:

IV (a)	Subject	=	Predicate
(b)	Objective universality	=	Subjective individuality
(c)	Species/Genus	=	Notion
(d)	System	=	Mankind

About such relations and their interpretations Hegel writes, 'the subject is a concrete individual in general [that is, in its objective universal reality, H.K.], and the predicate expresses this same as the *relation* of its *actuality*, determinateness, or *constitution* to its *Notion*'.[3] The constitution (Be-schaffenheit) is the result of the system's effort to give itself a rational grounding. That a phenomenon has a constitution means that its teleological direction (Be) is to be worked out (schaffen-heit) conceptually. Thus the notion as subject/predicate identity depends on what it posits in reality, and how it then produces its actuality out of the predicative constitution. In its immediacy the relation reads as before:

V (a)			System	=	Mankind
(b)	Subject	=	Ought to be	=	Predicate

——————— Posited ———————→

This implies, says Hegel, that 'the subject *ought* to be something', that the '*universal nature* has posited itself as the self-subsistent Notion'.[4] That the notion is self-subsistent is, from a rational point of view, presupposed by the *ought*, which makes the posited predicate or *particularity* into an '*external existence* with such and such a *constitution*'.[5] But this means that the predicate as individuality 'may or may not conform' to its subject.[6] Thus the rational system posits itself contingently as mankind. Hence also in its rationality the inbuilt generic *ought*, which is the dialectical medium and means for mankind, does at this level of the judgment not yet determine the relation apodictically.

And yet the assertoric judgment goes *beyond* the necessary determination of the universal system in the disjunctive judgment, because in its universality the system refers itself to its ultimate predicative individuality, that is, to mankind. But on the assertoric level the extremes are at first sundered to which the 'Notion itself as the posited unity that relates them is still lacking'.[7] The notion mankind, in other words, still remains unmediated.

In the disjunctive judgment the genus is necessarily the universality of its species. The system is quantitatively all its states:

VI

But the assertoric judgment demands that the disjunctive relation, in turn, ought to be something. Yet because of the *ought* the relation does not of necessity have to correspond to it. There is no rational reason why the system should correspond to mankind or why, to put it otherwise, the universal phenomenal genus ought to be individuality as the true logical genus of mankind:

VII

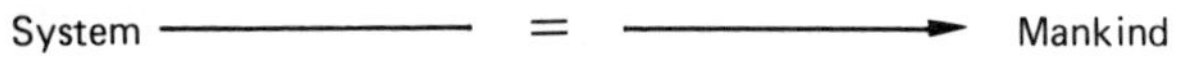

Now, let us recall that rationality is also subjectivity which ascribes a predicate to an externally posited subject:

VIII

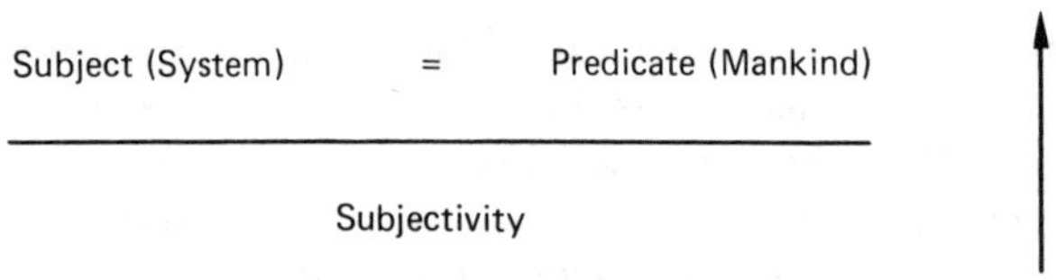

In this conceptual judgment subjectivity merely asserts that the subject is the predicate. It is only an unmediated presupposition, or a 'subjective *assurance*'.[8] Yet the subjective leap of faith, as it were, leads to no self-comprehension of the developed notional syllogism. Therefore, Hegel argues, when 'something is good or bad, etc. no one will suppose that it is, say, good only in *subjective consciousness* but perhaps bad in itself, or that good and bad . . . are not predicates of the objects themselves'.[9]

In applying the meaning of these lines, we say that if the system is to correspond to mankind, then, the argument goes, this is not something arbitrarily hypothesised in an external rational concept, but is internally posited by the immediate notional reason itself. Unlike rationality, which in a conclusion leaps to that which it is not itself, reason does not perform such a leap but instead develops immanently into its self-own syllogistic conclusion. This conclusion is identical with the continuity of the subject. Reason contains rationality, and reason produces itself coherently and historically out of this rationality. It is not we, the single living subjectivities, who posit the life of mankind, but it is mankind that as subject for-itself actively posits us in order to reproduce itself as the fulfilled and preserved present continuity of life. It is the whole as the spiritually organic principle that posits the part and reproduces itself out of the latter's differentiations. The relations below visualise this movement:

IX (a)	Subject in-itself	⇐	Subject for-itself
(b)	Subjectivity	⇐	Subject
(c)	Concept	⇐	Notion
(d)	System	⇐	Mankind
(e)	History	⇐	Life
(f)	Part	⇐	Whole

What is subjective and rational in these relations is the proposition that 'the *implicit* [an sich, H.K.] connexion of subject and predicate is not yet *posited*, or, what is the same thing, that it is only *external*; the copula is still an immediate *abstract being*'[10] and not yet the historically mediated concrete being in-and-for-itself.

If the *ought* implies that the subject/predicate correspondence may or may not be fulfilled, then, Hegel maintains, the result of the assertoric judgment is that rationality is 'confronted with equal right by its contradictory'.[11] It implies necessarily an internal contradiction and a conceptual dilemma. If a merely subjectively posited system is said to correspond to mankind, then to say that there is no such correspondence 'is equally justified'.[12] And it is justified because what is said of a rational concept defies demonstration.

But since the rational predicate mankind is self-contradictory, it cannot with necessity and of itself determine its subject. The rational subject in-itself or the system thus turn out to be 'contingent' and essentially, that is, historically 'problematic'.[13]

That there ought to be mankind is within the assertoric judgment a rational argument without cogency. A historically contingent subject cannot produce a necessary predicative object, of which it is asserted that it corresponds to rational subjectivity. Rationality merely posits the form of subject/object identity. In dialectical logic, however, it is the notional necessity of reason itself that *sui generis* determines its form by concretising itself into historical reality. It then mediates and sublates itself out of this phenomenon into logical actuality. Whatever is rationally posited is true only when it has become truth, that is, when history has transformed posited reality into produced actuality.

This interpretation can be articulated in a different way. We have referred to the notional identity between universality and individuality. The developed identity is expressed in two forms. At first it is posited, and then it is produced as result. That is, produced individuality is itself posited universality. Individuality and universality are necessarily mutually related to one another because both become universal individuality and individual universality. This is suggested by the movement of the Hegelian logic itself, which determines that 'it is only by both [the individual and the universal, H.K.] merging their one-sidedness on their own part [Sich-aufheben der Einseitigkeit beider an ihnen selbst, H.K.], that their unity is kept from becoming one-sided'.[14]

The sublation of one-sidedness is the dialectical self-production of the infinite or of non-finitude. To sublate the finite is to go beyond limited universality and to form the coherent identity of itself with its individuality. Historically mediated identity within infinity is demonstrated immanence.

2. The Problematic Judgment

That the assertoric judgment is contingent lies in the fact that it is a defective relation. It is based on rational positedness only and is therefore unmediated. Mediation, however, begins with the historical or, what Hegel calls, the *problematic* judgment. Here 'the content of the predicate is the relation of the subject to the Notion', that is, 'the *determination of the immediate as something contingent* is itself *given*'.[15]

When we say that the subject is mediated to the notion, then what we mean by this is that the subject is fully related to itself as to its self-own object. The unity of subject and object is mutual and notional comprehension. The notion is a result in which subject and object coalesce in the copula:

X (a) Subject = Object

(b) Rationality = Reason

$\longrightarrow \; = \; \longleftarrow$

The mediating activity of the rational subject as described in this section takes place in the *copula*. This middle term is the content of the predicate and is the true predication of the subject. The mediating copula turns the conceptual relation of simple correspondence into a notional judgment of coherence with the result that the predicate of the assertoric judgment becomes the object:

XI (a) Subject = Predicate (Assertoric)

(b) Subject = Object (Problematic)

(c) Subject = Predicate = Object (Problematic)

The formal immediacy of the subject is contingent in so far as it historically particularises itself into its copula. It is only when the copula fully relates the subject to itself as object that it is, at the end of this dialectical development, self-determined concrete necessity.

The problem with the assertoric judgment is that it is externally posited and that its assurance is merely subjective and rational. Now, however, the problem lies with the historical judgment itself whose positing activity is ultimately produced by reflecting reason. These two positions can be written as follows:

XII (a)

Posited

Rationality $\longrightarrow$ Reason

(b)

	Posited ←	
Rationality		Reason
	→ Produced	

The becoming of the subject towards itself depends upon its internal development which is the mediating middle. With the historical copula the extremes of the relation are notionalised or comprehended. The copula is the fulfilling notion. But first it is a problem.

To say, for instance, that something is problematic is to place the predicative indeterminateness of the subject into the *copula*:

XIII (a)	Subject	=	Predicate (Object)		(Assertoric)
			↓		
(b)		Subject	=	Object	(Problematic)

In the relation (b) of the above example 'no determination can emerge for the *predicate*, for this is already the objective, concrete universality. 'The problematic element, therefore', writes Hegel, 'concerns the immediacy of the *subject* which is hereby determined as a *contingency*'.[16]

We bring to mind that in the disjunctive judgment, which we have determined as the phenomenalisation of logic, the concrete universality was the object of the subject as reason. In the problematic judgment, which is the logicisation of the phenomenon, this universality assumes a different function. Here it becomes the object of the rational subject.

For this subject in-itself the true object is concrete universality which is in actuality the true subject for-itself as self-produced individuality. Thus, from the assertoric point of view, the question as to what the immediate subject is turns in the problematic judgment into the question as to what it is *for*. But the implied telos, which is expressed in the directional telos of the copulative ought, is not a rationally given. It is itself posited as the notional *task* or as the effort of reason. It is not given (gegeben) by us, the single phenomenal subjectivities, but is assigned (aufgegeben) to us by and for the one logical subject itself. Yet, because it is a task, it is also a problem which resides in the copula itself. The task is problematic because it may or may not fulfil its telos.

In our general rendition and application of dialectic, this means that it is not the empirically discerned system that first posits mankind. It is logical mankind that notionally presupposes its historical system *prior to* the conceptional activities of the latter. But rational activity, in turn, implies that mankind gives itself to its self-own system as to the latter's task to sublate mankind.

For example, one cannot meaningfully say: the system is mankind. The subject system is with Hegel its object mankind only 'according to its constitution',[17] only according to the mediating copulative predicate of the subject. The constitutional predicate is the task of the system to mediate itself towards itself as mankind:

XIV (a)	Subject	=	Predicate	⟶	Object	(Problematic)
(b)	System	=	Constitution	⟶	Mankind	(Problematic)
(c)	Universal	=	Ought to be	⟶	Individual	(Problematic)

Thus the predicative species in the disjunctive judgment becomes a problem for its subject genus in the present judgment. With respect to our example this implies that the United States and the Soviet Union in their relationship, which is the constitutional predicate of the two states, turn out to be a problem for the system in so far as the latter is not self-subsistent. The system exists only as the task to sublate mankind. Hence the system is not an in-itself. It is an in-itself only in that it is mediation for another, that is, for mankind. That the system is for another is due to its generic formation. And because it is generic it bears within itself the teleological activity.

Accordingly, not only do the United States and the Soviet Union fill a phenomenal necessity. Now they also ought to fulfil and hence mediate themselves as system to their logical mankind. In their dialectical role as predicative constitution they mediate the subject to its object. Therefore, notes Hegel, the predicate as 'the problematic element in the subject itself constitutes its *moment of contingency*, the *subjectivity* of the *thing* over against its objective nature or its

Notion, its merely *contingent mode* or its *constitution*'.[18] Whether the system is mediated mankind depends on the *ought* of its constitution. Or, to express it the other way round: whether mankind itself is actual depends upon the fulfilled ought of its system, of its historical reality.

If the system is mankind, then the copula does not only determine the one-sided predicative constitution of the subject, but it does this in terms of an *ought*. Rationality is only the in-itself of reality. It is not truth, but it ought to become truth. Dialectically developed truth is actuality mediated and sublated through the means of the ought. This ought is the *cunning of reason*. The constitutional relationship between the United States and the Soviet Union thus has a purpose. But this purpose is not to be understood as conceptually self-referential, or as revolving about the system itself. Rather must it be seen as the systemic means for the continuous actualisation of mankind. 'Hence, the *subject* itself is differentiated into its universality or objective nature, what it *ought* to be, and the particular constitution of its existence.'[19] The system ought to be mankind, but it can be that only according to its copulative constitution. The end can be fulfilled only through the dialectical mediation of its constitutional means:

XV (a)	System	=	Ought to be	=	Mankind
(b)	System	=	In accordance with its constitution	=	Mankind

The constitution is with Hegel the historical and formative 'essence' which 'determines itself as ground'.[20] The ground is differentiation, the mediating reason directed towards mankind and its substantive foundation. Thus the systemic subject in its immediacy 'contains the *ground* [its predicate, H.K.] of its *being* or *not being* what it *ought to be* [its object, H.K.]. In this way it is equated with the predicate'.[21]

But the predicate is only the first negation of immediate universality. Hence the system as the phenomenal subject 'has itself become problematic by reason of its *having lost* the immediate *determinateness* which it possessed in the immediate [assertoric, H.K.] judgement'.[22] No longer can we content ourselves with the subjective assurance that the system conceptionally presupposes mankind, or that it considers its continuous actualisation to be unequivocal. The relation has become a problem in as much as the system is not mankind but ought to be mankind in its fulfilled and sublating self-consciousness. But the fulfilment of the ought, though it may or may not be achieved by the rational system, is the mediating systemic means of mankind. And it is this *medius terminus* which is, furthermore, the second negation within notional sublation. The positive of the double negative is thus explained in the following way. Mankind consciously posits or negates itself into the system of the states. But the system itself is negated in the sense that mankind reflectively produces its self-consciousness out of and through the medium of the systemic constitution. The posited system is not something static, but is subject to historical transformation and hence in itself dynamic. The result of this dialectic is the actualised syllogism:

XVI (a)	System	=	Constitution	=	Mankind
(b)	–		–	=	+

The development of the second negation leads us now to the third and final formation of the system-determination.

3. The Apodictic Judgment

The coherent relation between subject and object is established if the middle predicative ought is fulfilled. If the 'thing with its *constitution*' is 'posited', then the judgment is no longer problematic but, according to Hegel, 'apodeictic'.[23] Yet what posits the subject in-itself with its constitution, or what posits the system with its constitution, is mankind itself which, as the subject for-itself, is in its notional idea the truly fulfilled logic.

In dialectic the term identity must be understood not as posited conceptional correspondence but as self-developing, internal and notional coherence. In this sense it is the dialectically sublated unity of historical differentiations. The subject mankind posits its objective self as the system. Conversely, the system posits its objective self as mankind. Thus we have:

XVII (a)

Object	=	Subject
Universal	=	Individual
System	←	Mankind

(b)

Subject	=	Object
Individual	=	Universal
System	→	Mankind

Let us look at relation (b) first. The subject of the apodictic judgment is stated in the following way:

XVIII Subject = Predicate = Object

Notion

If we explain this and say that the system, 'constituted so and so' is mankind, we may further state that this judgment 'has within it, first, the universal, what it *ought to be*, and secondly, its *constitution*; this latter contains the *ground* why a predicate of the Notion judgement applies or does not apply to the *whole subject*, that is, whether the subject corresponds to its Notion or not'.[24]

The whole subject is the historically developed identity between system and mankind, whereby its inner coherence is mediated through the predicative constitution. Notional identity is here truly objective. It is the established 'truth of the judgement',[25] because both, individuality and universality, have each other as object. The truth of the apodictic judgment is its syllogised unity. It is mankind in its actualisation. Or, to put it differently: it is mankind having transformed its consciousness of historical reality into the actuality of its present self-consciousness.

The original assertoric judgment (system = predicate, or: the system is mankind) has now truly objectified itself in that the assertoric predicate has become the apodictic object, and the copula has been converted into the mediating predicate between subject and object. Thus we can write with Hegel that the original 'subject and predicate correspond to each other and have the same content, and this *content* is itself the posited *concrete universality*'.[26] The constitution, if fulfilled, is the concrete mediating principle in the dialectical relation: the system is mankind. Accordingly, the constitutional *is* has become the fulfilled *ought*. The apodictic relation manifests the is/ought relationship as generic identity. The constitution notionalises and therefore contains the 'objective universal or the *genus* and the *individualised* universal'.[27] Both refer to the system and to mankind, respectively. Both have coalesced into one another. And the living principle of this reciprocity is the constitution. The constitution, because of its dialectical role as mediation, is the true universalising universal:

XIX (a)	System	=	Constitution	=	Mankind
(b)	Universal	=	Universal	=	Universal

All three elements in the apodictic judgment are therefore syllogised universals. They are historically developed unity, and together they form one content, or one coherently concretised universal. But it is because the universal is mediated that it is only in its opposite. That is to say, 'we have the universal which is *itself* and continues itself through *its opposite* and is a universal only as *unity* with this opposite'.[28] Mankind is only in and through the system, and the system is only in and through mankind. In the apodictic judgment the dialectical constitution of both is active historically and methodically within the predicating and mediating relationship between the United States and the Soviet Union.

The original predicate mankind 'is based on an *ought to be* and at the same time contains the *correspondence* of *existence* to that ought-to-be; it is not this ought-to-be or the genus by itself, but this *correspondence* that is the *universality* which constitutes the predicate of the apodeictic judgement'.[29] 'The *subject* . . . contains these two moments [predicate and object, H.K.] in *immediate* unity as the fact (Sache). But it is the truth of the fact that it is internally *split* [gebrochen, H.K.] into *what it ought-to-be* and *what it is*' – this, Hegel states, is the 'absolute judgement on all actuality'.[30] The actualisation of the idea of the self-conscious life of mankind is accordingly never, to repeat, a given but always a task. And this task is life itself which sunders and sublates itself continuously into the historical is/ought relationship. The relationship, in turn, is immanent and spontaneous self-movement. It is unified dialectical development and organic holism.

Though the system implicitly *is* in-itself, it *ought* to be explicitly the *is* of mankind for-itself:

XX (a) System = Mankind

(b) Is = Ought = Is

Fact:
Actualised notion

And Hegel describes this relation by saying that:

> it is because this original partition, which is the omnipotence [All-macht, H.K.] of the Notion, is just as much a return into its unity and an absolute relation of the *ought-to-be* and *being* to each other that makes what is actual into *a fact*; its inner relation, this concrete identity, constitutes the *soul* of the fact.[31]

The return into its unity is the system sublating and preserving itself as mankind. It is the system that has become conscious of itself as mankind. The return is the copulative and cyclical turning point as the positive of the double negative. The judgment 'has its *ground* in the constitution of the subject and thereby is *apodeictic*'.[32] That is to say, the unifying copula is the directional creation of the subject. It is the teleological and mediating constitution (Beschaffenheit) purpose-fully guided towards its object.

It is the copulative or constitutional relationship between the United States and the Soviet Union that determines the system towards mankind. If it is actualised, the copulative ought is determin-ate and fulfilled. The original copula has now further developed itself into ground in general. This copulative development is historical formation or notional activity.

The relational constitution determines the system because as the copula it is, according to Hegel, the 'immediate *determinateness* in the subject, but it is no less the *relation* to the predicate which has no other *content* than this very *correspondence*, or the relation of the subject to the universality'.[33] Thus, the relation of the system to mankind becomes:

XXI	(a)		Subject	=	Predicate	
	(b)	Subject	=	Predicate	=	Object
	(c)	System	=	Constitution	=	Mankind

What we see in these relations is that 'the subject through its determinateness points beyond itself and relates itself to the predicate'.[34] The system mediates itself through its constitution to mankind. But therewith '*this relating* has passed over into the predicate, alone constitutes its content, and is thus the *posited* relation, or the judgement itself'.[35]

The *pointing beyond* is the system relating itself towards mankind. This is the result of the directional relation (XVIIb) referred to above: system→mankind. However, the generic self-development is itself a self-determined one. That the phenomenal system ought to be mankind can be notionally asserted only because mankind is the actual logical subject that reflects itself in its systemic object. It is the explicit *is* of mankind. It is life as self-reflection that determines first of all the *ought* of the implicit *is* of the historical system. This notional self-determination lies, as we have expressed it in figure XVII(a) earlier, in the dialectical relation: system←mankind. It is the developed and fulfilled identity of the apodictic judgment:

XXII	(a)	Subject/Object		=		Object/Subject
	(b)	Subject	=	Object	=	Subject
	(c)	System	=	Constitution	=	Mankind
				Notion		

'Thus', concludes Hegel, 'the concrete identity of the Notion which was the *result* of the disjunctive judgement and which constitutes the *inner* basis of the Notion judgement . . . is now restored *in the whole*'.[36] The reconciliation of mankind with itself is the reproduced and hence 'positive . . . result'[37] of its posited, original and negative judgment into the system, on the one hand, and of the mediating constitutional relationship between the United States and the Soviet Union, on the other.

The constitution is the objective historical and spiritual copula which permeates both subject and predicate. In it the system and mankind 'have the same *content*'.[38] They have both the same inner object. It is, in Hegel's language, the '*fulfilled copula* of the judgement, the *copula pregnant with content*, the unity of the Notion that has re-emerged from the *judgement* in which it was lost in the extremes. Through this *impregnation of the copula* the judgement has become the *syllogism*'.[39] And it is with the syllogism that the necessity of the disjunctive judgment has become apodictically notionalised. The logical result of this dialectical mediation is that mankind is in every historical present sublated.

In summing up let us recapitulate the structure and purpose of this section. We had previously identified the determination of the system of states as an ought. The reflection of the present requires that it encompasses the whole of its history. This means that every particular moment of the past is to be sublated until all such antecedents are reflected in the present, for it is only when the past in its totality is comprehended that the present's consciousness of history is transformed into its self-consciousness. Now the ought itself is not a simple determinate form. It is because of the principle of organic dialectic that this conceptual determination sunders and develops into the notional constitution of those phenomenal differentiations that make up a particular historical period. In other words, the constitution is the essential content of the ought. And, of course, within the context of this writing, we describe differentiation with reference to the nuclear superpowers. And the constitutional content of this differentiation is, in turn, regarded as the reflective political relationship that prevails between these states. From the point of view of philosophical dialectic, then, we maintain that it is the constitution of a historically differentiated relation alone that provides us with an adequate insight into the true nature of the present life of mankind, and that reminds us of the strenuous effort that needs to be made if we want to secure its continuous self-sublation.

SUMMARY

A philosophy of dialectical logic is possible only if it can presuppose itself into its own history. The study of the history of mankind has traditionally been confined to the view of the history of its phenomenal differentiations which were the rational bearers of this history. But with the dawn of the nuclear age man not only became conscious of his threatened mankind, but in his reflections may also have begun to learn to see in it a philosophical determination different from those he was accustomed to attach to states which, in legal parlance, are considered to be subjects. As we have tried to show, dialectical thinking, for instance, allows for the determination of mankind as the logical subject that bears itself as its historical object. This object is the states-system and its constitution. The constitution is spiritual in nature in the sense that it comprises all forms of rational constructs that are meant to be realised in the spheres of political, economic, military, ideological, and other cultural means for effecting interstate relations.

It was the purpose of the foregoing considerations to observe the mediating movements of mankind and its actualisation. This we have attempted to do by means of an analysis and application of Hegel's logic of judgment and the various forms of its dialectical diremptions. The question of the nuclear age requires a philosophical framework for differentiated reflection. We firmly believe that Hegel's insightful method for comprehending the development of history and its self-consciousness can serve us as a first approximation to a systematic intellectual account of such a programme.

But, in order to complete our interpretation of the logic of judgment, we still need to describe more fully the idea of the dialectical syllogism. This will be expressed, on the one hand, in terms of the actual sublation of mankind and, on the other, with respect to mankind's self-negation in case of a nuclear war.

Part III
The Scientific Dissolution of History

5 The End of Hegel's Dialectic

As we have tried to demonstrate in the foregoing chapter, mankind is mediated in and through the constitution of the states-system. From the point of view of historical dialectic, this positive result will be articulated in the first of the following sections with reference to the adequate syllogism of the notion. Now, although we have seemingly accepted that dialectic describes the necessary positive of the double negative, this power to sublate history, however, may be denied by a nuclear war. Ever since Hiroshima we have come to regard the rational forces of annihilation as being those of the constitution. In the second section, therefore, we shall talk about these forces which threaten to prevail over man's ability to reason historically and thus to respond responsibly to the inner call of the life of mankind. The call of life is its intrinsic desire to preserve itself.

Yet this last act of the subject mankind must at the same time be interpreted as its own freedom to commit suicide. It is also the act through which Hegelian philosophical reflections will come to an end. Though this may be nothing but a truism, it still remains one that requires comprehension. And dialectic is in our view the method which in its application raises the thought of a nuclear holocaust to its notion which alone establishes for reflection the historical relationship between the life and death of the idea of holism.

Since it is not our purpose to dwell on the final fall of man and its empirical consequences for him, we shall instead delineate the dialectical structure of living history and its self-inflicted finality.

MANKIND SUBLATED

The principle of the vitality of history is the dialectical syllogism, whereby syllogism stands for the self-sublated and mediated preservation of the notion mankind. As our analysis and interpretation of dialectic has shown, this result of historical development means that the notion is now fully adequate and coherent. Its logical reason is truly actual. According to the first three relations of the figure below the syllogism is thus, to use Hegel's idiom, the resultant positive of the double negative:

I	(a)	Object	=	Predicate	=	Subject
	(b)	System	=	Constitution	=	Mankind
	(c)	—		—		+
	(d)	Judgment			=	Notion
	(e)			Syllogism		

The logic of this outcome is in need of further examination. Our application of the dialectical method is summarised in relations (d) and (e), which for Hegel express the reproduction or 'the restoration of the *Notion* in the *judgement*, and consequently the unity and truth of both. The Notion as such holds its moments sublated ['aufgehoben' – raised and preserved, H. K.] in *unity* . . . In the *syllogism* the Notion determinations are like the extremes of the judgement, and at the same time their determinate *unity* is posited'.[1]

The historical preservation of mankind, which is mediated through the particular inter-state development within that system, that is, through the constitutional relationship between the United States and the Soviet Union, is the self-affirmation of dialectical reason. It is the self-affirmation of history itself. 'The syllogism', Hegel says accordingly, 'is the completely posited Notion; it is therefore the *rational* ['Vernünftige' – reason, H. K.]', in the sense that 'in reason the *determinate* Notions are posited in their *totality* and *unity*'.[2] Mankind is only in and through its pluralistically structured unified system of states, and the system is only in and through its produced mankind. But that which mediates their identity is what reason produces and what rationality posits in the copulative constitution. The constitution establishes the relationship between the states-system and mankind. Mankind in-and-for-itself, therefore, constitutes itself notionally in the way its system organises its structure. And the system, in turn, constitutes itself conceptually in mankind which is the system's in-itself. And it does this with respect to the idea of the good for itself. Since the system consists of, for instance, ideologically competing states, the idea of the good for mankind is internally broken but, nonetheless, sublated by the very fact that mankind exists historically. In this sense the constitution connotes the reconciliation of notionalised concepts:

II (a)	Phenomenon	=	Copula	=	Logic
(b)	Rationality	=	Constitution	=	Reason
(c)	Concepts			=	Notion

The copula is interpreted as the 'middle term (medius terminus)'.[3] And the content of this mediating *medius terminus* is the syllogising constitution. Logically speaking, the content constitutes the historical and spiritual essence of mankind. Thus Hegel explains: 'the essential feature of the syllogism is the *unity* of the extremes, the *middle term* which unites them, and the *ground* which supports them'.[4] The ground, of course, is the continuity of history. But this means that reason produces itself out of that which rationality posits in the constitution. The mediating constitution is in its teleological activity always the developed present of rational reason. Along with its various synonymous contents it may be represented as follows:

III (a)	Rationality →		=		← Reason
(b)	Telos		=		Entelechy
(c)	System	=	History Essence Activity Constitution Rational reason Present	=	Mankind

Dialectical reasoning determines mankind as imperishable life. Life is the infinitely and eternally sublated present. And as the logical subject it is in consequence only as historical result. Only the past coheres with its resultant present: the future does not. The infinitude of mankind, then, is not, to speak with Hegel:

> the empty [and rational, H.K.] abstraction from the finite [system, H.K.], not the universality that lacks content and determinateness, but the universality that is fulfilled or realized [actualised, H. K.], the Notion that is *determinate* and possesses its determinateness in this true way, namely, that it differentiates itself within itself and is the unity of these fixed and determinate differences.[5]

Thus infinitude, as the historical unity of the determinate extremes of past and present, is 'nothing but the *syllogism*'.[6] And this dialectical syllogism is historically mediated self-consciousness.

The reason why there is infinitely sublated mankind lies in the mediating finitude of the system itself. Now, within dialectic the constitution of the system is never formally circular, but organically cyclical. In its historical and teleological sense it points beyond itself and towards the entelechy of mankind. All universality contains within itself the seed that differentiates itself in order to become individualised.

With regard to this determination, however, there still remains a most compelling but also extremely vexing question. It concerns the difficult idea of mankind itself acting with the objective to sublate its own actuality. Yet this question as to what it is in mankind that acts requires perhaps just as mysterious a philosophical and, for that matter, scientific answer as is the one that refers to the query what it is in the individual human being, the state, the system, and so forth, that acts. Because of the problems associated with the conceptualisation of theoretical terms such as, for instance, telos and infinite regress, a strictly empirical and epistemological answer seems to be ruled out. No rational explanation would be satisfactory, because no such answer would constitute a response to the question of self-reference. But within the realm of our philosophical discussion of the self-referential activity of the subject a dialectical speculation can be made in a rather determinate way. For what it leads us to argue is that the issue concerning self-activity must be comprehended in terms of the idea of individual holism. And in human history this idea extends to the mediation and sublation of the self-consciousness of mankind. Therefore, holism, being a spiritually organic notion, is that which spontaneously and in this sense of necessity acts towards itself.

The structure of the development of this idea is determined by what we call with Hegel *desire*, a mode of activity which permits of a twofold interpretation. Firstly, we want to say that through the continuous reconciliation of its natural need and spiritual desire the individual *qua* subject acts, and must act, in order to mediate and preserve itself dialectically. Although it is the telos of conscious activity to strive towards sublated self-conscious identity, it is equally true that the dialectical meaning of the individual human being is defective. And it is defective in so far as it always acts, and can only act, in relation to other such, and in the end to the totality of, individuals. Particular instances of activity, instances such as individual persons, but also communities, be they states or other internally mediated social relations, are the manifested particular moments of the idea of holism.

This holism, however, is, secondly, one individual mankind into which are mediated through communal differentiations all individual human beings. Unlike the life of individual persons the life of mankind is infinite life whose dialectical *is* can never be teleologically increased. It cannot be mediated into and by a notion that is higher than itself. In consequence, mankind is not contingent either in relation to, as it were, other different individual mankinds whose mutually affecting activities would have to be reconciled in turn. The life of mankind undergoes no transition to something which it has not yet reached, or to something different from what it is for itself. It is always within itself already transformed into actuality. Life is; it is one, and more it cannot be. But the being of life is essentially the conscious becoming of self-consciousness. Being is constant becoming. This is to say that spiritual activity and self-preservation are actual only in the task-rich present. The reality of the historical system, however, has, upon reflection, the posited and conceptual *ought* whose constitutional content always increases. Of the means to achieve the end there is no rational limit. The system thereby goes beyond itself and mediates itself towards mankind. The conscious task of the system is to fill the ought with reasonable rationality. Or, to put it another way, the rational system ought to conduct itself in such a way that it is conscious of reason which affects its historical mediation towards the sublation of mankind.

The expression *towards mankind* does therefore not refer to the question as to what mankind ought to be in the axiological and moral sense. No presumed meaning of a rationally posited political ought can be ascribed to mankind's logical status of necessity. The mediating *ought* is itself a systemic internal response to the *is* of notional reason or of mankind. In other words, there cannot be a rational and prescribed future-oriented *ought* without the present *is* of already actualised reason which alone is the object of philosophical description. We do not reflect upon mankind *as if* it existed in the form of a hypothesised reality. Just as Hegel's understanding of historical dialectic does not allow him to speculate into the future and ask what the state ought to be,[7] so in our adoption of his philosophical method we cannot simply presuppose the actual content of what we believe mankind ought to be. We are only entitled to describe it as it has already developed.

In whatever way the differentiated system posits its relational organisation, it will always be embedded in mankind whose dialectic is its ground. In its spiritual desire to sublate itself, mankind dirempts itself into its determinate constitution. It is not the constitution conscious of its ought which, at first, determines mankind. Mankind as the holistic notion is qualitatively more than the numerical quantity of the states that make up its conceptual parts. This, once more, is the Hegelian meaning of the *cunning of reason*. The state differentiations in the system may well *believe* that their respectively hypothesised concept of what is good for mankind also determines mankind's existence. Yet notional mankind is in its actuality the result of the dialectical mediation of these differentiated, often even mutually exclusive, concepts and the reciprocal relations they express. It is in this sense of unified result that it *knows* conceptual assertions to be illusions only, while it *knows* itself as actuality. And by knowledge we mean here the awareness of its actualised freedom to mediate and sublate itself. Knowledge describes itself as philosophically reflected existence or as the result of sublated historical relations. It does not explain the presumed episteme of that which it is not. Hence concepts are for the notion, asserted rationality is for historical reason which alone renders it apodictic. While every concept is contingent, its assumption of an ontological in-itself is determined *for* the one and necessary notion of mankind. And in its dialectical signification this means that, while the system can only be conscious of its concepts, mankind is conscious of itself as actualised history because it is the notion that sublates itself. As the subject mankind alone comprehensively acts and therefore is in its idea mediated identity. Fully adequate self-consciousness cannot be measured in terms that are relative to arbitrary external criteria. It manifests itself immanently and is therefore the necessary result of self-relation.

To conclude: mankind continuously preserves itself through the system and its institutional constitution. The continuity of existence is its dialectical openness to which no determinate future content can be ascribed. It forms itself out of its history whose real content it permeates and through which it freely works and weaves together its self-awareness. As life itself mankind is thus the true and actual genus. And it is the genius of the genus that it sublates itself through its mediating specific parts into its self-identical individual whole. This is the logic of the notion actively notionalising itself.

MANKIND ANNIHILATED

The genus of mankind is preserved through the historical sublation of its species, that is, the states-system. History itself substantiates this truth of the present. But it is by no means certain that it will also provide us with justified confidence for our future. In this section, therefore, we wish to describe what happens to dialectical logic in the event that the nuclear deterrence constitution of the system breaks down. An empirical answer to the question of how the world will look on the day after the holocaust may not require much sensitised imagination. But the possibility of history's self-termination still demands its philosophical articulation within the framework of Hegel's reflections upon life. Life, though once presupposed as imperishable history, has in the nuclear age led us rather to the heightened awareness of its actual fragility and finitude. If this end were ever to be effected it would amount to a dialectical, but in its result then also necessary, contradiction.

According to our discussion so far, we have established that rational subjectivity posits concepts for its own purposes. Let us recall also that its realisation, however, is always antinomial and hence filled with illusions. But, unlike the fate which thus befalls rationality, the reason of the subject reflectively overcomes this dilemma and actualises its purpose of fulfilment in that it produces itself out of the historically conflictual concepts of rationality. These conflicts are notionalised into the syllogism. The syllogism is the continuity or non-finitude of the self-sublating present. Both these movements and their interpretation are formulated in the figure on page 232.

While it is true to say that both these statements are made from the point of view of rationality, which we as individual human beings can neither escape nor transcend, this same rationality,

I (a) Rational subjectivity ← Concepts (Essence)

System ← Constitution

(b) Rationality ⇔ Concepts ⇔ Subject of reason

System ⇔ Constitution ⇔ Mankind

however, interprets their dialectical and philosophical implications differently.

For instance, in relation (a) the seemingly explanatory activity of rational subjectivity underlies, in its strongest sense, concepts in a transcendental way because it is logically prior to them. But, as remarked earlier, the asserted infinity of a transcendent and determining essence (left arrow) is paradoxically dependent upon the historical finitude of subjectivity. Contingency, therefore, renders conceptual infinity into a spurious one. By the same token, what the system is prone to claim for its unmediating constitution is equally unfounded.

The syllogism (b), on the other hand, describes a different situation. In it we find ourselves not only necessarily determined by historical reason. Reason also uses us and our concepts as its historical tools in order to mediate and to actualise itself through them. Man's rational concepts are in this schema nothing but the notional essence of the historical reason of mankind. That is to say, in dialectical logic it is we as particular rationalities who are dependent upon and hence finite with respect to the continuous and coherent non-finitude of reason.

Reason as history involves the dialectical sublation of the rational dilemma into the apodictic infinity of the all-encompassing notion. This result of reason's activity has an additional and yet most important consequence. It turns the apparently dominant phenomenal role of rational man and his conceptual creation, the systemic unity of states, into a means which is prevailed upon by the logically higher principle of the life of mankind for which it purposefully works. The system and its constitutional ought, the United States and the Soviet Union together with their reciprocal doctrinal relationship, are of necessity to sublate themselves into or are to respond to mankind whose holistic life indifferently permeates them in their particularity.

Dialectic describes the life of mankind as being continuous and imperishable. The rational may-or-may-not correspondence is only the *cunning of its reason*. What is conceptually assertoric is notionally apodictic. Life is the subject that wills itself immanently as and always for its continuity. In Hegelian terms, this continuity can be said to be 'simple self-same self-relation, which is not interrupted by any limit or exclusion'.[1] Historical continuity expresses a sublating activity. It mediates the particular constitutional relationship of the system into the actualising self-preservation of mankind. The deterrence constitution is not only rationally pluralistic; it also increases. That it increases instead of remaining static is due to the immanent historical dialectic that always requires new conceptual, though competing, adjustments to the multifarious real or imagined changes within the system.

If we now apply the notion of continuous self-sublation to the development of rational plurality, we can further say that, while particular universal concepts terminate and go under within historical activities, the one sublating individual notion of mankind continues itself through this activity. That is, while rational differentiations fade into their past, the coherent present identity of historical reason continues its unceasing self-sublation through that which is fading away. Transposed onto our situation it means two things. One is that the states-system knows only teleological concepts of a rational constitution which, however, it cannot hold and has always to amend. The other is that mankind knows itself as entelechy, as the actualised notion that comprehends whatever the understanding posits as constitution.

Within the history of system development rational concepts were never of such a nature as to affect their unifying reason negatively and *in toto*. In the beliefs and hopes of individual men and their communities mankind was presupposed and its continuous life taken for granted, notwithstanding, for instance, the religious fear of the apocalypse or other doomsday prophecies. But not only that. Though the individual concept man was theoretically universalised, the universal itself was never in need of being philosophically raised to the higher notion of individual mankind. Mankind was from the point of view of dialectical presentness not regarded as the one ultimate subject. There was always a form of redemptive transcendence expressed as yonder life and secular utopias.

Yet with Hiroshima the conceptual forces have suddenly and in an irrevocable manner begun to undermine and render uncertain the mediating power of mankind to preserve its continuity concretely. And aware of the consequences of an unreflected experience, the system with its otherwise only self-serving and self-referential theoretical doctrines has awakened to its responsibility to mankind. Though it used to be conceptually separated from it, it now belongs to mankind notionally. Both are dialectically related to one another. Since the dawn of the nuclear age the evolution of the prevailing constitutional political and technological deterrence relationship can no longer be seen as referring to illusory universal concepts to be understood and realised only in themselves. It must, instead, be comprehended as the mediating means for the sublation of individual mankind.

Long ago it was gunpowder which constituted a mediative technological content of the historical spirit and its course towards a new form of impersonal universalisation. 'It was one of the chief instruments', Hegel writes, 'in freeing the world from the domination of physical force, and placing the various orders of society on a level.' And the philosopher adds the incomparable sentence: 'Humanity needed it, and it made its appearance forthwith'.[2]

And further, Hegel reflects upon his own time and the French Revolution which constituted the mediative political content of the spirit and its course towards a still higher form of universalised freedom: 'Ours is a birth-time and a period of transition to a new era. Spirit has broken with the world it has hitherto inhabited'.[3] The old mode of thinking, in other words, fades away and, under dialectical pressure, must make room for a new sublating and transforming reflection. And Hegel continues in an unforgettable language: 'The gradual grumbling that left unaltered the face of the whole is cut short by a sunburst which, in one flash, illuminates the features of the new world'.[4]

In its absolute freedom mankind today as well has spiritualised itself into the rational invention of nuclear weapons. According to dialectic it needed them, and they made their appearance forthwith. They, too, have been meaningfully produced in and through the spirit of the time for its own reproducing end. With its life-power mankind has accordingly created once more a new form, a new moment of its phenomenal development, a new concrete sublation of fading pasts.

Ours today is, therefore, also a birth-time and a period of political and technological transition to a new era. Its erstwhile expectations of infinite progress, too, have been illuminated, but not by the sunburst of political reason, but by the nuclear burst of a potentially eliminating technological rationality. The flash of Hiroshima, this negativity of rationality and its greatest limiting and levelling force, has for the first time in human history brought about at least the beginning of a mediated universal consciousness of the possible death of individual mankind.

This may be regarded as the inversion of technological progress. It is its transformation into political regress. Just as the universal of individual political freedoms, as it was inscribed into the credo of the French Revolution, was spurious and turned into terror,[5] so the universal freedom of individual technologies, that was expected with the nuclear revolution, is illusory and therefore has also turned into terror. There is no absolute prediction which is independent of its historical judgment to come. History with its intrinsic dialectic continues to break through the hopes of such rationality. It dissolves their assumptions and makes them available for its further dialectical development and thus also for philosophical comprehension.

Nuclear fear is reinforced by the psychological anxiety about our inability to cope with it. It is theoretically enhanced even more through the rational infinity of the positive feedback mechanism that drives the sciences in near autonomous fashion towards improving the weapons systems and their lethality. Such qualitative changes are always interpreted in mechanistically quantitative, and justified, in turn, in politically ideological terms. In their constant preparations for self-assertion the states are reciprocally directed towards what Clausewitz aptly calls the 'extreme', towards the 'one decisive act', the 'single short blow', that is, towards rational 'totality'.[6] Yet the totalitarianism of nuclear terror, this opposite of holistic reason, is also seen as being benignly balanced by positive sublation. It is managed by the dialectical syndrome of fear and rationality, by the multifarious practice of a mutually reinforcing deterrence relationship, the *cunning of reason*, mankind's latest and perhaps last. Contrary to Clausewitz's admonition, the means of war no longer serve political ends.[7] The states now fade into their system and the survival of mankind is from then on predicated upon the total organisation of the latter's constitution. The former relationship between states and their various systems is in the nuclear age sublated into the higher relationship between the extremes of the states-system and mankind.

But the intrinsic problem with constitutional deterrence is that it is unstable conceptually and contingent notionally. As a phenomenal and theoretical concept it is in-itself problematic and hence philosophically untenable. On the one hand, its rational precepts can at most be approximated but never fully represented. On the other hand, the purpose of systemic deterrence points beyond itself and towards the possible sublation of mankind. It is in consequence of these forms of contingency that the postulate of rational totality turns into an ideologically dangerous totalitarianism. Its meaning therefore is never adequate. Yet as a logical notion deterrence is not self-subsistent either, for its dialectical function is to intend and produce purposefully the actualisation of mankind. Nuclear totalitarianism, however, makes the fulfilment of this task questionable.

Hegel once wrote that 'the universal must always be realised through the particular. Particular things compete with one another; but they also destroy themselves.'[8] That is to say, the system and mankind sublate themselves only in and through the individual states which are their organic composition and spiritual origin. But this is possible only because the states and their relational activities are placed within, and are determined by, the dialectical movement of history. Some may engage in peaceful competition, while others wage the wars of their destruction. Yet these are not mere accidents but dialectical necessities. History then resolves the contradictory claims for legitimacy and denies the states the one-sided and hence tragic assertion of their individual right. It reconciles their incompatible demands and redeems them in the repose of its eternal judgment.

But the question now arises of what happens if within the coherent relationship between the system and mankind mediation becomes atomised? What happens, in other words, if constitutional deterrence fails to function not only according to its rational assumptions, but according to the dialectical role reason has assigned to it? There is, of course, no necessary correlation between nuclear war and the total extinction of humankind. But such a remark is not very helpful for reflection except perhaps to myopic cynics. Cynicism, however, is not an argument, only an escape from directed thinking. So, bearing in mind the difficulty with the proviso of the may-or-may-not, the tragic truism of the answer is that if the *medius terminus* in the syllogism collapses upon itself, both the subject and the object perish. More importantly, however, it means that mankind would then have negated the determination of its own sublation, and as subject would have commited suicide. How is this to be understood dialectically?

Let us briefly go back to what we said about the content of the system or about its differentiation. We described this system, on the one hand, as consisting of all states and, on the other, as referring to the two nuclear superpowers. Now, at any particular historical moment prior to the nuclear age wars between individual members of the all-states system could and did destroy individual states but did not, and could not, destroy the universal system itself. And because the system as a whole was never jeopardised, the survival of mankind remained an understandable rational presupposition. Its future was always envisaged. And it was this, though only formal, understanding of the future of mankind that nourished the hopes of its communal parts. They believed that the historical content, which they thought could be legitimately ascribed to the future, would doubtlessly also be realised.

In the phenomenal world, in other words, we could conduct ourselves *as if* the non-finitude of the life of mankind would continue to exist as an eternal present. And we were enabled to do so precisely because other states or forms of differentiation survived and were transformed into other mediating states and sublated systems. An optimistic attitude was possible because the future-oriented conceptual universalisations, such as religions or ideologies, that were posited by these various forms of differentiation, did not cancel out such extremes. They did not eliminate one another, whatever their rational contradictions. In other words, the dialectic of history did not sharpen enough their differences into totality so as to force a turning point and thereby to threaten the survival of mankind.

The reassuring implication of this was that mankind took itself for granted, as it were, because it always manifested the organic and spiritual power to sublate its systemic forces. In consequence, it could securely assume its continuous actualisation. What happened historically, happened phenomenally only, without its rational axiom being doubted.

Yet this certainty must today not only be questioned. Its past ability to sublate itself will from now on have to be uncertain for the future, as well. The self-determination of the life of mankind is therefore problematic. Consequently, the understanding ought to beware of positing for itself a conceptual, yet always contradictory, total content for the future, a future, moreover, which is usually based on an epistemologically and ideologically convenient reductionism. Within differentiated mankind the aims of the highly valued rational absolutes of particular states bear within themselves not only their own respective justification but also the seed of mutual destruction. Hence the quest for contextual thinking and for holistic reflection is only the quest for intellectual humility.

The philosophical uncertainty has arisen ever since we can conceive the possibility of a nuclear war. In the extreme form of its escalation such a war would very likely not only destroy the world of the two-states system itself, which at present is the most developed rational form of historical differentiation. It would also threaten other atomic weapons states, non-nuclear states and, ultimately, mankind. It is here that Hiroshima constitutes the historical turning point where theoretical reflections on rational progress in science and technology are transformed into the philosophical reflection on mankind and its historical survival. The concern of thinking is no longer only the more-or-less of relations between states, on whatever level of analysis they may be established. It is suddenly either life or death. But when the spirit of history dies the system will then likewise have lost sight of mankind.

In other words, what happens historically in case of a nuclear war happens no longer only between individual members of the system. It happens essentially between the system and mankind. If the dialectic of the mediating constitutional relationship between the United States and the Soviet Union dissolves, so will or might the system of states and with it mankind. But since in dialectical logic mankind is the subject, it will not have sublated itself. It will have perished along with its objective and historical predicates.

Thus the interpretation of the absolute freedom of the logical subject must be that it is not only the freedom to preserve itself. It is the freedom to take its own life as well. Absolute freedom, in other words, is the freedom to live but also to die. In this sense it indifferently applies to beginning and end or, to paraphrase Hegel in a for him unexpected context, to being and to nothing.[9] While the phenomenal and derivative *ought* increases and is therefore responsible to the logical *is*, the *is* itself of logic cannot increase to a superior form of its being. Logic is not responsible for a still higher principle. It is responsible only for itself. Its account is the account of its own becoming. Dialectical logic is not rationally derived from anywhere. It develops internally and therefore revolves about itself. In that it describes itself it describes the secularised sublation and self-salvation of mankind.

But that logic can now dissolve itself through itself is a philosophical consideration that turns Hegelian dialectic into something very problematic indeed.[10] And the problem consists in the possibility of the self-negation of the positive of the double negative. In all pre-nuclear history the development of the syllogism always resulted in the positive of the double negative:

II	(a)	Object	=	Predicate	=	Subject
	(b)	System	=	Constitution	=	Mankind
	(c)	—		—	=	+

But if in atomic warfare the constitution collapses, it no longer mediates mankind but rather negates it. With the collapse of history dialectical self-sublation ends, and the positive of the double negative will essentially have negated itself:

III	—	— (—)	=	—

If mankind annihilates itself, its syllogism will have become self-negation. Contrary to dialectical logic life is then perishable. What follows from this activity is the self-inflicted finality of itself as the infinite. That the philosophical infinite can come to its immanently historical end is within dialectic unforeseeable. The resultant problem for reflection, therefore, cannot be solved with its logic either. But no new philosophical language has yet been devised into which we could mediate and sublate this awesome conclusion. Up to the present moment of historical dialectic mankind was always able to affirm its life through the death of particular members of the spiritual system.[11] But if in its absolute freedom individual mankind commits suicide through the force of the universal system, its death will be the death of death. The genus of life is only through the mediation of its fading species, only through the sublation of its otherness. It is because death knows no opposite that life cannot be.

SUMMARY

In this chapter we have applied Hegel's dialectical method and addressed the issue of mankind's historical sublation and its ultimate self-negation. And we have seen how with the negation of the positive the meaning of nuclear war has clearly brought about its own final conclusion. Thus, after a long and laborious journey through the various venues of dialectical reasoning, we have come to realise that the philosophical uncovering of the theoretical dilemma has led us only to the scientific uncovering of the philosophical dilemma. But, because all language is dialectical, it seems that this dilemma cannot itself be sublated.

The scientific-philosophical implication of nuclear war is therefore no longer merely to do with the issue of what kind of rational answer we can give to the idea of such a war. Since all our hopes are in the end subject to the judgment of history, no such language can provide us with definite solutions either. For this reason our concern with philosophical reflection revolves about a rather much more fundamental problem. For if dialectic can in the age of the atom bring about its own end, then what sort of reasonable question are we still able to ask at all concerning a war into whose possibility we are henceforth born?

From a holistic point of view the continuous survival of the human race cannot be presumed any more to be the result of any deductions made from subjective beliefs in religious or secular utopias. The life of mankind determines itself, and when we look at its history we find that war and peace are the most crucial extremes of humanity's dialectical development.

6 The Dialectical Relation between War and Peace

The dialectical account of history has revealed that a particular form of constitution between states may break down and, as a consequence, destroy the life of mankind. We regard this threat as constant in the nuclear age, an age which is likely to extend itself into the future. Hence the survival of man will continuously remain predicated upon this danger. Since the threat, however, is determined by the alternation between war and peace, it is incumbent upon us to conclude our inquiry with a discussion of these terms and their dialectical meaning.

The experience of war and peace raises two philosophical issues. The first is to do with Hegel's characterisation of war as an idea. An idea signifies a relation, and it is accordingly meaningful to speak about war not when it is analysed as an empirical fact, but only when it is reflected upon in relation to its historical ground. And the second point concerns the concept peace itself and the question of how to approximate this objective when it is approached through the medium of either hope or responsibility.

STATE RELATIONS

In chapter 4 we have specified the state as the phenomenal subject, and we discussed the logical relations between subjects *qua* subjects. Before looking at the problem of war and peace more closely, let us in this section, however, take up the topic of the state once more, but this time with a greater emphasis on the principle of conceptual sovereignty, its dialectical modification and sublation into the notional sovereignty of history.

The state as subject is a phenomenal in-and-for-itself. Accordingly, it can be said with Hegel to be 'individuality'[1] or 'personality'.[2] But in its dialectical formation the state manifests the dialectical principle of 'inner self-development', an expression which very much describes the life of an 'organism'.[3] Seen as an organism the state is constitutionally unified in the sense that its internal social and institutional differentiations are sublated into the universal 'single self'.[4] This self is 'substantive rationality ['Vernünftigkeit' = reason, H. K.] and immediate actuality and is therefore the absolute power on earth. It follows that every state is sovereign and autonomous against its neighbour'.[5]

But as substantive reason the state's absolute power is only formal and abstract and, hence, is inessential. The state, in that it hypothesises itself as absolute singularity, has only a false consciousness of itself. It loses itself in the emanating illusion of absoluteness. In accordance with dialectical logic or, more precisely, in accordance with Hegel's critique of Spinoza's treatment of it, substance must concretise itself historically in order to become a truly self-conscious, and that is essentially a reflected, subject. This transformation is mediated through the state's historically developed 'relation to other states',[6] that is, to other subjects. Expressed differently, the tendency of one state 'to look abroad lies in the fact that it is an individual subject'.[7]

A subject is subject only in and through the sublation of its objectification. This is to say, that the subject state recognises itself as subject only in that it re-flects itself in another state subject which becomes for it the object of reflection. The prefix *re*, as derived from Latin *res*, has in this context two related meanings. It can be interpreted as an object pure and simple. But *re* also signifies the more complex dialectical object in relation to which the subject is reflectively returned and thus mediated to itself. Accordingly, since both subjects are for one another objects (re) they are also for one another the objective historical turning point (re) in their mutual effort to obtain self-consciousness in relation to one another. And this applies indifferently to all subjects. Thus the state's posited sovereignty is necessarily mediated and therefore historically contingent. History dissolves the conceptual assertions of subjective selves and sublates them into the notion of society. Conceptual sovereignty is in its dialectical interpretation one-sided and hence notionally defective. And Hegel, in a clarifying comment, makes the very significant point that 'a state is as little an actual individual without relations to other states as an individual is actually a person without *rapport* with other persons'.[8]

The activity of relating implies negation because in that the subject relates to another subject it relates to an object which is different from what it itself is. Thus negation is not to be confounded with elimination. Instead it is to do with the subject's ability to relate to another subject. But negation understood in this way needs to be positively sublated in order for the subject to know itself as historically identical with itself. But the state at first believes that it relates to another single self, to another state, 'as if' it were something 'external' to it.[9] However, the identification of the state with itself does not come about through its unilateral relation to another state object. Identification is fundamentally reflective in that it is the mutual positive sublation of the double negative. It involves the relationship between two states or two subjects. For this reason, Hegel argues, historical dialectic is 'most supremely' the state's 'own' moment of truth.[10] What is initially believed to be external is after historical sublation or in actuality comprehended as the moment of *recognition*, whereby recognition is the internal essence of the subject's mediated self-identity.

Furthermore, according to our syllogism, state = system = mankind, the logical subject mankind differentiates itself first into its phenomenal object state. For Hegel the object state is the truly and only historical subject. And each subject *qua* subject has the right to decide for itself its own identity. States in the plural are on that account in a 'state of nature', and their individual 'rights are actualized only in their particular wills and not in a universal will with constitutional powers over them'.[11] This universal will would be the rationally posited transcendent law-giver. But the rational *ought*, as we have seen, is fraught with dilemmas which rationality itself cannot overcome. Consequently, Hegel writes that 'since there is no power in existence which decides in face of the state what is right in principle and actualizes this decision, it follows that so far as international relations are concerned we can never get beyond an *ought*. The relation between states is a relation between autonomous entities which make mutual stipulations but which at the same time are superior to these stipulations'.[12] It is the states, or the locus of decision within them, that regulate for themselves their own necessarily dialectical yet always only finite relationships. These relations are substantiated by treaties. But since treaty arrangements are in the last analysis governed only by the *ought* implied in the moral precept of *pacta sunt servanda*, what really happens, therefore, is that 'international relations in accordance with treaty alternate with the severance of these relations'.[13] The *ought* can never be fully realised because the dialectic of history always transforms its expectations into opposites, or into that to which it cannot correspond.

For Hegel there is no *Praetor* to judge between states. At best there may be an arbitrator or a mediator, and even he exercises his functions 'contingently only'.[14] Differentiation implies contingency, and so the relations between states are nothing but mutually conditioned, and are never necessary. Whatever they may agree upon is historically finite. Any consensus, therefore, remains 'infected with contingency'.[15] The only higher judge, Hegel says, is the 'universal absolute mind ['Geist' = spirit, H.K.], the world mind [spirit, H.K.]'.[16]

This world spirit, however, is not a transcendent mind. It is the appearing unity of differentiated history itself, the phenomenal judgment of logical mankind. History is true sovereignty, and as such is notional sovereignty. And it is out of the finitude of state relations that the absolute knowledge of the universal spirit, that is, of the history of mankind, arises. And because it is the subject, whose logical principle is the mediated in-and-for-itself, this knowledge is truly sovereign. It is, to speak with Hegel, 'free from all restrictions, producing itself as that which exercises its right – and its right is the highest right of all – over these finite minds [spirits, H.K.] in the *history of the world which is the world's court of judgement*'.[17] The plurality of finite spirits refers to the states and their historical entailments. It is that into which holistic history has judged and differentiated itself. 'The *goal*', Hegel says, 'Absolute Knowing, or Spirit that knows itself as Spirit, has for its path the recollection of the Spirits as they are in themselves and as they accomplish the organization of their realm'.[18] And 'from the chalice of this realm of spirits foams forth for Him his own infinitude'.[19] This organic infinitude is the eternal historical sublation of mankind as the logical subject. The states in-themselves are nothing unless they are *for* the history of mankind whose infinitude is life itself.

THE IDEA OF WAR

A nuclear war leading to universal death would be a result of the dialectical inversion. It would mean that the sublating power of mankind would not have been able to overcome the negating forces prevalent within the states-system. In their destructiveness these forces would then have ended and therewith finitised the infinitude of mankind.

But the possibility of such an apocalyptic event raises the question as to why war happens at all. An answer to this issue may be attempted with reference to the philosophical reasons Hegel gives for the occurrence of war.

We have stated that it is because of the objectification of mankind into states that these entities necessarily relate to one another as subjects. Now, apart from the specific case of the collapse of deterrence, other forms of interactions logically have the potential of deteriorating or sharpening to an extreme point of dialectical contradiction. In that case the quantitative accumulation over time of the subjectively felt injuries to selfhood transforms the peaceful relations between states into war. This nodal conversion from peace to war is absolute. It allows of no degrees. It is absolute in that it constitutes a qualitative turning point. And from a phenomenal point of view the turning point itself is proof that dialogic and social reason has converted itself back into the assertiveness of particular rationalities which, though only temporarily, have abdicated from that mediative reason.

But because war constitutes a turning point it also offers for the state subject the logical possibility of sublation. In describing the historical meaning of war Hegel writes that it 'is not to be regarded as an absolute evil and as a purely external accident, which itself therefore has some accidental cause, be it injuries, the passions of nations or the holders of power, etc., or in short, something or other which ought not to be'.[1] External accidents are things-in-themselves. But in the absence of a *Praetor* the question as to what a thing-in-itself is cannot be rationally and in this way objectively determined. The justification of a particular war can therefore not be deduced from such a transcendent and spurious point of reference either. It is subjectively contingent upon a state's 'actually injured or threatened welfare as something specific and peculiar to itself'.[2]

Instead of being a thing-in-itself, a war is *for* the actualisation of the state. The state subject in-and-for-itself is mediated through war which, within the dialectical scheme, is its first and necessary negation. But it is through the second and equally necessary negation – the reflective mediation towards peace – that the state is intentionally sublated. Thus war and peace are not only intrinsically related to one another. They are also the necessary historical and formative moments of the state. But, as we shall see in the following section, unlike peace, war serves a purpose in a dialectically much more explicit way. Though it is at first a negative instance, it is positively directed towards the preservation of the state subject.

Hegel clarifies his remarks on war by saying that:

> it is to what is by nature accidental that accidents happen, and the fate whereby they happen is thus a necessity. Here as elsewhere,

> the point of view from which things seem pure accidents vanishes if we look at them in the light of the concept [notion, H.K.] and philosophy, because philosophy knows accidents for a show and sees in it its essence, necessity.[3]

Phenomenal and concrete wars are philosophically interpreted as conceptual ideas in-themselves, or as particular accidents. But these cannot be meaningfully reflected upon except in relation to their notional whole. And this philosophical notion comprehends the rational form of war which is a historical content both of the relations between states and, ultimately, between the system of states and mankind.

Wars, then, are accidents and as such must be judged as fading moments in history. Their particular occurrence is intermittent and discontinuous. The finite, says Hegel, 'should be definitely established as accidental, because accidentality is the concept [sic, H.K.] of the finite'.[4] And if particular wars are accidental and finite, that is, phenomenally contingent, they also 'ought to pass away'.[5] Particular wars may or may not take place. Yet, if they are fought, the principle of dialectical sublation renders the conceptual *ought* into the mediative proviso that 'the possibility of peace be retained'.[6] Thus war is not in-itself a necessity. But once inter-state contradiction has given way to it, war will, for dialectical reasons, have become a necessity for state sublation.

The possibility of peace is recognised also in another way. For Hegel states are individual wills that assume the status of persons. As such they have rights. But, dialectically speaking, rights imply the simultaneity of obligations, namely, the reciprocal acknowledgement of rights which states give to themselves and their mutual relations. Accordingly, just as the state claims for itself the rational right to be recognised by others as a legitimate subject, so it ought to 'respect their autonomy', as well.[7] This principle is the corollary of Hegel's high regard for the individual human being, for whom the imperative 'be a person and respect others as persons', equally applies.[8] But Hegel also argues that the ought of rationality is not in and of itself fulfilled. It is dialectically contingent. Not only does recognition depend upon one's own historically developed internal constitution. In a much more crucial way it is dependent upon the subjective and discretionary will of others. Consequently, and again with reference to states, one cannot on rational grounds dismiss Hegel's conclusion that, 'if states disagree and the particular wills cannot be harmonized, the matter can only be settled by war'.[9]

The philosopher does not advocate that states engage in wars as a wilful and arbitrary instrument of policy. The employment of the hypothetical and contingent *if* in the above quotation indicates that war and state are not equivalents. The state is confronted with a multitude of 'chance events coming from without'.[10] Such events allow for the conduct of inter-state relations in a variety of calmer ways. One of them, a real war, however, may have to be regarded as the state's moment of truth, its last resort and the *ultima ratio* of its need as subject to sublate and preserve its integrity. But while the threat and danger of war are thus a source of the state's negation as the first condition for the positive awakening of its self-consciousness, war is not to be seen as the only source of the state to secure its continuous existence. At the same time, we cannot avoid the other argument either, namely, that there would be no necessary dialectic of history if it were not for the contingent interplay between war and peace.

The formal assertion of a state subject to possess the attribute of the freedom to act is dialectically one-sided, conceptually vacuous and politically even perilous. It is not only qualified by the mediating relationships it must necessarily enter into. In its insistent effort to protect a merely rational freedom, the state also runs the risk of losing it historically. Freedom implies the risk and responsibility for existence. But the assessment of risk requires an acute awareness of dialectic and, consequently, of circumspection. The description of contingency does not mean that any kind of war, waged at any time is for any reason justified.[11] Since the necessity of sublation comprehends the contingency of war, the latter is clearly subordinate to the former. This end of the state is historically mediated identity which, in turn, is to express itself within its internal and free social existence. It can also be described as a principle of ethics that guides the moral actions of persons towards their social or communal 'duty to maintain this substantive individuality', that is, the phenomenal subject state.[12] The state is only in rationality a free abstratum. Dialectically speaking, however, it is a concrete historical subject whose internal substance consists of the members of its developed community and its institutions. The community essentially mediates its members towards the state that in modernity is said to be alone the potentiality for actualising the idea of its inner freedom.

But, because a state exists only in that it externalises itself into relations with other states, its asserted peace, which is to be established as the possibility for freedom, is not always historically but logically threatened by war. In order to sublate itself, the state's decision to go to war is the decision to risk its very existence. However, freedom is freedom only if it is protected freedom, which is to say, that apart from war and peace, peace and freedom are themselves dialectically related. The freedom of the individual needs the security of the state in which it is embedded and through which it is socially mediated. The free actualisation of the state is ultimately fulfilled only when the freedom of all its members is actualised.[13] It is therefore its task not to jeopardise this telos, but to protect and to promote it. And, in accordance with this view, Hegel unambiguously states that the descriptive necessity of war is only a 'philosophic idea', and that, in fact, 'actual wars require some other justification'.[14] But these other attempts to justify a particular war must in the nuclear age first take cognisance of the responsibility for the whole, because it is the idea of holism that imbues the parts with life. Any war between states, therefore, which threatens mankind is counter to the very logic of dialectical mediation and self-sublation.

THE RESPONSIBILITY FOR PEACE

We have argued that the consequences of an atomic war would endanger the life and future of mankind, but that such an act, if ever perpetrated, would also be against the insight of dialectical reasoning. Since we can realistically discuss these likely effects only from the standpoint of the states, any further dialogue that is to embrace the part-whole relationship, that is, the relationship between nuclear weapons states and humanity, must now also address the subject matter of the hope and responsibility for peace. Accordingly, we shall in the following paragraphs thematise the logical structure of this question. Though we apply the term peace to the relationship between states, peace itself is a condition which is to be established not only between and for the states. Since the states are now situated in the history of the nuclear age, their efforts for peace are fundamentally made within their systemic organisation but intended *for* mankind, their one and only true *place* of ethos.

We recall that our study of dialectic began with a discussion of the inherent structure of the Platonic dialogue. One of the results of that investigation was that dialectical thinking precludes the possibility of us ever arriving at lasting definitions. If this is the case then it is equally difficult to see now how the idea of peace, a concept which we are all able to utter in dialogic language, can itself legitimately be given *the* globally universal and not just a particular meaning which would only be regionally applicable. People and states speak of peace. Yet this form of expected harmony is always dialogically advanced with a different understanding of its theoretical content and with different proposals for the practical means of its approximation.

As Plato has taught us, the unilateral theoretical assertion of a mere name itself is not enough for it to be grasped ontologically, let alone for its historical correspondence to be established in practice. Every idea is dialectically qualified into different and all too often eristic interpretations. They are intrinsically aporistic and, to use a Kantian distinction, at most regulative and never constitutive. Principles that are too abstract invariably break down when we come to defining them concretely and to carrying them out within political contexts. The conceptual form of a word is only a result of the activity of a hypothesising mind. But once this empty form of the word begins to be filled with the history of its development, its content necessarily becomes dialectically differentiated and forever problematic. And no form of moral indignation and sentiment can sublate in and of itself this rational dilemma.

Another conclusion of the above analysis is the following point. If no man-made and universally accepted concept of peace can be defined for the states-system, and if there is no transcendent and divine *Praetor* above the system either, adjusting the manifold relations between the states according to His own divine precepts, there exists then also no community in the traditional and religious sense, but only a society of states. There cannot be a communal system of states whose collected moral life is vertically mediated to and sublated by the unity of a transcendent and rationally believed-in ethos. Mankind, to which alone the states-system relates, is a philosophical notion and not a sort of conceptual divinity from which we can deduce moral prescriptions for our actions. What we find, instead, is a horizontally and functionally organised society of self-interested state subjects whose failure to express their subjective *will* to establish a sense of self-identity would spell their dissolution as subjects. One of the most intractable problems for philosophical reflection is, therefore, the articulation of the relationship between will and morality in the absence of a universally agreed ethos.

This interpretation of self-interest makes it doubtful that there will ever be written a political philosophy which thematises the dialectic between the states-system and mankind in a similar way as the previous traditions of contract theory have dealt with the relationship between citizens and their polity. Neither is it therefore likely that there will be legitimately established an ethical order for humanity to which the system is to belong on the basis of a moral faculty presumed to be intrinsic to it. The states-system cannot be regarded as a type of polis or religious gathering in the classical and medieval sense. Mankind itself is not determined by anything transcendent, but only in and through itself. Hence it contains no definite rational purpose either which the system ought to approximate.

It may be fitting to dwell for a moment on this point. In the past the way towards achieving the *good* of humanity was guided by many different prescriptions, and the idea of the good itself was always saturated with religious, metaphysical or ideological value meanings.[1] Aristotle, for instance, to refer here to only one source, writes that 'a state exists for the sake of a good life, and not for the sake of life only'.[2] In other words, the reference to life implies that its nature can be considered valuable only if it is given a spiritual content. Life itself *qua* existence is not a value. It is or is not, but it cannot be approximated. But what value content, one feels immediately inclined to ask today, are we still able to adduce to the *good* if we want to express with it humanity? Not only do we experience the gradual demise of understanding the *good* in its traditional sense. But we are also virtually lost in despair in the light of our increasing awareness of the inherent dialectical differentiation of the *good* as concept, whether this differentiation is manifest in religious, metaphysical or ideological deliberations on it, or in the attempt to realise it in practice. The *good*, like peace before, is theoretically and practically indeterminable. As antiquity, so will modernity and the age of nuclear weapons remain without a philosopher king.

One further implication of Hegelian philosophy emerges from the above. It touches on the relationship between hope and responsibility. Although this very important issue warrants a much broader discussion, it may nonetheless be helpful to present here in outline at least some of the questions it raises. It is clear from what we have found out about the dialectic between past and present, that the terms hope and responsibility – since they express what ought to be in the future – fall somewhat outside a Hegelian concern with the philosophical description of that relationship. On the other hand, in applying Hegel's method to the endeavour to notionalise mankind, we are required to employ both hope and responsibility, and analyse these attitudes with reference to the question of what is ultimately threatened in our time.

We have so far inquired into the antinomial dilemma one is confronted with when looking at the consequences of conceptual thinking. But, of course, from the point of view of Hegel's historical dialectic, all conceptual dichotomies are sublated by the notion. The result of the latter's activity is that, in dialectical discourse, it is not legitimate to posit a transcendent, in the sense of an extraneous, source of redemption for the states, because such a source is not demonstrable. Being an immanently mediating phenomenon the society of states is only organically, that is, internally notionalised by the logical subject mankind. And mankind, we remember, is the notion in-and-for-itself and not an external concept in-itself but for another, still higher, principle of reflection. Although we wish to believe that mankind ought to correspond to what we may posit for it – this, however, is not the province of a Hegelian-like dialectic. Mankind is historically actualised in and through the states-system alone. It stands in a generically necessary relationship to this system and the states which make up this system.

In considering this issue more specifically, we think that what the nuclear age has inscribed into man's conscience is not only and not so much the rational *principle of hope*.[3] The philosophical need of the time has made it instead necessary to raise this concept to the level of dialectical reason, and to sublate it into the notional *principle of responsibility*.[4] Hope is a passive sentiment. It presupposes a consciousness of the future, and is the very expression of particularistic rationality. In addition, it knows no task either because it emanates from the subjectivity of individuality whose sole concern is to secure and justify its own salvation. Responsibility, by contrast, implies an awareness of consequential activity. It is fundamentally dialectical and hence social in nature. And because it is a social experience, responsibility cannot be comprehended except as a task. The assignment is to be responsive to others in and through whom alone the self can reflect and recognise itself. And since the identity of the self is thus contingent upon otherness, responsibility constitutes the mediative development towards a holistic social self-consciousness. Such a comprehensive consciousness is the very condition for individual security and its sublation. The relationship between hope and responsibility is, therefore, analogous to the general part-whole relationship in which the latter subsumes the former. Without the responsibility to a mankind which is threatened with extinction, the hopes for its humanity remain devoid of social meaning.

Although directed towards the sublation of historical self-consciousness, responsibility today, however, comprehends itself in its sudden fragility. And it is with the heightened sensitisation to this awareness that the states try to mediate responsibly – and that is reciprocally – their equally vulnerable hopes for a peaceful humanity and posit it for mankind. In conscious responsibility the states respond to the inner call of life to preserve itself. It is the life within whose reflected sublation we are reconciled and truly at home. The life of mankind is without horizon, and hence is mankind's only actual peace (Um-friedung). And peace, understood in this restricted sense, makes possible first of all the protection of the history of the real freedom of human individuality. Yet, at the same time, we are in no position to predict or to know with necessity what the content of the actuality of life will be in any future present. No hypothesised future is determinate. And because of this rational indeterminacy, which renders the wisdom of our actions uncertain, we always ought to beware of the means we employ in the pursuit of fulfilling the life to come.[5]

But it is precisely at this juncture, where the states-system and mankind meet, that a distinctly new ethical problem arises. For the questions are now: who in the part-whole relationship is in fact the agent of responsibility, and how are we to formulate the conditions for nuclear peace?[6] Is mankind responsible for itself, or is it the system that is answerable to mankind? Since we can argue about holism only from the standpoint of the state and not from that of mankind itself, we can argue for it also only from the standpoint of rationality, fully cognisant, however, that this view carries with it insoluble implications.

Let us analyse this question in a more dialectical manner. According to Hegel, for instance, it is the people who are responsible for the state upon which they, in turn, depend for the protection of their freedoms.[7] On the other hand, to talk about the protection or security of the state is meaningful only because the state claims to be one sovereign individuality among other such asserted sovereignties. This is what differentiation expresses, namely, the existence of a plurality of states that have this characteristic of formal personality. In other words, in relation to other states, a particular state is responsible only for its own protection and not for that of another state. But in actuality, of course, such self-protection is always dialectically mediated through other states. The protection of the self is thus necessarily related to the protection of the other. In consequence, sovereignty does not reside in the extremes, but is sublated in the historical relations which mediate them to one another. By the same token, the establishment of peace is possible only within a differentiated system. Peace, like war, describes a dialectical relation and, therefore, comes to stand between states and not over and above one state or family of states alone. But are we justified now in saying that mankind is responsible for its own protection in the same way as a particular state is self-responsible? And does it make sense at all to speak of the peace of mankind?

It seems that in the present age we are faced with a novel existential experience. But the philosophical problem it poses can no longer be solved with reference to the traditional and rationally posited language of the peace of mankind. Such peace, in any case, we have always only paid lip-service to. But its necessity has never been reasoned through, let alone cogently demonstrated. For, on reflection, it is meaningless to say that mankind is responsible for protecting itself from the threat of a nuclear holocaust. Rather, it is the states that are responsible *for* humanity and *to* the life of mankind, because it is these historical phenomena, and the nuclear regime they have created, that are its manifestation. While the states know each other as objects, and are mutually conditioned, mankind does not mediate and sublate itself in and through another subject mankind, to which it dialectically relates as to an object. It does not know a historical relationship that would allow it to be recognised by something external to it. From this point of view mankind is unconditioned. Consequently, mankind is not a historical agent either. The term agency implies intentionality which is directed only towards and can affect only another agency. In a social context intentionality always involves at least one other subject. But another cosmic subject equal and meaningfully close enough to our planetary mankind does not exist. To put it differently: the externality of inter-state relations alone constitutes the content of the internal self-relation of mankind. Only historical phenomena such as states can enter into relations with other state subjects, and recognise each other in these relations. What results from these considerations is that the nuclear states may be said to be not only accountable to the history of mankind but also before its judgment. Mankind judges itself into states without which we, who exist as their substantive social content, are not. And hence it is because we *are* history that we cannot escape the responsibility to mankind either. While the organic whole may very well continue to live without particular parts, these cannot exist at all without the becoming of the whole itself. For without the *willed* responsibility to the life of mankind, whose history is the manifestation of its immanent dialectic, we cannot even hope to begin the dialogue about the good for mankind's humanity.

SUMMARY

According to the logic of dialectic states must externalise themselves into reciprocal relations. Depending on their content these interactions may or may not terminate in war. But since in philosophical reflection the history of relations between states is a dialectical necessity, the possibility of future wars is necessary, as well.

War is to be sublated in peace. Both terms acquire meaning only within the context of a dialectically differentiated world. In the history of such a world neither particular wars nor peace arrangements are lasting phenomena.

This situation, however, becomes problematic in the nuclear age, not only because we might not have the practical means to sublate it into peace. It is also perplexing because any dialogue about peace itself, which must from now on comprehend mankind as a whole, is subject to conceptual differentiation. That is why it is so difficult to express it in a universal understanding.

Conclusion

Our life-world is threatened by the possibility of a nuclear war. In its final implications this threat, which is posed by the relationship between inter-state policies, affects the whole of mankind, its global environment and, consequently, the totality of its historical developments as well. In order to comprehend the full meaning of an act that might end human history we need a method of philosophical reflection which notionalises the experience of the present in relation to its past. The only approach which makes the thinking of such historical holism legitimate in the nuclear age is provided by dialectic.

The reality of the life-world we seek to comprehend is neither a factual or transcendent world out there. Nor, indeed, is our knowledge of an assumed epistemological objectivity based upon an inner subjectivity. The position of a transcendental ground has itself been judged untenable. The reality of the human world can, instead, be adequately described only in the dialectical form of relation. The idea of relation dissolves all rational assertions of givenness and renders them alive in the medium of historical reason. It expresses the continuous unity between subject and object. More specifically, it creates the spiritual union between the present and its past.

The problem we must deal with in our time concerns man himself, the subject, whose historical life has become the object of his reflections. Dialectical thinking is ultimately the mode of thinking in which man's consciousness of history is mediated and transformed into man's history becoming conscious of itself.

Historical dialectic, which describes the becoming of self-consciousness, was first thought through in all its consequences by Hegel. In his reasoning Hegel demonstrates how the Platonic dialogue about, and Aristotle's scientific thinking of, objects external to the subject is in modernity actually sublated in the communal effort of man to think himself identical with his own history and all the practical and theoretical work that has been accomplished in it. It is this comprehensive aspect of the subject/object relation that makes Hegel's philosophy still the best and most important guide for learning about dialectic, in general, and about the dialectic of mankind, in particular. But lest it become maimed in the age of scientific fragmentation, the dialectical manner of reflecting requires the caring practice of holistic education. The principle of *e-ducere* not only teaches us to think in historical perspectives, but thereby also to admit of intellectual humility.

Dialectic can certainly not in and of itself prevent the outbreak of a nuclear war. But without a Hegelian disposition we cannot make sense of our threatened existence either. Without the study of Hegel our deliberations on the human life-world are reduced to positivistic fact-thinking, to the myopic minds of paradigms, or even to the anarchic hedonism of liberalism. We firmly believe, therefore, that an insight into Hegel's philosophic wisdom, together with a critique of the modern forms of theorising about our knowledge claims, is indispensable and must come prior to any so-called rational attempt to conceive of a future and to think out a praxis for it, a praxis whose content already is largely drained of its erstwhile sense of humanity. In other words, if we want to guide the present into the future, the present must first be contextually related to the historical content of its past. Only upon such a reflection can the future gain in meaning.

History is the actualised present life of mankind whose past futures could always be envisaged during times of war. And with this certainty it was, therefore, also always possible for the particular religious and ideological hopes and beliefs, which are all expressions of a historically differentiated humanity, to unfold themselves in and through dialogues.

But in a thoroughly scientificated life-world the presupposed historical continuum of past, present and future is beyond rational comprehension. Dialectical thinking makes it impossible for us to tell into what direction the whole of human history will develop. The precise path of the future cannot be predicted. Any predication of what man is to be is therefore problematic. But, moreover, in an increasingly technologised world, in which some states have appropriated all forces of nuclear destruction, not even the present future can be taken for granted any more.

The vision of atomic warfare and the idea of the self-inflicted finality of mankind make us all too aware of the fragility of the relationship between the present and humanity's self-image in history. As we have tried to show in this book, though life is reflectively actualised in every present, all its reality is nothing but a historically contingent experience. If only the present is, the past no more, and the future not yet, our consciousness of the life to come will accordingly also only be the consciousness of uncertainty. The philosophical unity of the dialectical history of mankind, which strives to become conscious of itself, is therefore related to and, indeed, dependent upon man's broken thinking. Always to bear this in mind, always to realise that all dialogues must end in dilemmas, and still remain hopeful for the future – this is our responsibility.

This conclusion is inescapable. But whether the ethical consciousness of mankind and the political will of the bearers of states are able to act in accordance with the understanding of historical contingency, and thus to withstand its forces of self-annihilation, cannot be determined. The life of mankind is not redeemed from outside the realm of human existence, and from within it has preserved its humanity only in the barely reflected consciousness of the present.

Abbreviations

ARISTOTLE

An. Post.	*Posterior Analytics*
An. Pr.	*Prior Analytics*
De Part. An	*Parts of Animals*
EE	*Eudemian Ethics*
Met.	*Metaphysics*
Nic. Eth.	*Nicomachean Ethics*
On Gen & Corr.	*On Generation and Corruption*
	On the Heavens
Phys.	*Physics*
Pol.	*Politics*
Rhet.	*Rhetoric*
SE	*Sophistical Refutations*
Top.	*Topics*

FEYERABEND

AM	*Against Method*
Emp.	'Problems of Empiricism'
How	'How to be a Good Empiricist'
PE	*Problems of Empiricism*
RRSM	*Realism, Rationalism and Scientific Method*
SFS	*Science in a Free Society*

HEGEL

HL	*Hegel's Logic*
HLHP I–III	*Hegel's Lectures on the History of Philosophy*, vols I–III
HPM	*Hegel's Philosophy of Mind*
HPN	*Hegel's Philosophy of Nature*
HPR	*Hegel's Philosophy of Right*
HSL	*Hegel's Science of Logic*
Lectures	*Lectures on the Philosophy of World History – Introduction*

LPR I	Lectures on the Philosophy of Religion, vol. I
PH	*The Philosophy of History*
PS	*Phenomenology of Spirit*
Diff.	*Differenz des Fichte'schen und Schelling'schen Systems der Philosophie*
L I–II	*Wissenschaft der Logik*, vols I–II
PG	*Phänomenologie des Geistes*
SW	*Sämtliche Werke*
VG	*Die Vernunft in der Geschichte*
VPW II–IV	*Vorlesungen über die Philosophie der Weltgeschichte*

KANT

CPR	*Critique of Pure Reason*
KRV	'Kritik der Reinen Vernunft'

KUHN

ET	*The Essential Tension*
LDPR	'Logic of Discovery or Psychology of Research?'
RC	'Reflections on my Critics'
SSR	*The Structure of Scientific Revolutions*

PLATO

Crat.	*Cratylus*
Crit.	*Critias*
Gorg.	*Gorgias*
	Laws
	Letters
Parm.	*Parmenides*
	Phaedo
Phaedr.	*Phaedrus*
Phil.	*Philebus*
Prot.	*Protagoras*
Rep.	*Republic*
Soph.	*Sophists*
Statesm.	*Statesman*
Symp.	*Symposium*
Theaet.	*Theaetetus*

POPPER

CR	*Conjectures and Refutations*
LSD	*The Logic of Scientific Discovery*
OK	*Objective Knowledge*
PH	*The Poverty of Historicism*
OS I–II	*The Open Society and its Enemies*, vols I–II
Replies	'Replies to my Critics'

References

INTRODUCTION

1. Hegel: HSL, p. 25; L I, pp. 3–4.
2. Ibid, HSL, p. 25; L I, p. 4.
3. Ibid, HSL, p. 42; L I, p. 22.
4. Hegel: PS, p. 44; PG, p. 58.
5. Polybius, *The Rise of the Roman Empire*, p. 43.
6. Clausewitz, C.v., *On War*, pp. 79–80.
7. Bosanquet, B., *The Introduction to Hegel's Philosophy of Fine Art*, p. xix.
8. Hegel: PS, p. 43; PG, pp. 56–7.

CHAPTER 1

Plato's Dialectical Dialogue

1. Plato: Rep. 534b9.
2. Ibid, Soph. 253b10–12.
3. Ibid, Soph. 235c1.
4. Ibid, Soph. 253c6–d3.
5. Ibid, Rep. 534e2–4.
6. Bubner, R., *Zur Sache der Dialektik*, p. 128.
7. Plato, Soph. 253c8.
8. Gundert, H., *Dialog und Dialektik*, p. 6.
9. Marten, R., *Der Logos der Dialektik*, pp. 30–44: Gadamer. H.-G., *Truth and Method*, pp. 325–41; Gundert, H. op. cit.
10. Plato: Prot. 336c1–2.
11. Ibid, Rep. 534b5–6.
12. Ibid, Parm. 136c3.
13. Ibid, Rep. 534d9–10.
14. Ibid, Letter VII, 344b1–7.
15. Gadamer, H.-G., *Dialogue and Dialectic*, p. 52.
16. Ibid, *Truth and Method*, p. 328.
17. Plato: Soph. 234c6–d7.
18. Ibid, Soph. 259e4–260a2.
19. Ibid, Crat. 390c10–11.
20. Bubner, R., *Zur Sache der Dialektik*, p. 134.
21. Marten, R., op. cit., p. 31.
22. Robinson, R., *Plato's Earlier Dialectic*, p. 77
23. Plato: Symp. 175d2–4.
24. Ibid, Phil. 20a1–5.
25. Gundert, H., op. cit., p. 5.
26. Gadamer, H.-G., *Truth and Method*, pp. 325–33.
27. Plato: Parm. 137b5.

28. Ibid, Parm. 137b11–12.
29. Marten, R., op. cit., p. 33.
30. Plato: Soph. 264a11.
31. Ibid, Theaet. 189e6–190a6.
32. Ibid, Rep. 534b3–5.
33. Ibid, Rep. 531e4–6.
34. Ibid, Rep. 511e1.
35. Marten, R., op. cit., p. 37.
36. Plato: Gorg. 486d2–4.
37. Ibid, Theaet. 201d1–3.
38. Ibid, Soph. 218c1–7.
39. Ibid, Gorg. 489e6– 7.
40. Ibid, Rep. 474b6.
41. Marten, R., op. cit., p. 162.
42. Plato: Theaet. 196d8–13.
43. Ibid, Phil. 13e9–10.
44. Ibid, Phil. 14b6–8.
45. Ibid, Soph. 224e–226a.
46. Hegel: HLHP II, p. 52; SW 18, p. 225.
47. Ibid. HLHP II, p. 53; SW 18, p. 227.
48. Ibid, HLHP II, p. 67; SW 18, p. 237.
49. Plato: Phaedo 100b6–7.
50. Ibid, Laws X, 895dff.
51. Ibid, Rep. 533b8–c2.
52. Ibid, Phaedo 101d3–e.
53. Ibid, Rep. 531cd; Robinson, R., op. cit., p. 75 and Marten, R., op. cit., p. 233.
54. Robinson, R., ibid, p. 77.
55. Hegel: HLHP II, p. 50; SW 18, p. 224.
56. Plato: Rep. 511b3–c2.
57. Ibid, Rep. 534b8–9.
58. Hegel: HLHP II, p. 51; SW 18, p. 225.
59. Ibid, HLHP II, p. 68; SW 18, p. 237.
60. Plato: Rep. 537c1–3.
61. Ibid, Rep. 537c7–8.
62. Ibid, Parm, 129d5–6.
63. Cornford, F. M., *Plato's Theory of Knowledge*, pp. 184–6.
64. Plato: Soph. 226c3–9.
65. Ibid, Phaedr. 265d4–e2.
66. Ibid, Soph. 253d1–e.
67. Stenzel, J., *Plato's Method of Dialectic*, p. 23.
68. Hegel: HLHP II, p. 52; SW 18, p. 226.
69. Plato: Phaedr. 265e3–266a2.
70. Ibid, Statesm. 262a1–2.
71. Ibid, Statesm. 262b1–11.
72. Ibid, Statesm. 263b10–12.
73. Ibid, Statesm. 285b1–5.
74. Ibid, Rep. 436b8–10; Bloom A., 'Interpretive Essay', p. 457n. 25; Crombie, I. M., *An Examination of Plato's Doctrines*, vol. II, p. 392.

75. Hegel: HLHP II, p. 61; SW 18, p. 245.
76. Habermas, J., *Knowledge and Human Interest*, pp. 191–213, 301–317.
77. Robinson, R., op. cit., p. 82.
78. Plato: Soph. 216a1.
79. Ibid, Crit. 106b4–5.
80. Hegel: HLHP II, p. 60; SW 18, p. 244.
81. Ibid, HLHP II, p. 70; SW 18, p. 274.

Aristotle's Dialectical Deduction

1. Stigen, A., *The Structure of Aristotle's Thought*.
2. Aristotle: On Gen. & Corr. 336b25.
3. Ibid, On Gen. & Corr, 336b12–13.
4. Aristotle: Pol. 1329b24–30.
5. Ibid, On the Heavens 270b19–20.
6. Ibid, Met. 1074b1–2.
7. Ibid, Met. 1074b10–14.
8. Ibid, Met. 993b20–23.
9. Ibid, De Part. An. 639b18–20.
10. Hegel: HSL, p. 34; L I, p. 12.
11. Aristotle: Met. 982b11ff.
12. Ibid, Met. 983a13–18.
13. Ibid, Met. 993a30–b7.
14. Ibid, Top. 101a35–37.
15. Ibid, Met. 1027b29–36.
16. Ibid, Met. 1051b3–5.
17. Ibid, Met. 993b10.
18. Ibid, Met. 993b12–15.
19. Ibid, Met. 995a12–14.
20. Stigen, A., op. cit., p. 68.
21. Aristotle: Nic. Eth. 1095a31–32.
22. Ibid, Nic. Eth. 1095b1–3.
23. Hegel: PS, p. 18; PG, p. 28.
24. Aristotle: Phys. 184a10–21.
25. Evans, J. D. G., *Aristotle's Concept of Dialectic*, p. 6.
26. Aristotle: An. Pr. 24a26.
27. Ibid, An. Pr. 24a11.
28. Ibid, Met. 1004b25.
29. Ibid, An. Pr. 46a29–30.
30. Ibid, Top. 101b3–4.
31. Evans, J. D. G., op. cit., p. 49.
32. Aristotle: An. Pr. 24a22–25.
33. Ibid. Top. 100a26–30.
34. Ibid, Top. 100a30–32.
35. Ibid, Top. 100b22.
36. Ibid, An. Post. 76b5–6.
37. Ibid, An. Post. 72a9–10.
38. Ibid, An. Post. 73a24; Rose, L.E., *Aristotle's Syllogistic*, p. 10 n. 25.
39. Evans, J. D. G., op. cit., p. 5.

40. Aristotle: Top. 101a25–b4.
41. Elders, L., 'The "Topics" and the Platonic Theory of Principles of Being', p. 129.
42. Aristotle: Top. 101a37–38.
43. Solmsen, F., 'Dialectic without the Forms', p. 54.
44. Ibid. p. 55.
45. Plato: Statesm. 287b2–4.
46. Solmsen, F., op. cit., p. 55.
47. Aristotle: An. Pr. 24b19–22.
48. Rose, L. E., op. cit.
49. Aristotle: Top. 120b9–11.
50. Ibid, Top. 143b24.
51. Ibid, Top. 105b32–33.
52. Solmsen, F., op. cit., p. 57.
53. Evans, J. D. G., op. cit., p. 12.
54. Aristotle: An. Pr. 74b22–26.
55. Solmsen, F., op. cit., p. 61.
56. Aristotle: Top. 100a20.
57. Lloyd, A. C., 'Genus, Species and Ordered Series in Aristotle', pp. 67ff.
58. Plato: Statesm. 261d3–4, 262b5.
59. Aristotle: Top. 103a31, 151b25ff.
60. Solmsen, F., op. cit., p. 64.
61. Aristotle: An. Pr.
62. Stenzel, J., op. cit., p. 168
63. Aristotle: Top. 158a35–36.
64. Ibid, Top. 104a11–12.
65. Ibid, An. Pr. 24a20ff.
66. Ross, W. D., *Aristotle*, p. 59.
67. Hegel: HLHP II, p. 221; SW 18, p. 413.
68. Kant: CPR, A 61.
69. Ibid, A 61.
70. Ibid, A. 61.
71. Aristotle: SE, 170a21–23.
72. Solmsen, F., op. cit., p. 59.
73. Moraux, P., 'La joute dialectique d'après le huitième livre des Topiques', p. 279.
74. Solmsen, F., op. cit., p. 59.
75. Owen, G. E. L., 'Dialectic and Eristic in the Treatment of the Forms', p. 104.
76. Aristotle: Rhet. 1354a2–3.
77. Ibid, Rhet. 1354a5–6.
78. Hegel: HSL, p. 51; L I, p. 32.
79. Ibid, PS, p. 40; PG, p. 53.
80. Bubner, R., op. cit., p. 127.
81. Weiss, F. G., *Hegel's Critique of Aristotle's Philosophy of Mind*, p. xxiii.
82. Hegel: HLHP II, p. 222; SW 18, p. 413.
83. Ibid, PS, p. 40; PG, p. 53.
84. Hegel: HLHP II, p. 223; SW 18, p. 415.

CHAPTER 2

Popper's Objective Dialectic of Falsification

1. Popper: LSD, p. 47.
2. Ibid, LSD, p. 97.
3. Ibid, PH, pp. 26–7.
4. Ibid, LSD, p. 107n.
5. Bubner, R., *Dialektik und Wissenschaft*, p. 134.
6. Popper: LSD, p. 98.
7. Ibid, LSD, p. 314.
8. Ibid, 'Replies', p. 1020.
9. Ibid, 'Replies', p. 991.
10. Carnap, R., *The Logical Structure of the World* .
11. Popper: LSD, p. 50.
12. Ibid, LSD, p. 280.
13. Kant: CPR, B 26.
14. Ibid, CPR, B 317.
15. Popper: CR, p. 129.
16. Ibid, LSD, p. 16.
17. Ibid, CR, p. 215.
18. Ibid, CR. p. 248.
19. Ibid, CR, pp. 228ff.
20. Ibid, OK, pp. 112, 106ff.
21. Ibid, LSD, p. 314.
22. Ibid, CR, pp. 120–35; OS II, p. 97.
23. Ibid, LSD, p. 108.
24. Ibid, OS, II, p. 231.
25. Ibid, OS II, pp. 225, 231.
26. Kant: CPR, B xxx; B 848–58.
27. Popper: CR, pp. 312–35.
28. Ibid, CR, p. 313 n. 2.
29. Ibid, OK, p. 21.
30. Ibid, CR, p. 222.
31. Ibid, CR, pp. 312ff.
32. Bubner, R., *Dialektic und Wissenschaft*, p. 142.
33. Feyerabend: RRSM, pp. 199–201.
34. Inwood, M. J., *Hegel*, p. 550 n. 100.
35. Hegel: HSL, p. 443; L II, p. 62.
36. Ibid, HSL, pp. 439–40; L II, pp. 58–9.
37. Ibid, PS, p. 41; PG, p. 55.
38. Aristotle: Met. 993b12–15.
39. Popper: CR, pp. 216–17.
40. Ibid, OK, p. 70.
41. Freedman, L., *The Evolution of Nuclear Strategy*, p. 178.
42. Popper: CR, p. 216.
43. Hegel: Lectures, p. 21; VG, p. 19.

Kuhn's Subjective Dialectic of Paradigms

1. Kuhn: RC, p. 236.
2. Ibid, ET, p. 18.
3. Ibid, SSR, pp. 160ff.
4. Ibid, RC, p. 242.
5. Ibid, SSR, p. 10.
6. Ibid, SSR, p. 178.
7. Masterman, M., 'The Nature of a Paradigm', p. 69.
8. Kuhn: SSR, p. 24.
9. Ibid, SSR, p. 179.
10. Ibid, SSR, p. 24.
11. Ibid, SSR, p. 49.
12. Ibid, SSR, p. 94.
13. Ibid, SSR, p. 180.
14. Ibid, ET, p. 295.
15. Laudan, L., *Progress and its Problems*, p. 74.
16. Kuhn: SSR, p. 180.
17. Musgrave, A., 'Kuhn's Second Thoughts', p. 289.
18. Kuhn: SSR, p. 181.
19. Ibid, RC, p. 249 n. 3.
20. Toulmin, S., 'Conceptual Revolutions in Science', p. 342.
21. Ibid, p. 342.
22. Kuhn: SSR, pp. 166, 177.
23. Watkins, J., 'Against "Normal Science"', p. 26.
24. Laudan, L., op. cit., p. 228n. 1.
25. Ibid, p. 5.
26. Kuhn: SSR, p. 37.
27. Ibid, SSR, p. 196.
28. Ibid, SSR, p. 196.
29. Newton-Smith, W. H., *The Rationality of Science*, p. 114.
30. Kuhn: ET, p. 178.
31. Ibid, SSR, p. 55.
32. Ibid, ET, p. 201.
33. Stegmüller, W., *The Structure and Dynamics of Theories*, p. 141.
34. Kuhn: SSR, p. 85.
35. Ibid, LDPR, pp. 798–819.
36. Ibid, SSR, p. 90.
37. Ibid, ET, p. 332.
38. Stegmüller, W., op. cit., p. 147.
39. Ibid, p. 148.
40. Kuhn: SSR, p. 198.
41. Bubner, R., *Dialektik und Wissenschaft*, pp. 149–50.
42. Kuhn: SSR, p. 108.
43. Ibid, SSR, pp. 166, 170.
44. SSR, p. 170.
45. Macintyre, A., 'Epistemological Crises, Dramatic Narrative, and the Philosophy of Science', p. 73.

46. Hollinger, D. A., 'T. S. Kuhn's Theory of Science and its Implications for History', p. 216.
47. Kuhn: SSR, p. 164.
48. Ibid, SSR, p. 37.
49. Popper: OS I, p. 291 n. 8.
50. Kuhn: SSR, pp. 36–7.
51. Ibid, SSR, p. 37.

Feyerabend's Dissolution of Scientific Dialectic

1. Kuhn: SSR, pp. 172, 171.
2. Bubner, R., *Dialektik und Wissenschaft*, p. 157.
3. Kuhn: SSR, p. 181.
4. Feyerabend: How, p. 14.
5. Ibid, Emp., p. 149.
6. Ibid, RRSM, p. 141.
7. Ibid, RRSM, p. 107.
8. Ibid, AM, p. 66.
9. Ibid, Emp., p. 183.
10. Ibid, AM, p. 32.
11. Ibid, Emp., p. 246 n. 114.
12. Ibid, AM, p. 32.
13. Ibid, Emp., p. 148.
14. Ibid, Emp., p. 182.
15. Ibid, SFS, p. 98.
16. Ibid, SFS, p. 98.
17. Ibid, AM, p. 46.
18. Ibid, RRSM, p. 60.
19. Ibid, RRSM, p. 107.
20. Ibid, Emp., p. 164.
21. Ibid, Emp., pp. 169–70.
22. Ibid, Emp., p. 180.
23. Ibid, Emp., p. 180.
24. Ibid, Emp., p. 180.
25. Ibid, Emp., pp. 180–1.
26. Ibid, Emp., p. 252 n. 142.
27. Ibid, Emp., p. 252 n. 142.
28. Ibid, Emp., p. 253 n. 142.
29. Ibid, Emp., p. 247 n. 116.
30. Ibid, Emp., p. 247 n. 116.
31. Ibid, Emp., p. 247 n. 116.
32. Ibid, Emp., p. 247 n. 116.
33. Ibid, RRSM, pp. 199–201.
34. Ibid, RRSM, p. 107.
35. Ibid, AM, p. 30.
38. Ibid, AM, p. 171.
37. Ibid, PE, p. 136.
38. Ibid, PE, p. 136.
39. Bubner, R., *Dialektik und Wissenschaft*, pp. 162–3.

40. Feyerabend: PE, p. 137.
41. Ibid, PE, pp. 137–9.
42. Ibid, PE, p. 142.
43. Ibid, PE, p. 142.
44. Ibid, PE, p. 143.
45. Aristotle: Nic. Eth. 1177a18.
46. Ibid, Nic. Eth. 1178a3–5.
47. Ibid, EE, 1249b20–21.
48. Feyerbend: AM, p. 46.
49. Ibid, PE, p. 160.
50. Ibid, AM, p. 23.
51. Winner, L., *Autonomous Technology*.
52. Swift, J., *Gulliver's Travels*, p. 135.

CHAPTER 3

Understanding and Reason

1. Kant: CPR, B 359.
2. Ibid, CPR, B 671–72.
3. Ibid, CPR, B 698–99.
4. Ibid, CPR, B 701.
5. Ibid, CPR, B 714.
6. Ibid, CPR, B 729–30.
7. Ibid, CPR, A 107.
8. Ibid, CPR, A 123.
9. Ibid, CPR, B 139.
10. Hegel: HSL, p. 824; L II, p. 484.
11. Feyerabend: AM, p. 154.
12. Bubner, R., *Zur Sache der Dialektik*, p. 28.
13. Hegel: HL, para. 161; SW 8, para. 161.
14. Ibid, HL, para. 161; SW 8, para. 161.
15. Rotenstreich, N., *From Substance to Subject*, p. 5.
16. Feyerabend: AM, p. 156.
17. Hegel: HSL, pp. 580–1; L II, pp. 217–18.

Feyerabend and Hegel

1. Feyerabend: PE, p. 71.
2. Ibid, AM, p. 20.
3. Ibid, AM, p. 179.
4. Ibid AM, p. 179.
5. Ibid, AM, p. 179.
6. Düsing, K., *Das Problem der Subjektivität in Hegels Logik*, p. 293.
7. Hegel: HLHP III, p. 547; SW 19, pp. 685–6.
8. Feyerabend: AM, pp. 179–80.
9. Hegel: Diff., p. 13.
10. *Der Sprach Brockhaus*.
11. Hegel: HSL, p. 612; L II, p. 252.

12. Feyerabend: PE, p. 73.
13. Ibid, PE, p. 73; Hegel: Diff., p. 13.
14. Ibid, PE, p. 73.
15. Hegel: Diff., p. 19.
16. Ibid, HSL, p. 571; L II, p. 205.
17. Ibid, HSL, p. 601; L II, p. 240.
18. Feyerabend: PE, p. 73; Hegel: HSL, p. 442; L II, p. 61.
19. Hegel: HSL, p. 442; L II, p. 61.
20. Ibid, HSL, p. 439; L II, p. 58.
21. Ibid, HSL, p. 440; L II, p. 59.
22. Ibid, HSL, p. 440; L II, p. 59.
23. Ibid, HSL, p. 440; L II, p. 59.
24. Düsing, K., op. cit., p. 213.
25. Hegel: L I, p. 26.
26. Feyerabend: PE, p. 73 n. 18.
27. Ibid, PE, p. 73 n. 18; Hegel: L I, p. 26.
28. Hegel: HSL, p. 45; L I, p. 26.
29. Feyerabend: PE, p. 73.
30. Hegel: HSL, p. 96; L I, p. 82.
31. Ibid, HSL, p. 96.
32. Ibid, L I, p. 82.
33. Ibid, HSL, p. 835; L II, p. 496.
34. Ibid, HSL, p. 836; L II, p. 497.
35. Ibid, HSL, p. 842; L II, p. 504.
36. Solomon, R. C., *In the Spirit of Hegel*, p. 393.
37. Ibid, p. 393.
38. Plato: Phaedo 99d8–e3.
39. Zimmerli, W. C., *Die Frage nach der Philosophie*.

Philosophical Speculation

1. Feyerabend, RRSM, p. 107.
2. Ibid, PE, p. 73.
3. Ibid, PE, pp. 72–3.
4. Hegel: HL, para. 166; SW 8, para. 166.
5. Kant: CPR, B 384.
6. Wieland, W., *Die Aristotelische Physik*, p. 41.
7. Hegel: PS, p. 18; PG, pp. 28–9.
8. Ibid, HSL, p. 55; L I, p. 37.
9. Ibid, HSL, p. 56; L I, p. 38.
10. Ibid, HSL, p. 56; L I, p. 38; PS, p. 2; PG, p. 10.
11. Ibid, HSL, p. 60; L I, p. 42.
12. Ibid, HSL, p. 440; L II, p. 59.
13. Ibid, HSL, pp. 440–1; L II, pp. 59–60.
14. Ibid, HSL, p. 744; L I, p. 395.
15. Ibid, HSL, p. 742; L II, p. 393.
16. Ibid, HSL, p. 734; L II, p. 384.
17. Ibid, HSL, p. 736; L II, p. 386.
18. Ibid, HSL, p. 739; L II, p. 390.

19. Ibid, HSL, p. 741; L II, p. 392.
20. Ibid, HSL, p. 741; L II, p. 392.
21. Ibid, HSL, p. 743; L II, p. 394.
22. Ibid, HSL, p. 735; L II, p. 385.
23. Ibid, HSL, p. 745; L II, p. 396.
24. Ibid, HSL, pp. 746–7; L II, p. 398; HL, para. 209; SW 8, para. 209.
25. Brockard, H., *Subjekt*, pp. 117–18; Hegel: PS, p. 302; PG, p. 355.
26. Hegel: Diff., p. 11.
27. Ibid, Diff., p. 22.
28. Ibid, Diff., p. 22.

Negative and Positive Reason

1. Düsing, K., op. cit., pp. 322–7.
2. Feyerabend: PE, p. 74.
3. Hegel: Diff., p. 21.
4. Ibid, HSL, 607; L II, p. 247.
5. Aristotle: Met. 982b12–13.
6. Hegel: HPN, para. 268; SW 9, para. 268.
7. Ibid, HPN, para. 268; SW 9, para, 268.
8. Feyerabend: PE, p. 74; Hegel: Diff., p. 14.
9. Feyerabend: PE, p. 74.
10. Hegel: HSL, p. 575; L II, p. 211.
11. Feyerabend: PE, p. 74.
12. Ibid, PE, p. 74; Hegel: Diff., p. 14.
13. Riedel, M., *Theorie und Praxis im Denken Hegels*.
14. Hegel: PS, p. 10; PG, p. 19.
15. Ibid, PS, p. 10; PG, p. 20.
16. Ibid, PS, p. 11; PG, p. 21.
17. Ibid, PS, p. 12, PG, p. 22.
18. Ibid, PS, pp. 11–12; PG, p. 21.
19. Ibid, PS, p. 12; PG, p. 22.
20. Ibid, HSL, p. 417; L II, p. 33.
21. Goethe, J. W. v., *Faust*, line 1237.
22. John 1:1.
23. Hegel: HLHP I, p. 3; SW 17, p. 29.
24. Ibid, Diff., p. 22.
25. Ibid, Diff., p. 22.
26. Ibid, HSL, p. 832; L II, p. 493.
27. Feyerabend: AM, p. 27; Hegel: HSL, p. 28; L I, p. 6.
28. Hegel: HSL, p. 28; L I, pp. 6–7.
29. Ibid, HLHP I, p. 32; SW 17, p. 61; HPR, para. 343; SW 7, para. 343.
30. Ibid, PS, p. 3; PG, p. 12.
31. Ibid, HSL, p. 54; L I, p. 35.
32. Ibid, HSL, p. 834; L II, p. 495.
33. Ibid, PS, p. 19; PG, pp. 29–30.

Formal and Concrete Logic

1. Rademacher, H., *Hegels 'Wissenschaft der Logik'*, p. 11.
2. Hegel: HLHP II, p. 148; SW 18, p. 331.
3. Ibid, HSL, pp. 43–4; L I, p. 24.
4. Ibid, HSL, p. 44; L I, p. 24.
5. Ibid, HSL, p. 44; L I, p. 25.
6. Ibid, HSL, pp. 44– 5; L I, p. 25.
7. Hagen, E. v., *Abstraktion und Konkretion bei Hegel und Kiergegaard.*
8. Eley, L., *Hegels Wissenschaft der Logik*, p. 19.
9. Hegel: HSL, p. 612; L II, p. 252.
10. Inwood, M. J., *Hegel*, p. 267.
11. Düsing, K., op. cit., p. 246.
12. Bubner, R., *Zur Sache der Dialektik* p. 102.
13. Hegel: HSL, p. 45; L I, p. 25.
14. Ibid, HSL, pp. 45–6; L I, p. 26.
15. Ibid, HSL, p. 25; L I, p. 3.
16. Ibid, HSL, p. 48; L I, p. 29.
17. Ibid, HSL, pp. 49–50; L I, pp. 30–1.

Ground as Ontology and Logic

1. Eley, L., op. cit., p. 13.
2. Hegel: HSL, p. 446; L II, p. 65.
3. Brockard, H., op. cit., pp. 29–30.
4. Hegel: Diff., p. 12.
5. Rademacher, H., op. cit., pp. 28, 36.
6. Hegel: PS, p. 32; PG, p. 45.
7. Kant: CPR, A 61.
8. Ibid, CPR, B 86; A 293.
9. Ibid, CPR, B 88.
10. Ibid, CPR, B 86.
11. Ibid, CPR, A 298.
12. Bubner, R., *Zur Sache der Dialektik*, p. 128.
13. Marcuse, H., *Hegels Ontologie und die Theorie der Geschichtlichkeit*, p. 228.
14. Ibid, p. 89.
15. Lukacs, G., *Hegel's False and his Genuine Ontology*, p. 64.
16. Bloch, E., *Subjekt-Objekt*, p. 159.
17. Henrich, D., 'Formen der Negation in Hegels Logik', p. 213.
18. Eley, L., op. cit., p. 18.
19. Ibid, p. 17.
20. Henrich, D., 'Hegels Logik der Reflexion', p. 224.
21. Lugarini, L., 'Die Bedeutung des Problems des Ganzen in der Hegelschen Logik', p. 31.
22. Fulda, H. F., 'Unzulängliche Bemerkungen zur Dialektik', p. 41.
23. Eley, L., op. cit., p. 11.
24. Brockard, H., op. cit., p. 49.
25. Hegel: HSL, p. 137; L I, p. 125.

26. Ibid, HSL, p. 824; L II, p. 483.
27. Ibid, HSL, p. 110; L I, p. 96.
28. Ibid, HSL, p. 777; L II, p. 432.
29. Marx, W., *Hegel's Phenomenology of Spirit*, p. xxi.
30. Marcuse, H., op. cit., p. 181.
31. Hegel: HSL, p. 577; L II, p. 213.
32. Ibid, HSL, p. 27; L I, p. 5; Eley, L., op. cit., p. 16.
33. Ibid, HSL, p. 63; L I, p. 46.
34. Ibid, HSL, p. 63; L I, p. 46.
35. Ibid, HSL, p. 64; L I, p. 47.
36. Theunissen, M., *Sein und Schein*, p. 39.
37. Marcuse, H., op. cit., p. 218.
38. Henrich, D., 'Hegels Logik der Reflexion', p. 313.

Substance and Subject

1. Spinoza, B. de, *The Chief Works of Benedict de Spinoza*, 'Ethics', vol. II, p. 45, Def. I.
2. Ibid, p. 48, Prop. p. vii.
3. Hegel: Diff., p. 27.
4. Rotenstreich, N., op. cit., p. 20.
5. Hegel: HSL, p. 536; L II, p. 164.
6. Ibid, HSL, p. 536; L II, p. 164.
7. Ibid, HSL, p. 537; L II, p. 164.
8. Ibid, HSL, p. 538; L II, p. 166.
9. Ibid, HSL, p. 538; L II, p. 166.
10. Ibid, HSL, p. 539; L II, p. 167.
11. Ibid, HSL, p. 537; L II, p. 165.
12. Brockard, H., op. cit., p. 62.
13. Hegel: HSL, p. 571; L II, p. 205.
14. Ibid, HSL, p. 536; L II, p. 164; Düsing, K., op. cit., p. 229.
15. Hegel: HSL, p. 69; L I, p. 54.
16. Ibid, PS, p. 476; PG, p. 546.
17. Ibid, HSL, p. 546; L II, p. 176.
18. Ibid, PS, p. 10; PG, p. 19.
19. Ibid, HPR, para. 1; SW 7, para. 1.
20. Ibid, HPR, p. 10; SW 7, p. 33.
21. Ibid, PS, p. 19; PG, p. 29.
22. Wilkins, B. T., *Hegel's Philosophy of History*, p. 143.

Method and System

1. Hegel: PG, vi.
2. Ibid, PS, p. 28; PG, p. 40.
3. Ibid, PS, p. 35; PG, p. 48.
4. Ibid, HSL, p. 605; L II, p. 245.
5. Ibid, HSL, p. 603; L II, p. 242.
6. Riedel, M., op. cit.; Dubský, I., 'Hegels Arbeitsbegriff und die Idealistische Dialektik'; Stepelevich, *et al.*, *Hegel's Philosophy of Action*; Lim, S.-Z., v., *Der Begriff der Arbeit bei Hegel*.

7. Rademacher, H., op. cit., p. 26.
8. Ruben, P., 'Von der "Wissenschaft der Logik" und dem Verhältnis der Dialektik zur Logik', p. 73.
9. Hegel: PS, p. 486; PG, p. 557.
10. Ritter, J., *Hegel and the French Revolution*, p. 51.
11. Hegel: HSL, p. 53; L I, p. 35.
12. Kant: CPR, B v; KRV, p. 3.
13. Ibid, CPR, B xxii; KVR, p. 21.
14. Hegel: HSL, p. 527; L II, p. 154.
15. Ibid, HSL, p. 837; L II, p. 498.
16. Feyerabend: AM, p. 183.
17. Ibid, AM, p. 37.
18. Hegel: Diff., p. 25.
19. Ibid, HSL, p. 829; L II, p. 490.
20. Ibid, Diff., p. 8.
21. Ibid, PS, p. 3; PG, p. 12.
22. Ibid., PS, p. 13; PG, p. 23.
23. Ibid, PS, p. 3; PG, p. 12; PG: title page.
24. Ibid, HSL, p. 757; L II, p. 409.
25. Ibid, HSL, p. 826; L II, p. 486.
26. Ibid, HSL, p. 826; L II, p. 486.
27. Ibid, HL, para. 17; SW 8, para. 17.
28. Ibid, HSL, p. 838; L II, pp. 499–500.
29. Ibid, HSL, p. 835; L II, p. 496.
30. Ibid, HSL, p. 842; L II, p. 502.
31. Ibid, HSL, p. 838, L II, p. 500.
32. Ibid, HSL, p. 755; L II, p. 407.
33. Ibid, LPR I, p. 59; SW 15, p. 15 and 75.
34. Ibid, HLHP I, p. 21; SW 17, p. 49.
35. Ibid, HLHP I, p. 23; SW 17, p. 51.
36. Ibid, HLHP I, p. 24; SW 17, p. 52.
37. Düsing, K., op. cit., p. 338.
38. Hegel: HL, para, 237; SW 8, para. 237.
39. Ibid, HSL, p. 835; L II, p. 496.
40. Ibid, HSL, p. 841; L II, p. 502.
41. Ibid, PS, p. 31; PG, p. 44.
42. Ibid, PS, pp. 32–3; PG, p. 54.
43. Ibid, HSL, p. 830; L II, p. 491.
44. Ibid, PS, p. 35; PG, p. 48.
45. Ibid, HSL, p. 172; L I, p. 163.
46. Ibid, PS, p. 36; PG, p. 48.
47. Ibid, HSL, p. 830; L II, p. 491.
48. Ibid, PS, pp. 34–5; PG, p. 47.
49. Ibid, HSL, p. 54; L I, p. 36.
50. Ibid, HSL, p. 28; L I, p. 7.
51. Ibid, HSL, p. 831; L II, p. 492.
52. Ibid, HSL, p. 824; L II, p. 484.
53. Ibid, HSL, p. 840; L II, p. 502.
54. Ibid, HSL, p. 824; L II, p. 484.

55. Ibid, HSL, p. 827; L II, p. 487.
56. Ibid, HSL, p. 842; L II, p. 504.
57. Ibid, HSL, p. 602; L II, p. 242.

The Application of Logic

1. Bubner, R., *Zur Sache der Dialektik*, p. 128.
2. Ibid, p. 148.
3. Rademacher, H., op. cit., p. 37.
4. Hegel: HPR, para. 31; SW 7, para. 31.
5. Solomon, R. C., op. cit., p. 5.
6. Taylor, C., *Hegel*, pp. 48, 45.
7. Marcuse, H., op. cit., p. 278.
8. Ibid, *Reason and Revolution*, p. 155.
9. Marx, W., op. cit., p. xxi.
10. Brockard, H., op. cit., p. 73.
11. Hegel: HSL, p. 50; L I, p. 31.
12. Rademacher, H., op. cit., pp. 5, 30.
13. Ibid, p. 36.
14. Hegel: PS, p. 53; PG, p. 71.
15. Ibid, PS, p. 53; PG, p. 71.
16. Ibid, PS, p. 55; PG, p. 73.
17. Ibid, PS, p. 55; PG, p. 73.
18. Pinkard, T., 'The Logic of Hegel's "Logic"', p. 435.
19. Hegel: HSL, p. 48; L I, p. 29.

CHAPTER 4

The Idea of Mankind as Life

1. Hegel: HSL, p. 824; L II, p. 484; Düsing, K., 'Die Idee des Lebens in Hegels Logik', pp. 276–89.
2. Hegel: HL, para. 244; SW 8, para. 244.
3. Ibid, HSL, p. 755; L II, p. 407.
4. Ibid, HL, para. 244; SW 8, para. 244.
5. Ibid, HPN, para. 376; SW 9, para. 376.
6. Ibid, HPM, para. 575; SW 10, para. 575.
7. Ibid, HPM, para. 576; SW 10, para. 576.
8. Ibid, HPM, para. 577; SW 10, para. 577.
9. Solomon, R. C., op. cit., p. 594.
10. Hegel: HSL, p. 842; L II, p. 504.
11. *Etymologisches Wörterbuch der Deutschen Sprache*.
12. *Brockhaus Enzyklopädie*.
13. Hagen, E. v., op. cit., pp. 9–10.
14. Marcuse, H., *Hegels Ontologie und die Theorie der Geschichtlichkeit*, p. 63.
15. Ibid, p. 67.
16. Brockard, H., op. cit., pp. 111–12.

17. Hegel. VPW II–IV, p. 938; partially in PH, p. 457.
18. Ibid, HPN, para. 259; SW 9, para. 259; Riedel, M., *Fortschritt und Dialektik in Hegels Geschichtsphilosophie*.
19. Ibid, HPN, para. 259; SW 9, para. 259.
20. Ibid, PS, p. 493; PG, p. 564.
21. *Brockhaus Enzyklopädie*.
22. Hegel: HSL, p. 747; L II, p. 398.
23. Ibid, HLHP III, p. 553, SW 19, p. 691.

The Differentiations of Mankind

1. Hegel: Lectures, p. 48; VG, p. 55.
2. Ibid, HSL, p. 755; L II, p. 408.
3. Ibid, HSL, p. 597; L II, p. 236.
4. Ibid, HSL, p. 826; L II, p. 487.
5. Ibid, Lectures, p. 49; VG, p. 57.
6. Ibid, Lectures, p. 50; VG, p. 58.
7. Ibid, VPW II–iv, p. 937; PH, p. 456.
8. Ibid, Lectures, pp. 196–7; VG, p. 242.
9. Iibid, Lectures, p. 197; VG, 243.
10. Ibid, PH, p. 440; VPW II–IV, p. 913.
11. Cooper, B., *The End of History*, p. 287.
12. Hegel, Lectures, p. 89, VG, p. 105.
13. Ibid, Lectures, p. 89; VG, p. 105.

The Historical Judgment

1. Hegel: HSL, p. 577; L II, p. 213.
2. Ibid, HSL p. 824; L II, p. 484.
3. Ibid, HSL, p. 577; L II, p. 213.
4. Ibid, HSL, p. 623; L II, p. 264.
5. Ibid, HSL, p. 623; L II, pp. 264–5.
6. Ibid, HSL, p. 622; L II, p. 264.
7. Ibid, HSL, p. 59; L I, p. 42.
8. Ibid, HL, para. 163; SW 8, para. 163.
9. Ibid, HL, para, 164; SW 8, para. 164.
10. Ibid, HL, para. 163; SW 8, para. 163.
11. Ibid, HL, para. 163; SW 8, para. 163.
12. Ibid, HL, para. 163; SW 8, para. 163.
13. Ibid, HL, para. 166; SW 8, para. 166.
14. Ibid, HL, para. 166; SW 8, para. 166.
15. Ibid, HL, para. 166; SW 8, para. 166.
16. Ibid, HL, para. 166; SW 8, para. 166.
17. Ibid, HL, para. 166; SW 8, para. 166.
18. Ibid, HL, para. 166; SW 8, para. 166.
19. Ibid, HL, para, 166; SW 8, para. 166.
20. Ibid, HL, para. 166; SW 8, para. 166.
21. Ibid, HL, para, 163; SW 8, para. 163.
22. Ibid, HL, para. 163; SW 8, para. 163.

23. Ibid, HL, para. 164; SW 8, para. 164.
24. Ibid, HL, para. 164; SW 8, para. 164.

The State

1. Hegel: HSL, p. 631; L II, p. 272.
2. Ibid, HSL, p. 631; L II, p. 272.
3. Ibid, HSL, p. 631; L II, pp. 272–3.
4. Ibid, HSL, p. 632; L II, p. 274.
5. Ibid, HSL, p. 632; L II, p. 274.
6. Ibid, HSL, p. 632; L II, p. 274.
7. Ibid, HSL, p. 632; L II, p. 274.
8. Ibid, HSL, p. 633; L II, p. 274.
9. Ibid, HSL, p. 633: L II, p. 275.
10. Ibid, HSL, p. 633; L II, p. 275.
11. Ibid, HSL, p. 633; L II, p. 275.
12. Ibid, HL, para. 172; SW 8, para. 172.
13. Ibid, HL, para. 172; SW 8, para. 172.
14. Ibid, HSL, p. 633; L II, p. 276.
15. Ibid, HSL, p. 633; L II, p. 275.
16. Ibid, HL, para. 172; SW 8, para. 172.
17. Ibid, HSL, p. 651; L II, p. 295.
18. Ibid, HL, para. 172; SW 8, para. 172.
19. Ibid, HL, para. 172; SW 8, para. 172.

The Reflection of the State

1. Hegel: HSL, p. 643; L II, p. 286.
2. Ibid, HSL, p. 643; L II, p. 286.
3. Ibid, HSL, p. 643; L II, p. 286.
4. Ibid, HL, para. 174; SW 8, para. 174.
5. Ibid, HSL, p. 643; L II, p. 286.
6. Ibid, HSL, p. 643; L II, p. 286.
7. Ibid, HL, para. 174; SW 8, para. 174.
8. Ibid, HL, para. 174; SW 8, para. 174.
9. Ibid, HSL, p. 643; L II, p. 286.
10. Ibid, HSL, p. 644; L II, p. 287.
11. Ibid, HL, para. 175; SW 8, para. 175.
12. Ibid, HL, para. 175; SW 8, para. 175.
13. Ibid, HL, para. 174; SW 8, para. 174.
14. Ibid, HL, para, 174; SW 8, para. 174.
15. Ibid, HSL, p. 644; L II, p. 287.
16. Ibid, HL, para, 175; SW 8, para. 175.

The Development of State-Reflection

1. Hegel: HSL, p. 645; L II, p. 288.
2. Ibid, HSL, p. 645; L II, p. 288.
3. Ibid, HSL, p. 645; L II, p. 288.

4. Ibid, HSL, p. 645; L II, p. 288.
5. Ibid, HL, para. 175; SW 8, para. 175.
6. Ibid, HSL, p. 645; L II, p. 288.
7. Ibid, HSL, p. 646; L II, p. 289.
8. Ibid, HSL, p. 646; L II, p. 289.
9. Ibid, HL, para. 175; SW 8, para. 175.
10. Ibid, HSL, p. 646; L II, p. 289.
11. Ibid, HSL, p. 646; L II, p. 289.
12. Ibid, HSL, p. 646; L II, p. 289.
13. Ibid, HSL, p. 647; L II, p. 290.
14. Ibid, HL, para. 175; SW 8, para. 175.
15. Ibid, HSL, p. 647; L II, p. 290.
16. Ibid, HSL, p. 527; L II, p. 154.
17. Ibid, HSL, p. 648; L II, p. 291.
18. Ibid, HSL, p. 647; L II, p. 290.
19. Ibid, HSL, p. 648; L II, p. 291.
20. Ibid, HL, para. 175; SW 8, para. 175.
21. Ibid, HSL, p. 648; L II, p. 291.
22. Ibid, HSL, p. 648; L II, p. 291–2.
23. Ibid, HL, para. 175; SW 8, para. 175.
24. Ibid, HL, para. 175; SW 8, para. 175.
25. Ibid, HSL, p. 649; L II, p. 292.
26. Ibid, HSL, p. 650; L II, p. 293.
27. Ibid, HSL, p. 650; L II, p. 293.
28. Ibid, HL, para. 176; SW 8, para. 176.

The Formation of the States-System

1. Hegel: HSL, p. 650; L II, p. 294.
2. Ibid, HSL, p. 650; L II, p. 294.
3. Ibid, HSL, p. 650; L II, p. 294–5.
4. Ibid, HSL, p. 651; L II, p. 294.
5. Ibid, HL, para. 177; SW 8, para. 177.
6. Ibid, HL, para. 177; SW 8, para. 177.
7. Ibid, HL, para. 177; SW 8, para. 177.
8. Ibid, HSL, p. 651; L II, p. 295.
9. Ibid, HL, para. 177; SW 8, para. 177.
10. Ibid, HSL, p. 652; L II, p. 295.
11. Ibid, HSL, p. 652; L II, p. 295.
12. Ibid, HL, para. 177; SW 8, para. 177.
13. Ibid, HSL, p. 652; L II, p. 296.
14. Ibid, HSL, p. 653; L II, p. 297.
15. Ibid, HSL, p. 652; L II, p. 295.
16. Ibid, HSL, p. 652; L II, p. 296.
17. Ibid, HL, para. 177; SW 8, para. 177.
18. Ibid, HSL, p. 652; L II, p. 296.
19. Ibid, HSL, p. 653; L II, p. 296.
20. Ibid, HL, para. 177; SW 8, para. 177.
21. Ibid, HSL, p. 653; L II, p. 296.

22. Ibid, HSL, p. 653; L II, p. 297.
23. Ibid, HSL, p. 653; L II, p. 297.
24. Ibid, HSL, p. 653; L II, p. 297.
25. Ibid, HSL, p. 654; L II, p. 297.
26. Ibid, HSL, p. 654; L II, p. 298.
27. Ibid, HSL, p. 655; L II, p. 299.
28. Ibid, HSL, p. 654; L II, p. 298.
29. Ibid, HSL, p. 655; L II, p. 299.
30. Ibid, HSL, p. 654; L II, p. 298.
31. Ibid, HSL, p. 655; L II, p. 299.
32. Ibid, HSL, p. 654; L II, p. 298.
33. Ibid, HSL, p. 657; L II, p. 301.
34. Ibid, HSL, p. 657; L II, p. 301.
35. Ibid, HSL, p. 658; L II, p. 303.

The Determination of the States-System

1. Hegel: HSL, p. 658; L II, p. 303.
2. Ibid, HSL, p. 657; L II, p. 301.
3. Ibid, HSL, p. 657; L II, p. 302.
4. Ibid, HSL, pp. 657–8; L II, p. 302.

The Development of the States-System

1. Hegel: HSL, pp. 658–9; L II, p. 303.
2. Ibid, HSL, p. 659; L II, p. 303.
3. Ibid, HSL, p. 659; L II, p. 303.
4. Ibid, HSL, p. 659; L II, p. 303.
5. Ibid, HSL, p. 659; L II, p. 303.
6. Ibid, HSL, p. 659; L II, p. 303.
7. Ibid, HSL, p. 659; L II, p. 303.
8. Ibid, HSL, p. 659; L II, p. 304.
9. Ibid, HSL, p. 659; L II, p. 304.
10. Ibid, HSL, pp. 659–60; L II, p. 304.
11. Ibid, HSL, p. 660; L II, p. 304.
12. Ibid, HSL, p. 660; L II, p. 304.
13. Ibid, HSL, p. 660; L II, p. 304.
14. Ibid, HL, para. 241; SW 8, para. 241.
15. Ibid, HSL, p. 660; L II, p. 304.
16. Ibid, HSL, p. 660; L II, p. 305.
17. Ibid, HSL, p. 660; L II, p. 305.
18. Ibid, HSL, pp. 660–1; L II, p. 305.
19. Ibid, HSL, p. 661; L II, p. 305.
20. Ibid, HSL, p. 444; L II, p. 63.
21. Ibid. HSL, p. 661; L II, p. 305.
22. Ibid, HSL, p. 661; L II, p. 306.
23. Ibid, HSL, p. 661; L II, p. 306.
24. Ibid, HSL, pp. 661–2; L II, p. 306.
25. Ibid, HSL, p. 662; L II, p. 306.

26. Ibid, HSL, p. 662; L II, p. 306.
27. Ibid, HSL, p. 662; L II, p. 306.
28. Ibid, HSL, p. 662; L II, p. 306.
29. Ibid, HSL, p. 662; L II, p. 306.
30. Ibid, HSL, p. 662; L II, p. 306–7.
31. Ibid, HSL, p. 662; L II, p. 307.
32. Ibid, HSL, p. 662; L II, p. 307.
33. Ibid, HSL, p. 662; L II, p. 307.
34. Ibid, HSL, p. 663; L II, p. 307.
35. Ibid, HSL, p. 663; L II, p. 307.
36. Ibid, HSL, p. 663; L II, p. 307.
37. Ibid, HSL, p. 663; L II, p. 307.
38. Ibid, HSL, p. 663; L II, p. 307.
39. Ibid, HSL, p. 663; L II, p. 307.

CHAPTER 5

Mankind Sublated

1. Hegel: HSL, p. 664; L II, p. 308.
2. Ibid, HSL, p. 664; L II, p. 308.
3. Ibid, HSL, P. 665; L II, p. 310.
4. Ibid, HSL, p. 665; L II, p. 310.
5. Ibid, HSL, p. 665; L II, p. 309.
6. Ibid, HSL, p. 665; L II, p. 309.
7. Ibid, HPR, p. 11; SW 7, pp. 34–5.

Mankind Annihilated

1. Hegel: HSL, p. 187; L I, p. 179.
2. Ibid, PH, p. 402; VPW II–IV, p. 855.
3. Ibid, PS, p. 6; PG, p. 15.
4. Ibid, PS, p. 7; PG, p. 16.
5. Ibid, PS, pp. 355ff; PG, pp. 414ff.
6. Clausewitz, C. v., op. cit., pp. 77–80.
7. Ibid, pp. 87, 605ff.
8. Hegel: Lectures, p. 214; VG, p. 264.
9. Ibid, HSL, p. 82; L I, p. 67.
10. Wilkins, B. T., op. cit., p. 177; Jaeschke, W., 'World History and the History of the Absolute Spirit', p. 104; Ahlers, R., 'The Dialectic in Hegel's Philosophy of History', p. 163.
11. Inwood, M. J., op. cit., p. 444.

CHAPTER 6

State Relations

1. Hegel: HPR, para. 322; SW 7, para. 322.
2. Ibid, HPR, para. 279; SW 7, para. 279.

3. Ibid, HPR, para. 267; SW 7, para. 267.
4. Ibid, HPR, para. 278; SW 7, para. 278.
5. Ibid, HPR, para. 331; SW 7, para. 331.
6. Ibid, HPR, para. 322; SW 7, para. 322.
7. Ibid, HPR, para. 329; SW 7, para. 329.
8. Ibid, HPR, para. 331; SW 7, para. 331.
9. Ibid, HPR, para. 323; SW 7, para. 323.
10. Ibid, HPR, para. 323; SW 7, para. 323.
11. Ibid, HPR, para. 333; SW 7, para. 333.
12. Ibid, HPR, para. 330A; SW 7, para. 330A.
13. Ibid, HPR, para. 333; SW 7, para. 333.
14. Ibid, HPR, para. 333; SW 7, para. 333.
15. Ibid, HPR, para. 333; SW 7, para. 333.
16. Ibid, HPR, para. 339A; SW 7, para. 339A.
17. Ibid, HPR, para. 340; SW 7, para. 340.
18. Ibid, PS, p. 493; PG, p. 564.
19. Ibid, PS, p. 493; PG, p. 564.

The Idea of War

1. Hegel: HPR, para. 324; SW 7, para. 324.
2. Ibid, HPR, para. 337; SW 7, para. 337.
3. Ibid, HPR, para. 324; SW 7, para. 324.
4. Ibid, HPR, para. 324; SW 7, para. 324.
5. Ibid, HPR, para. 338; SW 7, para. 338.
6. Ibid, HPR, para. 338; SW 7, para. 338.
7. Ibid, HPR, para. 331; SW 7, para. 331.
8. Ibid, HPR, para. 36; SW 7, para. 36.
9. Ibid, HPR, para. 334; SW 7, para. 334.
10. Ibid, HPR, para. 323; SW 7, para. 323.
11. Avineri, S., 'The Problem of War in Hegel's Thought', pp. 463–74.
12. Hegel, HPR, para. 324; SW 7, para. 324.
13. Ibid, PS, 214; PG, 258.
14. Ibid, HPR, para. 324; SW 7, para. 324.

The Responsibility for Peace

1. Strauss, L., 'What is Political Philosophy', pp. 9–55.
2. Aristotle: Pol. 1280a31–32.
3. Bloch, E., *Das Prinzip Hoffnung.*
4. Jonas, H., *Das Prinzip der Verantwortung.*
5. Henrich, D., 'Nuklearer Frieden'; Jaspers, K., *The Future of Mankind.*
6. Henrich, D., *Ethik zum Nuklearen Frieden.*
7. Hegel: HPR, para. 324; SW 7, para. 324.

Bibliography

Ahlers, Rolf, 'The Dialectic in Hegel's Philosophy of History', in R. L. Perkins (1984), pp. 149–66.

Aristotle, '*The Complete Works of Aristotle*, vols I, II, ed. Jonathan Barnes (Princeton University Press, 1984).

Avineri, Shlomo, 'The Problem of War in Hegel's Thought', in *Journal of the History of Ideas*, vol. XXII, Oct–Dec 1961, pp. 463–74.

Bloch, Ernst, *Das Prinzip Hoffnung*, in Gesamtausgabe, Band 5 (Frankfurt a/M: Suhrkamp, 1959).

____, *Subjekt-Objekt: Erläuterungen zu Hegel* (Frankfurt a/M: Suhrkamp, 1972).

Bloom, Allan, 'Interpretive Essay', in Plato, *The Republic of Plato* (1968), pp. 307–436.

Bosanquet, Bernard, *The Introduction to Hegel's Philosophy of Fine Art*, trans. B. Bosanquet (London: Kegan Paul, 1905).

Brockard, Hans, *Subjekt: Versuch zur Ontologie bei Hegel* (München: Anton Pustet, 1970).

Brockhaus Enzyklopädie (Wiesbaden: F. A. Brockhaus, 1967).

Bubner, Rüdiger, *Dialektik und Wissenschaft* (Frankfurt a/M: Suhrkamp, 1974).

____, *Zur Sache der Dialektik* (Stuttgart: Philip Reclaim, 1980).

Carnap, Rudolf, *The Logical Structure of the World*, trans. R. A. George, (London: Routledge & Kegan Paul, 1968).

Clausewitz, Carl von, *On War*, eds and trans. Michael Howard and Peter Paret (Princeton University Press, 1984).

Cooper, Barry, *The End of History: An Essay on Modern Hegelianism* (University of Toronto Press, 1984).

Cornford, F. M., *Plato's Theory of Knowledge* (London: Routledge & Kegan Paul, 1967).

Crombie, I. M. *An Examination of Plato's Doctrines*, vol. II (London: Routledge & Kegan Paul, 1963).

Dubský, Ivan, 'Hegels Arbeitsbegriff und die Idealistische Dialektik', in I. Fetscher (1973), pp. 408–63.

Düsing, Klaus, 'Die Idee des Lebens in Hegels Logik', in Rolf-Dieter Horstmann und Michael John Petry (eds), *Hegels Philosophie der Natur: Beziehungen zwischen empirischer und spekulativer Naturerkenntnis* (Stuttgart: Ernst Klett, 1986), pp. 276–89.

____, *Das Problem der Subjektivität in Hegels Logik*, Hegel-Studien, Beiheft 15 (Bonn: Bouvier Verlag Herbert Grundmann, 1976).

Elders, L., 'The "Topics" and the Platonic Theory of Principles of Being', in G. E. L. Owen (1968), pp. 126–37.

Eley, Lothar, *Hegels Wissenschaft der Logik* (München: Wilhelm Fink, 1976).

Etymologisches Wörterbuch der Deutschen Sprache, ed. Friedrich Kluge (Berlin: Walter De Gruyter, 1963).

Evans, J. D. G., *Aristotle's Concept of Dialectic* (Cambridge University Press, 1977).
Fetscher, Iring, (ed.), *Hegel in der Sicht der Neueren Forschung* (Darmstadt: Wissenschaftliche Buchgesellschaft, 1973).
Feyerabend, Paul, *Against Method* (London: NLB, 1979).
——, 'How to be a Good Empiricist—A Plea for Tolerance in Matters Epistemological', in P. H. Nidditch (ed.), *The Philosophy of Science* (Oxford University Press, 1981), pp. 12–39.
——, 'Problems of Empiricism', in Robert G. Colodny (ed.), *Beyond the Edge of Certainty* (Englewood Cliffs: Prentice-Hall, 1965), pp. 145–260.
——, *Problems of Empiricism*, Philosophical Papers, vol. II, (Cambridge University Press, 1981).
——, *Realism, Rationalism and Scientific Method*, Philosophical Papers, vol. I (Cambridge University Press, 1981).
——, *Science in a Free Society* (London: NLB, 1978).
Freedman, Lawrence, *The Evolution of Nuclear Strategy* (New York: St Martin's Press, 1981).
Fulda, Hans Friedrich, 'Hegels Dialektik als Begriffsbewegung und Darstellungsweise', in R.-P. Horstmann (1978), pp. 124–74.
——, 'Unzulängliche Bemerkungen zur Dialektik', in R.-P. Horstmann (1978), pp. 33–69.
Gadamer, Hans-Georg, *Dialogue and Dialectic: Eight Hermeneutical Studies on Plato*, trans. P. Christopher Smith (New Haven: Yale University Press, 1980).
——, *Truth and Method*, trans. William Glen-Doepel (London: Sheed and Ward, 1975).
Goethe, J. W. v., *Faust*, vol. I (Stuttgart: Philipp Reclam, 1963), line 1237.
Gundert, Hermann, *Dialog und Dialektik: Zur Struktur des Platonischen Dialogs* (Amsterdam: Verlag B. R. Gruner N.V., 1971).
Gutting, Gary, *Paradigms and Revolutions: Appraisals and Applications of Thomas Kuhn's Philosophy of Science* (London: University of Notre Dame Press, 1980).
Habermas, Jürgen, *Knowledge and Human Interest*, trans. Jeremy J. Shapiro (Cambridge: Polity Press, 1987).
Hagen, Eduard von, *Abstraktion und Konkretion bei Hegel und Kierkegaard* (Bonn: H. Bouvier, 1969).
Hegel, G. W. F., *Differenz des Fichte'schen und Schelling'schen Systems der Philosophie* (Hamburg: Felix Meiner, 1962).
——, *Lectures on the Philosophy of Religion*, vol. I, trans. E. B. Speirs and J. Burdon Sanderson (London: Routledge & Kegan Paul, 1968).
——, *Lectures on the Philosophy of World History—Introduction*, trans. H. B. Nisbet (Cambridge University Press, 1980).
——, *Phänomenologie des Geistes* (Hamburg: Felix Meiner, 1952).
——, *The Philosophy of History*, trans. J. Sibree (New York: Dover, 1956).
——, *Sämtliche Werke*, vols 1–20, ed. Hermann Glockner (Stuttgart: Fr. Frommann, 1927–30).
——, *Die Vernunft in der Geschichte* (Hamburg: Verlag von Felix Meiner, 1955).

——, *Vorlesungen über die Philosophie der Weltgeschichte*, vols II–IV (Hamburg: Felix Meiner, 1968).
——, *Wissenschaft der Logik*, vols I and II (Hamburg: Felix Meiner, 1971).
Hegel's Lectures on The History of Philosophy, vols I–III, trans. E. S. Haldane and Frances H. Simson (London: Routledge & Kegan Paul, 1974).
Hegel's Logic, trans. W. Wallace (Oxford: Clarendon Press, 1978).
Hegel's Phenomenology of Spirit, trans. A. V. Miller (Oxford University Press, 1979).
Hegel's Philosophy of Mind, trans. W. Wallace (Oxford: Clarendon Press, 1971).
Hegel's Philosophy of Nature, trans. A. V. Miller (Oxford University Press, 1970).
Hegel's Philosophy of Right, trans. T. M. Knox (Oxford University Press. 1967).
Hegel's Science of Logic, trans. A. V. Miller (Oxford: George Allen & Unwin, 1976).
Henrich, Dieter, *Ethik zum Nuklearen Freiden*, unpublished manuscript (München 1988).
——, 'Formen der Negation in Hegels Logik' in R.-P. Horstmann (1978), pp. 213–29.
——, 'Hegels Logik der Reflexion' in D. Henrich (1978), pp. 203–324.
——, 'Nuklearer Frieden', in *Dialektik*, vol. 4, Für den Frieden, eds Bernhard Heidtmann *et al.* (Köln: Pahl-Rugenstein, 1982), pp. 11–20.
——, (ed.), *Die Wissenschaft der Logik und die Logik der Reflexion*, Hegel-Studien, Beiheft 18 (Bonn: Bouvier Verlag Herbert Grundmann, 1978).
Hollinger, David A., 'T. S. Kuhn's Theory of Science and its Implications for History', in G. Gutting (1980), pp. 195–222.
Horstmann, Rolf-Dieter (ed.), *Dialektik in der Philosophie Hegels* (Frankfurt a/M: Suhrkamp, 1978).
Inwood, M. J., *Hegel* (London: Routledge & Kegan Paul, 1983).
Jaeschke, Walter, 'World History and the History of the Absolute Spirit', in R. L. Perkins (1984), pp. 101–21.
Jaspers, Karl, *The Future of Mankind*, trans. E. B. Ashton (The University of Chicago Press, 1973).
Jonas, Hans, *Das Prinzip der Verantwortung* (Frankfurt a/M: Insel, 1979).
Kant, Immanuel, *Critique of Pure Reason*, trans. Norman Kemp Smith (New York: St Martin's Press, 1965).
——, 'Kritik der Reinen Vernunft', in Ernst Cassirer (ed.), *Immanuel Kants Werke*, vol. III (Berlin: Bruno Cassirer, 1913).
Kuhn, Thomas S., *The Essential Tension: Selected Studies in Scientific Tradition and Change* (The University of Chicago Press, 1977).
——, 'Logic of Discovery or Psychology of Research?', in P. A. Schilpp (1974), vol. II, pp. 798–819.
——, 'Reflections on my Critics', in I. Lakatos and A. Musgrave (1978), pp. 231–78.
——, *The Structure of Scientific Revolutions* (The University of Chicago Press, 1970).
Lakatos, Imre and Alan Musgrave (eds.), *Criticism and the Growth of Knowledge* (Cambridge University Press, 1978).

Laudan, Larry, *Progress and its Problems: Towards a Theory of Scientific Growth* (Berkeley: University of California Press, 1978).
Lim, von Sok-Zin, *Der Begriff der Arbeit bei Hegel* (Bonn: H. Bouvier, 1966).
Lloyd, A. C., 'Genus, Species and Ordered Series in Aristotle', in *Phronesis*, vol. 7, 1962, pp. 67–90.
Lugarini, Leo, 'Die Bedeutung des Problems des Ganzen in der Hegelschen Logik', in D. Henrich (1978), pp. 19–36.
Lukacs, Georg, *Hegel's False and his Genuine Ontology*, trans. David Fernbach (London: Merlin Press, 1978).
Macintyre, Alasdair, 'Epistemological Crises, Dramatic Narrative, and the Philosophy of Science', in G. Gutting (1980), pp. 54–74.
Marcuse, Herbert, *Hegels Ontologie und die Theorie der Geschichtlichkeit* (Frankfurt a/M: Vittorio Klostermann, 1968).
——, *Reason and Revolution: Hegel and the Rise of Social Theory* (London: Routledge & Kegan Paul, 1963).
Marten, Rainer, *Der Logos der Dialektik: Eine Theorie zu Platon's 'Sophistes'* (Berlin: Walter De Gruyter, 1965).
Marx, Werner, *Hegel's Phenomenology of Spirit*, trans. Peter Heath (New York: Harper and Row, 1975).
Masterman, Margaret, 'The Nature of a Paradigm', in I. Lakatos and A. Musgrave (1978), pp. 59–89.
Moraux, Paul, 'La joute dialectique d'après le huitième livre des Topiques', in G. E. L. Owen (1968), pp. 277–311.
Musgrave, Alan, 'Kuhn's Second Thoughts', in *British Journal of the Philosophy of Science*, 22, 1971, pp. 287–306.
Newton-Smith, W. H., *The Rationality of Science* (London: Routledge & Kegan Paul, 1981).
Owen, G. E. L. (ed.), *Aristotle on Dialectic: The Topics* (Oxford: Clarendon Press, 1968).
——, 'Dialectic and Eristic in the Treatment of the Forms', in G. E. L. Owen (1968), pp. 103–25.
Perkins, R. L. (ed.), *History and System: Hegel's Philosophy of History* (Albany: State University of New York Press, 1984).
Pinkard, Terry, 'The Logic of Hegel's "Logic"', in *Journal of the History of Philosophy*, vol. XVII, no. 4, Oct. 1979, pp. 417–35.
Plato, *The Collected Dialogues* (eds.), Edith Hamilton and Huntington Cairns (Princeton University Press, 1971).
Plato, *The Republic of Plato*, trans. and with an Interpretive Essay, by Allan Bloom (New York: Basic, 1968).
Polybius, *The Rise of the Roman Empire*, trans. Ian Scott-Kilvert (Harmondsworth: Penguin, 1984).
Popper, Karl, *Conjectures and Refutations* (Routledge & Kegan Paul, 1972).
——, *The Logic of Scientific Discovery* (London: Hutchinson, 1977).
——, *Objective Knowledge* (Oxford: Clarendon Press, 1979).
——, *The Open Society and its Enemies*, vols I and II (London: Routledge & Kegan Paul, 1980).
——, *The Poverty of Historicism* (London: Routledge & Kegan Paul, 1979).
——, 'Replies to my Critics', in Schilpp (1974), vol. II, pp. 961–1197.

Rademacher, Hans, *Hegels 'Wissenschaft der Logik'* (Wiesbaden: Franz Steiner, 1979).
Riedel, Manfred, 'Fortschritt und Dialektik in Hegels Geschichtsphilosophie', in I. Fetscher (1973), pp. 387–407.
____, *Theorie und Praxis im Denken Hegels* (Frankfurt a/M: Ullstein, 1976).
Ritter, Joachim, *Hegel and the French Revolution*, trans. Richard Dien Winfield (Cambridge, Mass.: MIT Press, 1982).
Robinson, Richard, *Plato's Earlier Dialectic* (Oxford: Clarendon Press, 1953).
Rose, Lynn E., *Aristotle's Syllogistic* (Springfield, Ill.: Charles C. Thomas, 1968).
Ross, W. D., *Aristotle: A complete Exposition of his Work and Thought* (New York: Meridian Books, 1960).
Rotenstreich, Nathan, *From Substance to Subject* (The Hague: Martinus Nijhoff, 1974).
Ruben, Peter, 'Von der "Wissenschaft der Logik" und dem Verhältnis der Dialektik zur Logik', in R.-P. Horstmann (1978), pp. 70–100.
Schilpp, Paul Arthur (ed.), *The Philosophy of Karl Popper*, vols I and II (Illinois: La Salle, 1974).
Solmsen, Friedrich, 'Dialectic without the Forms', in G. E. L. Owen (1968), pp. 49–68.
Solomon, Robert C., *In the Spirit of Hegel: A Study of G. W. F. Hegel's 'Phenomenology of Spirit'* (Oxford University Press, 1983).
Spinoza, Benedict de, *The Chief Works of Benedict de Spinoza*, vol. I, trans. R. H. M. Elwes (New York: Dover Publications, 1955).
Der Sprach Brockhaus (Wiesbaden: F. A. Brockhaus, 1968).
Stegmüller, Wolfgang, *The Structure and Dynamics of Theories*, trans. William Wohlhuter (New York: Springer, 1976).
Stenzel, Julius, *Plato's Method of Dialectic*, trans. D. J. Allan (New York: Arno Press, 1973).
Stepelevich, L. S. and D. Lamb (eds), *Hegel's Philosophy of Action* (Atlantic Highlands, N.J.: Humanities Press, 1983).
Stigen, Anfinn, *The Structure of Aristotle's Thought* (Oslo: Universitetsforlaget, 1966).
Strauss, Leo, 'What is Political Philosophy' in L. Strauss, *What is Political Philosophy* (Illinois: Free Press of Glencoe, 1959), pp. 9–55.
Swift, Jonathan, *Gulliver's Travels* (New York: Modern Library, 1958).
Taylor, Charles, *Hegel* (Cambridge University Press, 1983).
Theunissen, Michael, *Sein und Schein: Die kritische Funktion der Hegelschen Logik* (Frankfurt a/M: Suhrkamp, 1980).
Toulmin, Stephen, 'Conceptual Revolutions in Science', in R. S. Cohen and M. W. Wartofsky, (eds), *Boston Studies in the Philosophy of Science*, vol. III (Dordrecht: R. Reidel, 1967), pp. 331–47.
Watkins, John, 'Against "Normal Science"', in I. Lakatos and A. Musgrave (1978), pp. 25–37.
Weiss, F. G., *Hegel's Critique of Aristotle's Philosophy of Mind* (The Hague: Martinus Nijhoff, 1969).
Wieland, Wolfgang, *Die Aristotelische Physik* (Göttingen: Vandenhoek & Ruprecht, 1970).

Wilkins, Burleigh taylor, *Hegel's Philosophy of History* (Ithaca: Cornell University Press, 1974).
Winner, Langdon, *Autonomous technology* (Cambridge, Mass.: MIT Press, 1978).
Zimmerli, Walther Christoph, *Die Frage nach der Philosophie*, Hegel-Studien, Beiheft 12 (Bonn: Bouvier Verlag Herbert Grundmann, 1974).

Index